Pinches of Salt, Prisms of Light

"You are the salt of the earth. But if the salt loses its saltiness, how can it be made salty again? It is no longer good for anything, except to be thrown out and trampled by men. You are the light of the world. A city on a hill cannot be hidden. Neither do people light a lamp and put it under a bowl. Instead they put it on its stand, and it gives light to everyone in the house. In the same way, let your light shine before men, that they may see your good deeds and praise your Father in heaven."

—Matthew 5:13-16

Pinches of Salt, Prisms of Light

Copyright © 1999, Carmen Leal and Eva Marie Everson

Cover illustration by Esther Horvath

Canadian Cataloguing in Publication Data

Leal, Carmen
    Pinches of salt, prisms of light: ordinary people, extraordinary stories

ISBN 1-55306-012-1

    1. Devotional literature, Canadian (English). 2. Christian life. I. Everson, Eva Marie II. Title.

BV4515.2.L43 1999   242   C99-900811-0

Living Hope, Inc.
P.O. Box 952163, Lake Mary, FL 32795-2193 USA
Tel: (407) 328-0981 • Fax: (407) 328-7810
E-mail: Carmen@Leal.com
Internet: www.Carmen.Leal.com

Printed in Canada
by

Essence
PUBLISHING

$\mathcal{D}$edication

This book is dedicated to...

two great examples of "salt and light" in my life:
my grandmother, Elma Purvis, and my brother, Van Purvis.
I love you both immeasurably! —*Eva Marie Everson*

And...

to my family. We never had much money,
but my father, Lucien, and my mother, Barbara,
raised eight character-filled children. Because of their salt and
light in our lives as children, they and Kevin, Eric, Debbie,
Diane, Patricia, Michael and Merrill continue to influence
my life and the lives of countless others.
I truly thank God for you all. —*Carmen Leal*

Contents

Acknowledgements

Writing and compiling the stories in *Pinches of Salt, Prisms of Light* has been a true labor of love. Throughout the course of a year, this book was conceived of, worked on, cried over, and eventually finished. We owe our thanks to many for making this possible. We received encouragement, help, and support from all quarters, and are grateful to all who had anything to do with this book. We would especially like to thank:

Our Heavenly Father, for His constancy and for leading us down the paths to this place and these people. You are awesome!

Eva Marie's husband, Dennis, and their three children, Chris, Ashley, and Jessica. Thank you for your unfailing belief in her and in this book, and in what God wants to do in her life.

Carmen's two patient sons, Nicholas and Justin, whose intelligence and laughter always encourage her.

Our parents. Parents are some of the most important people in our lives and we have some of the best!

Eva Marie's parents, Preston Purvis and Betty Purvis, who loved her work when it was nothing more than scribble, understood it when she was going through her "dark period," and cheered it when she began writing for God. (I love you with all my heart!)

Carmen's parents, Lucien Leal and Barbara Leal, who continue to be a source of inspiration.

JoAnn Zarling, our editor, who has worked tirelessly through great illness and pain because she loves God and us. You are one of the most gifted people we know, JoAnn.

Dr. Joel Hunter, Senior Pastor at Northland, A Church Distributed; Orlando Rivera, our Missions Pastor; Northland's Foundation for the Arts Board of Directors; and the staff and congregation of Northland, A Church Distributed. You have consistently encouraged us, and our hearts cry out with a resounding, "Thank you!"

Esther Horvath, our talented artist with a generous heart. We sincerely hope that you, our readers, have heard the same "Come inside and see the Lord" whispers that we heard when we first beheld this painting. Thank you, Esther.

Lelania Farenkoph, another gifted graphics artist and good friend. Lelania has designed our "salt and light" logo which you see between each story. She spent countless hours creating the finest design for our book. Thank you, dear friend.

There are special people in our lives who we thank from the bottom of our hearts:

Eva Marie's students at Life Training Center, the recipients of her daily devotional Debbie's Place, her "Little WoWo," and Mr. & Mrs. Huie Harris for their supportive prayers and belief in her talent.

The staff at Island Lake Center, who have given Carmen's husband, David, extraordinary care, allowing her to have worry-free time to write. You have our sincere gratitude.

Charlene and Gary, Carmen's two special friends, who have been a tremendous support, and friends to David. Thank you.

About the Artist

To me, doorways are mysterious, inviting, and personal. Each one is like a story waiting to be told, an invitation to be accepted.

As the daughter of Ukrainian immigrants living in quiet poverty, I wasn't any different than our neighbors. We all struggled daily to put a few potatoes or some oatmeal on the table, and to keep from being evicted.

My mother had never gone to school, my father had been apprenticed to a cabinetmaker to learn his trade. To them, my art was useless because it couldn't provide food, clothes, or shelter. But my teachers told me that the little clay house I formed in kindergarten and the old oak tree I painted during a free art workshop were "good." They told me I had a "gift." But I thought the teachers surely must be mistaken, because my mother always mumbled something in Ukrainian about "messing around" as she threw my creations in the trash.

Yet I continued to find art effortless, comfortable, and satisfying. And then I met the One who is effortless, comforting, and eternally satisfying. I was sixteen when I heard the Lord tell me that He was here to love me and care for me. He told me to go forth, to find Him, and to worship Him. Since this journey began, I've learned more and more just how God wants me to trust only Him.

I majored in fine arts throughout high school and college, married, and started our family. I also refined my skills at portraiture. Yet God continued to place other work in my life, postponing the time when I could paint as much as I desired. It wasn't until I gave up "making it happen," and totally trusted Him, that the Lord began blessing me with one beautiful project after another, including mural projects of entire rooms and even entire houses!

I love this creative work I do and the enjoyment it gives to others. All my gratitude and praise, I give to my Creator.

Having my art on the cover of this book of stories is both special and humbling. Each story in *Pinches of Salt, Prisms of Light* is a doorway into learning something about yourself and the world around you. They are doorways to a closer relationship with God. I hope reading this book gives you as much enjoyment as I got from painting the cover picture.

Esther Horvath

Preface

The Hawaiian "aloha" is a word that so aptly describes Northland, A Church Distributed in Orlando, Florida.

Everyone has heard it sometime or another. Most people think that "aloha" means "hello," or "good-bye." But it means much more than that. Besides "hello" and "goodbye," the Hawaiian English dictionary has over thirty meanings for the word. Some of these include charity, mercy, befriend, affection, love, hello, farewell, pity, endearing, friendship, sympathy, and hospitable. In other words, "aloha" is another very appropriate word for "salt and light." To "have aloha" *is* to "be salt and light."

When Carmen thought she left aloha in Hawaii, she found that Central Florida and Northland, A Church Distributed have, in their own way, just as much aloha as any tropical paradise.

Northland, A Church Distributed does more than teach about "salt and light," it exudes love and care to its surrounding community in the quintessence of what Christ Jesus meant when He taught about the Christian's "salt and light" to a dying world.

For one year, Senior Pastor Dr. Joel Hunter taught on that subject. But this church goes beyond that. Northland is there for the community as a whole. They listen non-judgementally to the problems of whomever desires their help, then they find the best way to provide that help. They've been known to assist their people with monetary help in cases where there is illness or hunger, or whatever else is needed.

Each quarter, Northland has a "car-care day" for single moms. Volunteers, some of them professional auto repair people, do oil changes and minor checkups. One month, a group of children and moms even did a service project by washing cars belonging to single parents. Besides having a benevolence fund, Northland has a food bank, a tie in with a local employment agency, and an extensive counseling program. They support many charities throughout Central Florida, and they have an ever growing missions focus that sends "aloha" around the world. The services themselves are filled with "aloha," as are the Bible studies and small home groups.

Of course, Northland is only one church that is spreading salt and light throughout Central Florida and beyond. *Pinches of Salt, Prisms of Light* is a book of stories. Each story represents an ordinary person who is part of his or her own church, each being "salt and light" in the world.

Alexander Graham Bell said, "When one door closes, another opens; but we often look so long and so regretfully upon the closed door, that we do not see the one which has opened for us."

How appropriate that the cover art for this book is a doorway. We invite you to open the door and explore the many others that our writers have opened—and the times of another door closing.

We hope you will enjoy reading these extraordinary stories as much as we enjoyed writing and compiling them.

Aloha,

Eva Marie Everson
Carmen Leal

Foreword

Our church, Northland, A Church Distributed, spent the entire year of 1998 helping people fathom what Jesus meant when He described His followers as the "salt and light of the world" (Matthew 5:13-16). It's not that the people of Northland are so dull that it took them a year to get it. For something to become a part of us, it takes time to weave it into our character.

To be salt and light in the world, you have to be in the world. Your relationships must not be merely the religious kind.

In fact, too much salt spoils, rather than flavors. Too much light blinds, rather than reveals. Our Lord was saying that influence, rather than dominance, is the way to best minister to others.

Since the beginning of time, man has loved stories. We love them even more when they are personal, when they apply to us and to our own lives. They give us more than just information; they open our hearts. Stories that come from everyday life, like the parables that Jesus told, transform our perspectives. They "in-form" us in ways that other forms of communication can't. That's what I like about stories!

Stories influence and add pleasure, insight, and motivation to our lives. They are relational; they inspire us to be loving rather than preachy. Many of the stories in this book are not overly religious, some aren't "religious" at all. But they are real. They are just what God can use to mold all of us into better servants.

One of the greatest things about God is that He came down to live with us. The more we focus on His awesomeness in worship and praise, the more we will see Him in our everyday lives.

The more we see Him in our everyday lives, the better influences we will be for Him in the world.

These stories will be a blessing to you, and through you, to others.

Joel Hunter
Senior Pastor of Northland, A Church Distributed

Salt and Light In Family

"I will open my mouth in parables, I will utter hidden things, things from of old—what we have heard and known, what our fathers have told us. We will not hide them from their children; we will tell the next generation the praiseworthy deeds of the Lord, His power, and the wonders He has done."

—Psalm 78:2-4

"Sometimes the poorest man leaves his children the richest inheritance." —Ruth E. Renkel

More Than An Heirloom

SUSAN CHESSER BRANCH

Fifteen of us crammed into my Grandma Chesser's tiny one-bedroom apartment. Even after her death at the age of eighty-one, her apartment was as it had always been—as neat as a pin. She was meticulous about her meager possessions, tidy to a fault, and practical about what she needed and didn't need. With such a limited amount for storage, we thought that most of her keepsakes were long gone, thrown away or given away out of necessity. But as drawers were opened and boxes searched, a whole mansion of memories unfolded before our eyes.

Dozens of pictures and letters spilled out of small shoe boxes. Grandma had utilized every available space in her tiny apartment; we found boxes under her bed, hidden behind blankets, and stacked in closets. I even unearthed some cards and letters with my childish handwriting, my first attempts at letter writing. Stacks of letters, cards, all kinds of papers, all blended together. In that stack were report cards from the 1930s, World War II ration books, postcards from forgotten vacations.

Cries of delight rang out when my sister and cousins found long forgotten handmade gifts, gifts made fifteen, twenty years ago. I found practically all of the gifts I had made for her, too, all that I could remember. Simple boxes and trinkets most people would have thrown out one week later, she kept safely tucked away for her pleasure.

All those gifts: needlework, shellacked plaques with trite sayings, macramed potholders, and scores of other items made by grandchildren filled the spaces of her home. I remember giving her gifts and crayon pictures and she would smile pleasantly. She was never one to make a "big fuss." She was quiet, austere, she dressed simply, almost plain, never drawing attention to herself. The most unusual part of her appearance was her hair; she hadn't cut it for years and years and wore it in a single braid wrapped around her head. Only at night would we see the long silver mane. I could never understand why she cut it after all those years. Her only explanation was that it was too hard to take care of.

Box after box, we searched in wonder. There were crocheted baby hats, leaving us to wonder whose tiny heads they fit at one time. Seven sons had been born to my grandparents, two of the little boys dying at young ages. She never said much about the two sons who never grew up.

Nestled with the pair of wire-rimmed eyeglasses she must have worn when she was a teenager were rusted fish hooks, probably my grandfather's. She had even saved his old shaving cup, razor, and razor strap. His death came at the beginning of their "good years," after all the sons had left home and life was slowing down. She stoically lived another twenty years without him, yet I always knew she missed him.

In her jewelry box, scattered among the costume jewelry, was a rock. It wasn't a pretty, fancy rock; just a small, gray, rough stone. But it had my father's name on it, written in his own childish handwriting in black ink. As he rubbed and examined it, his eyes searched the stone for details of its past. He couldn't remember its importance, but she must have. He was her youngest son, the one she tended to "spoil."

We laughed when we discovered a paint-by-number picture hidden behind a door. I claimed it as mine, but my brother later corrected me saying it was his. Why either of us would want to claim it, I don't know. Possibly the ugliest painting in the world, yet she saved it. From a distance, it looked like a dog; closer up, it was a swamp of mottled green and brown paint.

I saw the valentines first. It was like finding treasure. All different sizes of bright red cards, circa 1930s vintage. Chubby-cheeked children, angelic faces, with cute cartoon sayings: "How's chances?" "You've got me all busted up over you!" Most were addressed to my father, each from a different girl. There were a few re-addressed to another brother, apparently some early attempts at recycling.

But mostly, we found letters. Page after page that recounted everyday life, heartaches, and unexpected joys.

"I think the kids have the flu."

"Guess we'll be coming home for Christmas."

"We're having pretty good weather today."

"I'm tired of camp and I want to come home."

Grandma faithfully answered every letter, even the ones from summer camp.

I have heard many stories of relatives fighting tooth and nail over an antique bedroom suite, a piano, or a diamond ring. Grandma wasn't able to hand down valuable heirlooms like that, but what we found were more valuable than Victorian pianos. Her memories were her keepsakes, important enough to save for years, even as long as fifty years. Maybe, on her loneliest nights, these were the things that gave her the most pleasure.

"The joys of parents are secret, and so are their griefs and fears."
—Francis Bacon

Yellow Ruffles

CARMEN LEAL

"But Mama, I don't have a present." My four-year-old voice quivered as huge tears pooled their way down my chubby cheeks. "I don't even have money to buy something for Daddy."

"Honey, you don't need to buy anything to give a gift. You can do a favor for someone you love, or even give them something special of yours you think they might like."

Daddy's birthday finally arrived, complete with homemade cake and ice cream. With a large family such as ours, birthdays were the only times we had ice cream. It was always the same flavor—Neapolitan. Instead of scooped onto plates, we enjoyed this treat cut into squares, and we usually fought for the slab with the least vanilla. Today, though, the ice cream didn't matter! I had finally thought of a gift for Daddy, something I valued more than just about anything I owned.

While Daddy smiled and complimented each of his numerous offspring on their offerings, I hopped from one foot to the other in anticipation. My tousled curls bounced in rhythm as I danced and chattered about the room.

Daddy's large brown hands shook the childishly wrapped box as he laughingly guessed at its content. "Is it a car? I know! It must be a ship, and we can sail off together."

"No, Daddy," I squealed. "It's too small to be a car or a ship."

As the smudged paper came off the crushed box, the lid fell off, revealing yellow fabric. Daddy's resonant laughter boomed through the too small living room, while my sister's shrill giggles nearly drowned out another brother's chuckle. Why was every-one laughing at my gift? I ran upstairs into hiding.

My mother followed me and quietly sat down on my bed. "What's wrong, Carmen?"

"Daddy didn't like my gift. He laughed at me and so did everyone else. Even you. You said I could give Daddy something of mine I liked best of all. I never even wore those panties before. He doesn't like them and he doesn't like me," I sobbed.

"Honey, those yellow panties with all the ruffles are beauti-ful, but daddies don't usually wear ruffled panties, and they real-ly are very tiny."

The party was ruined for me as I remembered their respons-es. I stayed in my room and cried myself to sleep. The yellow panties were never mentioned again.

One day, when I was nine, I peeked into the french doors of my parents' bedroom. Through the sheer curtains and small window pane, I saw my dad in a burgundy suit wearing a hat curved downward toward his handsome features. He stooped, defeatedly, and carefully placed his clothing in a scarred, leather suitcase.

At the time, I didn't know about divorce; it was quite rare in the 1960s, especially in Catholic families with eight children. Without even knowing the word, I sensed that life as I knew it was changing. My father was leaving because he didn't love me enough.

Just as I turned to leave, a flash of yellow caught my eye. The ruffled panties! I knew then just how much Daddy loved my gift. More than that, I understood how much he loved me. With all the memories Daddy could have packed in that suit-case as he started his new life, he chose that scrap of yellow fab-ric. It was the last item Daddy placed on the pile before he closed the lid.

Thank you for keeping my gift, Daddy. I love you, too.

"God could not be everywhere, and therefore he made mothers."
—Jewish Proverb

Blessed Stillness

JoAnn Zarling

I wanted to scream in frustration! My five-year-old son had just tumbled headlong down the front steps and was sobbing in pain and fright. His little elbow was bleeding profusely from a cut, and even from where I sat by the window, an angry-looking bump on his tiny forehead was already visibly swelling. I saw that he wasn't severely injured, but he was badly shaken, bruised, and frightened. He needed reassurance, and there were injuries to tend, a little body to comfort, and tears to kiss away.

But I couldn't go to him. My body could not respond to the screaming in my mind. Paralysis from the stroke which wreaked havoc in my life kept me imprisoned in my wheelchair, and I could not run to my hurting child with motherly comfort and caring. My left side was a useless mass of unfeeling flesh and bone that did nothing but weigh me down.

So it was Cyndy, our fourteen-year-old daughter, who ran outside to pick up Roddy's trembling little body. She carried him tenderly upstairs and cuddled him for a minute before bringing him to me. My right arm could still hold him, and I cooed into his little ear as Cyndy's gentle ministering soothed the sting in his elbow.

For what seemed to be the millionth time, I silently prayed, "Lord, help me! Show me how to make the best of this situation and be the kind of mother I need to be. I feel so utterly useless!"

My stroke was the result of a blood clot in the brain. It was caused by severe head injuries sustained in a freakish accident when I fell out of a second-story window while washing it.

Throughout my illness, God had held me close. In the constant enforced quietness of my world when first stricken with this horrible thing, I had taken shelter in His protective nearness. I was totally dependent upon Him for everything from companionship to comfort.

In the beginning, before I let God communicate His loving nearness to me, I was terrified. It didn't take Him long, though, to let me know that He was right there beside me and would remain there. He would be my guide through the uncertain future. As a young mother of four growing children, I had some very understandable questions about not only my future, but also my husband's and my children's.

Slowly, I gained strength. My thought processes were sometimes painfully jumbled, sometimes not. The frustration of trying to move limbs that no longer felt part of me would have been unbearable but for the Lord's presence. He shouldered my cares and stopped my frightened tears in the middle of those long, lonely nights as I lay helpless in the hospital and later the rehabilitation center.

Numerous Bible verses that I once memorized were lost to me, yet in one way or another, God brought to mind just what I needed, at the times I most needed it. Somehow, He always communicated the words that He wanted me to recall, and transmitted all the strength and comfort needed to survive the trauma of a life turned up-side-down.

So as I sat "uselessly" in my wheelchair, with my precious youngest child snuggled in my lap, a verse flashed into my mind. ""My grace is sufficient for you, for My power is made perfect in weakness" (2 Corinthians 12:9).

At that precise moment, Roddy looked up at me with absolute love and trust in his huge, wet brown eyes. "Mommy, you feel so nice to me when I hurt."

Useless? Me? No, I wasn't useless at all. God, in His wisdom, even used the very *feel* of me to comfort my child. My loving, caring presence did for my little boy what God's constant presence does for me.

That was many years ago, and much has happened since then. My little boy is now a big, handsome man. Today I can sometimes walk short distances within the house with crutches, and I thank God for that once un-looked for ability. There are still things that make me feel "useless," but not often. Because I will never forget the lesson my Lord taught me all those years ago. He will use me in any capacity He can, if and when I let Him. Like Paul, I have learned the wisdom of being content in whatever state I find myself.

I believe that God uses the happenings in life, whether good or bad, for my good and His glory. I do not believe that these life-altering catastrophes were results of His "zapping" me. The fact is that He has blessed me unspeakably in the ample time I've had to "be still" and know that He is God. How great God is!

"I love you not only for what you are, but for what I am when I am with you." —Roy Croft

Mother

ELLY LeBLANC

What dreams did you have that you put aside for me?
What promises, made to yourself, that you never got to see?
In the beginning of life I demanded, you gave

For everything I asked, you gave
Your infinite wisdom, you gave, even without asking!

Of course, I didn't always listen!
That is how we are set-up,
To live and learn from mistakes we make,
Triumphs accomplished, love forsaken.

Yet still I falter, still I wade
Through life's oft muddied waters;
Teetered on the edge
I hold my breath and say to myself,
What would you do?

Suddenly, as if my life to the present replays through my memory
I remember things you taught me,
Words you gave in comfort,
Tears you dried and wounds you healed,
I'm up to your knees again, I feel picked up, and held.

Instantly I'm focused,
The inner child still there can see again!
You are the strongest person I will ever know
You are and always will be constantly with me
I ache to do half as well as you, if the time comes.

Yours is the only love unquestioned
That is always tested
Unconsciously that is, for what do we know?
You are selfless, there is no hidden agenda
Such an altruistic act no one could seek.

Your omniscience, patience, and understanding
Will be forever with me,

I return daily now, in my reflection
I love you, Mother,
I owe you everything!

"Where is home? Home is where the heart can laugh without shyness. Home is where the heart's tears can dry at their own pace."
—Vernon G. Baker

I'll Love You Forever

CARMEN LEAL

One evening, I was playing Monopoly with a family friend and my sons, fourteen-year-old Justin and sixteen-year-old Nicholas. The game was going smoothly until Justin, in a characteristic, major capitalistic move, wanted to buy several properties from his brother. This coup, if he could coerce his brother into selling, would give him a monopoly; one entire city block.

This was bad news for the other three players in the game; I was perilously close to bankruptcy. So Justin offered his brother an obscene amount of money, to no avail. When that didn't work, he switched to incentives, including, "You'll never have to pay me rent if you land on these." Nicholas, child of my heart during that hard-fought Monopoly game, persisted in saying, "No."

Finally, Justin looked at his brother, often the source of such conflict and jealously in his life, and smiled. "Please let me buy them from you, Nicholas. If you do, I'll love you forever."

Nicholas' face melted, and we all broke into laughter. Their completed transaction soon forced me into bankruptcy, and the game eventually ended with Justin the undisputed real estate mogul, despite not charging his brother rent.

Sometimes, life is challenging at best and a nightmare at worst. But whenever I see my kids together, so handsome and strong and so close to being on their own, I hear Justin saying, "But I'll love you forever!" I know it's true and those words get me through one more rough day.

"There was a time when father amounted to something in the United States. He was held with some esteem in the community; he had some authority in his own household; his views were sometimes taken seriously by his children; and even his wife paid heed to him from time to time." —Adlai E. Stevenson

The Man

EVA MARIE EVERSON

My friends called Daddy "The Man" long before "You da man!" ever became a popular catch phrase. When it came to law enforcement, Daddy was a natural. Love for his work ran through his veins thicker than blood ever could. When I was born, Daddy worked as a license examiner with the Georgia State Patrol. He became a patrolman a few years later and, in 1968, graduated from the FBI Academy in Washington, D.C. When he returned to Georgia, he took a job with the Georgia Bureau of Investigation, first as a Special Investigator and later in the GCIC (Georgia Crime Information Center).

In the early 1970s, when Mr. Jimmy Carter was Governor of our great state, the GCIC obtained a new administrator, Mr. Beardsley. Something between Mr. Beardsley and Daddy didn't quite gel, so working with him was an exercise in faith. When Mr. Beardsley decided that Daddy should take a transfer from our hometown of Sylvania (where Daddy had been stationed for nearly twenty years) to the remote town of Alma, the true test of Daddy's faith began.

Not wanting the transfer had nothing to do with lack of respect for authority. My mother had been ill for several years and was under the constant care of physicians; her doctors were adamant that she should not move from the area. Also, my parents did not want to uproot my brother and me. Given these two factors, Daddy refused the transfer.

Mr. Beardsley was not pleased. In what could only be a power play, he sent my father "on the road" for an "undetermined" amount of time. I remember Daddy standing in the middle of our knotty-pine kitchen, telling Mama that he would only be home once every three weeks or so. "If he had poured hot water over me, it couldn't have been any more of a shock," he said. And so he packed his bags and began "living" in State Patrol offices.

When Daddy came home for a day or two, I'd run through the house as soon as I heard the back door open and fling myself into his arms. Daddy's hugs were desired bear hugs, in spite of the fact that the handle of his gun dug painfully into my flesh. Over Mama's delicious, home-style dinner, we listened attentively as he told us of his travels, and how much he missed us... especially at night. "I don't know why Mr. Beardsley has chosen to do this," he said. "But every morning and every night I read the twenty-seventh Psalm. It gives me the courage and strength to get through this. And I know that one day God will bless me and change this man's heart."

From that day on, I read Psalm twenty-seven on a daily basis, allowing it to penetrate my heart and mind. I believed the words, even though I saw no evidence of the promises found there.

One afternoon, after a year had gone by, Mama was outside in the yard. Having just killed a snake with her shovel (an act she would later call prophetic), she was still excited when she ran in to answer the ringing telephone.

"Hello?"

"I just got the word," Daddy said from the other end. "I'm coming home. This time for good."

Daddy was right. God was true to His promises. I had learned a lesson that I would never forget. Today, if you turn to the twenty-seventh Psalm in my Bible, you will see written in bold letters, "Daddy's Psalm." Every time I see those words, I remember.

"The cure for all the ills and wrongs, the cares, the sorrows, and the crimes of humanity all lie in the one word love. It is the divine vitality that everywhere produces and restores life."
—Lydia Maria Child

Expressions of Love

KEN SHEARS

After many years of what seemed, at the time, over-whelming personal difficulty, our daughters are now able to relate much better to their mom. Maybe it's because Rose is so incapacitated and relies totally on them when we visit her or bring her home from the nursing home.

Jackie, our youngest daughter, constantly refers to her mom as "sweet," and she loves her very much. She also laments not having a mom that she can share her triumphs and tragedies with on a normal basis. Still, Rose and I are so fortunate; as a result of the pain caused by Huntington's Disease, Jackie and her older sister are close in ways that transcend sisterhood. Only now, they also correct any erroneous memories I may have of how she did her housekeeping, and a myriad of other details that spring from their youthful impressions of their mother before she became ill. They're beginning to realize what they owe their mom.

We have, like all families, shed many a tear over our losses. But we are also blessed by the wonderful memories we made before Rose became ill.

There's a term in the Christian teen community, "WWJD." It stands for "What Would Jesus Do?" For our children, it's WWMD or, "What Would Mom Do?" Our kids constantly correct my memories about what their mom liked to eat and how to fix it. I'm a terrible cook, and boy, do they let me know when I fall short of the mark!

Our house is full of the crafts that Rose created, offering unbroken links to her love and kindness. These are silent icons of her attention to details we rarely noticed at the time, but which now stand as beacons of her love and care for all of us.

We are blessed to have reached the point where we can meaningfully return the love she so richly deserves. Even though Rose is now in a condition that some would call helpless, she is still the focal point of our family.

Last year, I was hospitalized because of cancer for a total of two months. I had two radical procedures performed during that time, and for a while, things were "touch and go." Looking back, what I remember most vividly was the comfort of having my children, people from my church, and even hospital staff simply hold my hand.

But in a twist of fate, I was most comforted by my wonderful Rose, whom I'd had to place in a nursing home just a few months before. I'd visited her a few days prior to my last hospitalization, and not even sure she would understand what I was trying to tell her, I bluntly explained my situation. She quietly leaned forward and pressed her forehead against mine. Though Huntington's Disease has almost totally robbed her of speech, this expression of her love did more to erase my despair than any words she could have spoken.

We are continually learning to share our feelings, to show our love. I sincerely believe that however difficult it may be, honestly and simply sharing your feelings for another's suffering is a precious gift that outlasts all the tears and fears.

"The mother's heart is the child's schoolroom."
—Henry Ward Beecher

I Have Learned a Great Thing

JULIA ARRANTS

from the grandmothers in quiet sandalled feet,
from the old ones moving in silence,
through foreign lands of laundry
I have learned a great thing.

In the vastness where one word is spoken
they look from the window
and light the same candles,
and tell the same story
from the hidden pith of the world;
the heart of all secrets
what a wind,
yes, what a rain.

"To live is to suffer; to survive is to find meaning in suffering."
—Viktor Frankel

Adversity Equals

TIFFANY JOHNSON, AGE 12

It finally happened. I had a little brother! Little did I know what that first week would be like. I had been an only child for eight years, so I had no idea what little kids were like. I will never forget that week.

We were living with my maternal grandparents at the time. My grandfather has always been, well, you might say, "in love with the Lord." He has Multiple Sclerosis and has been in a wheelchair since I was born. For years, my grandmother has cared for him. When we moved into the house to help with his care, we were not aware that it would probably help us more than him.

My PaPa was overjoyed by the birth of my brother. However, shortly after Cory's birth, my PaPa went into a coma that lasted for nine days and eight nights. He had "live in" nurses, and his room was a tangle of IV machines, heart monitors, and a whole mess of other equipment. Somehow I knew that if I was with him he would know I was there. I combed his hair, washed his face, and did whatever the nurses would let me do. During this time, I watched what the nurses were doing, and I learned a lot. Twice the doctor came to the house and told us that he did not think my PaPa would live through the night. On the eighth night, the nurse swore that she saw an angel sitting next to my grandfather. She said that God was in the room. We knew that PaPa was probably with God and expected that in the morning he would be gone.

The next morning, he woke up.

This experience really made me stronger emotionally, because I am very close to my PaPa. I learned how to trust and care even when things don't look so good. Because of that, I am also closer to my brother. Sometimes I think things are awful and bad and then I remember that something good can happen. If it weren't for the support of my friends, family, and church, my grandfather probably would not be here today and I would not be who I am. Through the hardest of times, I grew. I learned that strength and motivation can come from times that seem hard. I learned where to put my heart and trust. For those who were with me—no, with us—and the fact that they cared, I am very grateful.

"All that I am, or hope to be, I owe to my angel mother."
—Abraham Lincoln

My Marvelous, Mystifying Mama

M. ELDRED MANN

Mama. How shall I describe her? She was an enigma, a catastrophic force, a peacemaker, a visionary, and an elocutionist all rolled into one.

She was born at the turn of the century, in the piney-woods territory (later a part of Fort Stewart, Georgia) at Lida, a small rural community owned by her father and appropriately named for her. Granddaddy was a progressive farmer and large landowner who kept a general store. Old-timers, spitting tobacco juice, lounged lazily on the store's sunny porch and occasionally sipped a five-cent Coca cola or hand-pumped gasoline at thirteen cents a gallon for their "tin Lizzy" Model T Fords. Legend has it that these cars had acquired this nickname in the deep South because anyone with a length of hay wire and a piece of tin could supposedly repair them easily, regardless of what was wrong.

Before school age, Mama had early shown a penchant for mimicry. She was especially good at imitating the hard-shelled Primitive Baptist preachers who, filled with the Holy Spirit, spewed forth the doctrine of their religion in such a profusion of sing-song revelation that an auctioneer would have some difficulty in keeping pace with them. Oftentimes, Mama would be lifted bodily and placed upon a tree stump to entertain crowds with her characterizations. Her voice would take on a quivering tremelo, apropos to the preachers, as she began to chant, "Pre-destination of the saints of the Lord...." All eyes were riveted on her; she, reveling in this recognition and basking in the glory of others' praise, was the center of attention—and she loved it!

Mama was an avid reader, an excellent student, steeped in the traditional mastery of Latin, and, though she was not an acclaimed virtuoso, she played an acceptable violin, piano, and organ. She had a beautiful alto voice, but her forte was elocution. When she gave a reading, she tenaciously held the audience in the palm of her hands. They laughed hilariously at her antics, or shed silent tears as she swayed them through her verbal depictions. At times, she performed at the school auditorium during the amateur shows for talented townfolk; invariably she took home the first prize. My father was not especially happy with her participation in these programs, and he disgustedly referred to them as "when Lida Mae was up there showing her rear end." (His terminology was not quite so nice as mine.) She won awards in school and medals in District Meets for her elocutionary speeches. Once, she even entered the State Meet. Though she was not the state winner, the judges sought her out to explain that she was definitely the most talented speaker there, but they had to disqualify her since her speech was too long. My Mama had not been aware of this restrictive limit in performance time.

Undoubtedly, Mama had the best set of lungs for effective voice projection I have ever heard. When we children were away playing with neighboring friends, near five o'clock p.m. she would stand on our back porch, and, taking a deep breath, she began her litany of calling her children home. "Durell, Eldred, James, Burney Ann—oooo.... (her voice rose in an increasing crescendo on the "OO") Come home!" The next day at school, I would be jokingly assailed by friends who lived at least a mile away from us, giving their imitation of Mama. Today, fifty years later, I occasionally see childhood playmates who cannot resist smiling in remembrance of this.

Mama had a definite flair for comedy. Nothing pleased her more than to send her listeners into uncontrollable mirth or "belly" laughs. She had a quick wit in repartee, and in declining years, every doctor's office that she frequented with me in attendance was an opportunity to entertain. I'd shrink into silence, wishing I could crawl into the nearest hole while she questioned startled patients, relentlessly cajoling them into smiles. Within fifteen minutes, she'd know practically every person's name, where they were from, who their parents were, what hobbies they had, and the symptoms of their illnesses. Once we were in a doctor's office in Savannah, Georgia, where Mama had again placed herself as the center of attention. I happened to notice an old gentleman sitting in the corner who had not said a word. It was evident that he preferred a quiet waiting room, as did I.

"I think I'm going to buy me a red dress. I'm getting old enough to wear bright colors without undue attention," Mama said, finishing her statement.

The old gentleman spoke up, "You know why women wear red dresses, don't you?" His tone inferred that only fast, sexy women wore noticeably loud colors.

"Of course I do," Mama retorted.

"Why?"

I presume he thought he'd embarrass her into silence. Not my Mama! Instantly, without hesitation, she pitched in, ready for battle. "To cover their nudity!"

Mama was a grand cook. The beds, on occasion, might go unmade until after lunch, or the floors could do with a little better sweeping, but on the buffet would be a huge chocolate-nut cake or a buttery pound cake, gourmands' delights, fantastic in their regal beauty and taste. Or there might be a platter of fudge—thick, moist, creamy smooth, never grainy or hard—or a plate of divinity topped either by a pecan half or a maraschino cherry that almost took one's breath away in succulent ecstasy.

When feasting on the ambrosial fare of the gods, who would notice an unmade bed? Recently, my sister and I listed the many desserts my mother had so lovingly prepared for our enjoyment. We easily recalled thirty-three. This was astronomical for the early 1900s, as the average family had only pound cake, sweet-in' bread (made with syrup), a hard sugar cookie, or an egg custard pie. Of course, there was the traditional fruitcake at Christmas, if the family could afford such a luxury.

I believe that Mama often spoke without thinking. I cannot comprehend her intentionally being cruel, but she was sickeningly frank, almost brutal at times. She justified this trait as being honest. Never, and I do mean never, would she ever stoop to anything even remotely akin to a "little white lie." Once, she was standing before the dresser combing her long hair which she plaited and criss-crossed in the back. Daddy, who was home because of heart trouble, asked where she was going. Without thinking (surely her mind was on something else), she spoke, "To town to buy a new black dress to wear at your funeral." I recoiled in shock.

Another time, when she awoke from minor surgery, she told her doctor that she didn't care what other people thought. She thought that he was a good doctor and she loved him. I shrieked, "Mama!" It never crossed her mind how she had indirectly maligned him; she thought she had been complimenting him.

She was honest almost to a fault. A half hour after my father died, she called the Georgia Power Company to come read our meter. She wanted Daddy's funds to pay for the electricity up until his death, but she would pay from her private income the charges for the remainder of the month. She had similar arrangements concerning the telephone bill and all other utilities. She did not want to cheat her children out of their rightful share of the estate. This compulsion for honesty was almost too persnickety for me.

Mama loved her black 1957 Chevrolet and proudly drove it to the grocery store and to church. She was a terrible driver, but in our little countrified town, where maybe five cars would pass the house during a day in the '60s, she survived. I once watched her back out of our driveway onto the road without looking back to see if another car were near. I yelled, "Mama, you didn't even look!"

Her cool reply was, "My neck's too short. I can't look back."

She exasperated me. She tickled me. She amazed and inspired me. She was an amalgamation that elicited varied conflicting emotions within me. She purposefully would annoy me by putting ragged linens on my bed. This was her way of attempting to humble me. I was always, according to Mama, trying to rise above my rearing.

I learned many vital lessons from her, but the most profitable one which stands out predominately in my memory was an incident with our neighbor about Mama's chickens. It happened during the depression years when nobody had a superfluity of anything. We had a sufficiency of food and never went to bed hungry, but we were the exception to the rule in this regard.

Our next door neighbors complained constantly that our chickens were getting out of the chicken yard and ruining their lawn. We tried everything to restrain them. Closing the door of the fowl-house after our chickens had gone to roost, I chased them out, one by one, as Mama clipped the feathers off one wing. This overbalanced them, and they could not fly over fences. Hoping to stop up the holes, we took scrap pieces of wood and drove them into the ground among the strands of wire fencing. Whatever we did, a few of those chickens always seemed to end up in the neighbor's yard. During the depression years, when providing daily food for a family was a main concern, it simply was not possible or feasible to build a new fence.

Daddy borrowed a car, and we made a trip to bring our paternal grandmother back with us for an extended visit, getting back home just before dark. Lying on the ground in our chicken yard were seventeen dead hens. The neighbors had slipped over while we were away and poisoned our chickens with arsenic, which they had purchased at a local drug store. Those seventeen hens represented seventeen meals of either chicken and dressing or chicken and dumplings, as well as our daily eggs.

The way Mama handled this situation demonstrated to me how Christians should conduct themselves. She disliked throwing food scraps wastefully on the ground; so she asked the people who had been responsible for the killing of the chickens if she could feed the scraps from our table to their chickens. This became Mama's accustomed habit for many years. To me, this was one of the most magnanimous gestures I had ever witnessed. How could Mama forgive such a hostile transgression and return good for evil? Silently, I blessed her for demonstrating so clearly how to incorporate the teachings of the Bible into a person's daily life. She was, in my eyes, the embodiment of the Golden Rule of doing unto others as you would have them do unto you.

When she was eighty-one, Mama died in intensive care from a massive cerebral stroke. Just minutes before her death, she carried on a slurred conversation with my sister and her husband. Mama asked if they knew what a baker's dozen was. In the less avaricious business world of the yesteryears, the baker always put in thirteen doughnuts or cookies, one for good measure, as he did not want to appear too mercenary. Then Mama's speech became more halting and softer, almost a whisper. "I wonder how the old saying of not giving a tinker's damn originated...." I was feeding her jello and chicken broth when she began to cough. I watched the heart monitor. From ninety-two beats a minute, it plummeted in seconds to thirty-six. We were asked to leave as the nurse attempted to revive her. On my way to the waiting room, I turned around for a final look at my beloved mother. There was a faint smile on her face. She would no longer feel excessive heat or cold; she would not have to be lifted and tugged about or fed blended food; she was free at last from pain and suffering. She had worked conscientiously and steadily all her life. She ate no bread of leisurely idleness. She had endured hardships and deprivations, and she had reared a family, often sacrificing her own comforts in order that her children could have more, and I thank God that He gave me such a mother. Lives there another one like her? I wonder.

Salt and Light In the Neighborhood

"The entire law is summed up in a single command: love
your neighbor as yourself."

—Galatians 5:14

> *"The best portion of a good man's life is his little, nameless,*
> *unremembered acts of kindness and of love."*
> —William Wordsworth

A Simple, Uncelebrated Kindness

Eva Marie Everson

It all began with a jar of pickles. As Dave struggled to open the tightly sealed jar he had just taken from his refrigerator, he asked himself, "If, as a young man in my forties, I have difficulty opening a jar of pickles, how much more trouble would I have with it if I were seventy... or eighty...?"

From that thought was born a desire to help the elderly. Not so much with the larger issues that confront senior citizens, but with the little things. After all, there are services that provide the elderly with meals, with transportation to and from medical appointments, with personal care assistance, etc. But who do they call if they simply need a jar of pickles opened?

Dave's heart saw a big picture; an organization headed by himself that would assist with these particular needs. But Dave's reality got in the way: his job demanded almost continual travel for most of the week. His idea would have to wait.

Or would it?

One day, as Dave dragged heavy trash cans to the curb in front of his quiet neighborhood home, he happened to glance over at the house two doors down from his. This home was owned and occupied by Mr. Frieberg, an elderly gentleman rarely seen by the neighbors. Again, Dave asked himself, "As strenuous as this daily job is for me, how much more so if I were Mr. Frieberg?"

Without another thought, Dave strode over to Mr. Frieberg's yard and pulled his heavy trash cans to the curb. Early the next morning, immediately after the city sanitation truck made its rounds and while the rest of the world slumbered on, Dave quietly returned his neighbor's cans to their place before hauling in his own.

Since then, months have passed. Twice a week, when Dave is in town, he performs this ritual. Should he be away, his wife does it for him.

And Mr. Frieberg? Well, Mr. Frieberg doesn't know who is performing these kindnesses. Just who is doing them is not important. The important thing is that he knows that the simple, uncelebrated kindness is being done.

"Have you had a kindness shown? Pass it on." —Henry Burton

Just Pass It On

NINA SNYDER

"You may lose this baby," Dr. Murray told me. "Don't lift anything. You can't do any more ironing or you'll go into premature labor again—and I might not be able to stop it next time."

Although I didn't know how I was going to comply, I agreed to do everything in my power not to risk my unborn baby's life. I left the doctor's office feeling that my world was wobbling off course. When my husband, Tom, came home from work that night, we wrestled with Dr. Murray's warning and what it would mean over the next three months. We could send our fifteen-month-old toddler, Judy, to stay with my parents in Miami for the duration of my pregnancy, but, even so, how could I manage my other responsibilities at home without lifting anything over one pound in weight—shopping, cooking, cleaning, laundry, ironing… ironing.

The ironing dilemma seemed to be unsolvable. No-iron fabric had not been developed yet, and everything came through the wash in a wicked mass of wrinkles. Tom could handle much of my work load, but certainly not all—definitely not the ironing. We couldn't afford to hire anyone. What was I going to do?

"We'll manage," Tom said.

My parents drove up to Orlando the next weekend. After a brief visit, they packed Judy's clothes and as many of her toys as they could fit into their car. I didn't cry until they and Judy drove out of sight. I wouldn't see her again until the baby was born.

A few days later, Tom and I attended a political action meeting. During the break, Cathy, a woman I had recently met, asked me how I was feeling.

"O.K.," I said. Then I told her the problem I'd been having with premature labor. "My first pregnancy lasted seven months and my second pregnancy ended in miscarriage. Now, my doctor says I possibly could lose this baby. Tom is able to take care of much of my work at night and on the weekends, but I still don't have a solution to the ironing problem."

"Oh," Cathy said. "I'll do your ironing for you."

"I can't let you do that," I said. I hardly knew her. How could I expect a stranger to take on such a burden?

"Why not?" she asked. "I'll come over to your house this week and pick up your ironing. When I'm finished with it, I'll return it to you and pick up another load."

"I can't afford to pay you. It's out of the question."

"I don't want you to pay me," she said. "I will do it as unto the Lord."

"Well, I don't know what to say. Thank you." I had no idea what she meant by "as unto the Lord."

And so she came. Every week Cathy picked up a laundry basket of clean but crumpled clothing and exchanged it for a gift of beautifully pressed garments on hangers. Every delivery brought me a fresh wave of guilt.

"How can I ever repay you?" I wailed one day.

"The way you can repay me is to pass it on," she said.

"Pass it on?"

"Yes. I told you that I was doing this for you as unto the Lord. One day you will run into someone who needs a helping hand. Then, you can meet that person's need as unto the Lord."

I still didn't know what "as unto the Lord" meant, but I did understand what she was saying about passing it on.

"That sounds good to me," I said. "But I still wish I could do something for you."

"You will be doing something for me if you'll just pass it on."

A few years later, I entered a new experience with the Word of God. I began to read the Bible as never before, hungrily and with understanding. Then one day, I came across Jesus' words, "If you have done it unto one of these the least of my brethren, you have done it unto me." Ah! Mystery solved. That's what she meant.

And yes, I have encountered several needs where I have been able to lend a helping hand. When they asked me, "How can I ever repay you for your kindness?" I repeated what Cathy told me thirty-five years ago: "Just pass it on."

"The true calling of a Christian is not to do extraordinary things,
but to do ordinary things in an extraordinary way."
—Dean Stanley

Love For Eternity

CARMEN LEAL

My friend Sarah's son, Michael, has emotional problems diagnosed as most closely resembling Attention Deficient Disorder (ADD). Raising a child with Attention Deficient Disorder is difficult enough when there are two committed, loving parents working together. The problems that face single parents trying to cope with ADD children, though, can be more than overwhelming.

It was evident that Michael's behavior and the constant need to arrange for after-school care for him distressed Sarah a lot. I saw she needed help and told her I'd be happy to pick him up from school each Wednesday during the school year and take him to the Awana program at my church. It was out of my way and I did have to rearrange my schedule, but the results were well worth it!

Michael loved Awana. His behavior improved and Sarah knew that for one day a week, she had free childcare on which she could depend. More importantly, Michael invited Jesus into his heart and has begun to tell others about Jesus.

It wasn't a big sacrifice on my part and did not cost me one penny. However, the love that was shown to this family made an impact that will last for eternity.

"No act of kindness, no matter how small, is ever wasted."
—Aesop

Salt and Socks

EVA MARIE EVERSON

"Hey." I heard the voice of my husband from the other side of the bed.

I opened one eye and peered at the digital bedside clock. It was a few minutes past 3 a.m.

"Hey," I returned groggily.

"What are you doing?"

My brow furrowed. "Sleeping?"

"I don't want to worry you or anything...."

I immediately sat up and turned. My spouse of twenty years was lying flat on his back, his eyes fixed on the ceiling. "What's wrong?" I asked anxiously.

"The room is spinning," he said.

The nurse in me rose to the occasion. "When did this start?"

"About a month ago."

"Excuse me?"

"Off and on for about a month."

"I mean, when did it start tonight?"

"About half an hour ago." He swallowed hard. I watched a flash of fear cross his face.

Thirty minutes later I was helping him dress for a trip to the emergency room. I slipped into a pair of jeans and a tee shirt, then stepped into my nearby sandals. Before we left, I ran into the home office and zipped out a prayer request e-mail to all Debbie's Place* recipients.

Hours later, my husband lay on a gurney in a drug-induced

sleep, and I was scrunched in an uncomfortable corner chair, trying to rest my head against the cold metal countertop. I was worried, exhausted, bored, and very cold. A nurse had given me a blanket, but my feet were chilled to the bone because I was wearing sandals.

I closed my eyes briefly but opened them again when I heard movement in the room. Peeping around the doorway was my friend (and recipient of Debbie's Place) Kirstin.

"Hey," I whispered as I rose to greet her. She escorted me to a visitor's area where her husband waited, and we spoke about my husband's condition in hushed tones for a few minutes.

"But what about you?" Kirstin asked softly, in her thick German accent.

"I'm fine," I replied. "Just a little bored, and my feet are cold."

After we said goodbye, I watched them leave through the exit doors before returning to my still sleeping husband. No more than ten minutes later, Kirstin again stood in the doorway, extending a bag from her hand.

"Here," she said with a smile. "We got you some magazines and a couple of pairs of socks."

I was overwhelmed! So many times we ask, "What can I do for you?" without truly expecting an answer. But Kirstin and her husband didn't ask. They saw the need and met it. It was a random act of kindness. It was salt and light.

*For more information about Debbie's Place, see "Salt and Light In Cyberspace."

"There are two ways of spreading light; to be the candle or the mirror that reflects it." —Edith Wharton

Saltines

CAROLYNN J. SCULLY

I had heard from two different friends that I should meet Lynn. Both knew we would become good friends, but the meeting never seemed to come about until we moved to our new home, yet God had planned that our lives should be entwined. We became backyard neighbors and awed at the coincidences that brought us together.

Lynn has four children, two girls and two boys, and at the time, I had two girls. Her youngest son, Brock, is a year younger than my oldest daughter, Erin. She had already walked before me as a mom, and her walk with the Lord's Spirit was years ahead of mine. She became my mentor. I was at her back door whenever questions surfaced or my life seemed to be in a disaster; she consistently turned my eyes to the Lord and our hearts to prayer.

Hospitality seemed to be her gift, though she constantly said she had to work very hard at it. She held weekly Bible studies for women in her home, and her door was always open to anyone dropping by. She loved children, and because of her quick smile, gentle voice, and open arms, they loved her.

Lynn was a saltines and Kool-Aid mom. Whenever children visited her home, she offered saltine crackers as a snack. The children soon learned where the saltines were located and she allowed them freedom to help themselves.

One summer, when Erin was seven and Briget was four, Lynn decided to have a Bible study for the children of the neighborhood. Once a week, they cheerfully toted their Bibles to fellowship with friends, memorize Scripture, get hugs from Lynn, and lots of saltines and Kool-Aid. It wasn't long before their group was known as the "Saltines." Friendships grew and feuds were dissolved through Lynn's faithful teaching and loving that summer.

As the school year loomed ahead, the children begged Lynn not to quit having the Saltines Bible study. She accepted their challenge by challenging them to be responsible—to get themselves to her house early, before school, once a week. When they did, she fed them breakfast, and they feasted on the Word until it was time for hugs, and off to school they would go. Reports from mothers throughout the neighborhood were the same; the children never fussed about the early day, and most were happy to get themselves out the door on "Saltines" day.

Our neighborhood was united because of Lynn and God's presence in her life. It was sad when the time for the Saltines Bible study ended, and even sadder when we had to move. But her salt is still tasted after these many years. I have often desired the gifts she had, but Lynn would be the first to encourage me to be salt and light where God intended, using the gifts He has given to me.

"For me—to have made one soul
The better for my birth;
To have added one flower
To the garden of the earth...." —Edwin Hatch

Diana's Green Thumb Ministry

CARMEN LEAL

"Hi, Darlin'. You mind if I plant some flowers 'round your tree?" Diana's honey-sweet voice called as I walked back from the mailbox.

"Oh, that's fine, Diana. Whatever you want. I just don't have any money for flowers."

How could I think about flowers when I was worrying about unpaid medical bills and car payments? We live in a pleasant subdivision, and as much as I want to keep my yard looking attractive, I don't have the time, tools, or energy to make it a priority.

"Oh, don't bother about money. Your yard will look nicer when I'm done."

I went about my routine and didn't think more about the yard. Diana is exactly the sort of neighbor we all remember while growing up—and who is next to impossible to find in the suburbia of the nineties. She moved from Dallas a year before, and believes her ministry is the neighborhood.

No sooner had she moved in, Diana began walking the subdivision, learning about the families in each of the 197 homes. Along with learning names, ages, jobs, and hobbies, came the prayer requests. Diana began to pray for the neighborhood with the goal of winning Remington Oaks for Christ.

She ran for the Neighborhood Board, a thankless job

nobody really wants to do, and began to make a difference. Soon she had pinpointed all the Christians and had them praying for those in need, too. It wasn't long before people—including non-Christians—began calling Diana with their prayer requests.

Diana, a lover of beauty, delights in the outdoors. An offer of a few flowers soon grew to shrub-pulling, hedge-clipping, and trimming trees. Eventually, Diana started to cut my grass, since I didn't own a lawn mower. She even talked my neighbor, Keith, into cutting my grass when he did his.

As I've been known to kill even silk plants, I find someone who enjoys yard work an enigma. My yard isn't the only one to benefit from her tender care, either. Diana goes from house to house, doing what she does best—getting to know people, praying for them, and making yards beautiful. Definitely, Diana's ministry is to beautify the neighborhood with grace and good will.

As I see Diana scurrying about with a pair of clippers tucked under one arm—all four-foot-eleven of her—I know God is hard at work in Remington Oaks via Diana's "green thumb" ministry.

"Gratitude is the fairest blossom which springs from the soul."
—Henry Ward Beecher

I Thank Thee, God

BARBARA PUGH

"I thank Thee, God, for loving souls
Who help us to attain our goals;
The ones who with kind word or deed
Buoy up our spirit, meet our need
To talk of things both great and slight;
For these I thank Thee, God, tonight."

Salt and Light In Friendship

"A *friend loves at all times*." —Proverbs 17:17

"A friend is someone who makes me feel totally acceptable."
—Ene Riisna

Friendship

CAROLYNN J. SCULLY

True Friendships
Reap Lasting Rewards worth
Security, love, intimacy, and growth.
Friends care, Encourage, listen, and
Tenderly touch a deep Need in our soul; so that
We can Dream and reach
For the Success that
Seems Hopeless, yet,
Because of the Insistence of a friend,
We Persevere.

"Jesus made it clear that the most important thing in the world is our relationship to God and others. When we achieve that, everything good will follow." —Norman Vincent Peale

Dear Tash

A LETTER BY KATIE L. DAVIS

As I sit here reflecting back, I can't recall ever thanking you. How could such a thing have gone unrecognized and unrewarded? You saved my life. Yet I can't remember ever once saying the simple words, "Thank you."

I know I'm truly lucky to have a friend who cared as much as you, and I know I didn't make it easy. I remember all the times you invited me to church, and I remember all the excuses I came up with to avoid going. So why was it that I finally accepted your invitation that morning? I'll tell you.

You always seemed to have everything in your life figured out—or at least things weren't forever falling apart around you. You exuded a calmness and security that I admired. I never knew exactly where you got it, but I knew you had it.

Then there was the way you talked about church and the others in the youth group. You sounded like you were from a totally different world than the one I was in, but still, I admired it. However, the one fear that kept me inside my world was the one that kept me outside yours: I had a deep fear that if I walked through the doors of the church, everyone inside would see right through me. They'd see the things I'd done and turn me away. The world I was in at the time accepted me the way I was; the way they had made me. Just the simple fear that yours wouldn't kept me away.

So I went on living my life in the dark, watching you live yours in the sunlight and always wondering if that sunlight would someday be mine. I knew "the way," because you'd shown it to me many times, but it wasn't until that morning that I finally decided to take it. I remember it well.

Everyone was so nice. No one seemed to look down on me, even if they could see right through me. No one cast me out because I wasn't just the same as they were. They accepted me, but not in a way I'd ever been accepted before. It wasn't because I was like them. I was accepted because I was myself.

So I kept going back, enjoying the sunlight I'd so often admired and longed for. Then I made the best decision of my life. I chose to accept Jesus Christ as my Lord and Savior, and to receive the gift of eternal life. I was saved, and I owed it all to you. So, now as I look back and realize I never thanked you for it, I'm sorry it took me so long.

Thank you from the bottom of my heart for caring enough about me to bring me out of the darkness and into the sunlight. I love you.

Katie L. Davis

"We ourselves feel that what we are doing is just a drop in the ocean. But the ocean would be less because of that missing drop."
—Mother Teresa

The Cereal and Milk Miracle

CARMEN LEAL

As a single mom, I panicked every month when bill paying time reared its ugly head. How could I spread so little money so far? It was routine for my children to preface each request for whatever they wanted or needed to buy with, "Mom, I know you don't have the money but..." and I grew increasingly frustrated at having to say no.

I vividly remember one harried day. Everything that could go wrong went wrong from the moment I awoke. That afternoon, I heard the phone ringing as I rolled into the driveway, so I dashed into the house to answer it. It was Melanie, my friend from Los Angeles.

"What are you doing at 4:12 this afternoon?" she asked.

"Going crazy, trying to figure out what to fix for dinner," I retorted.

"Why not meet the 4:12 American Airlines flight from L.A.? There's a box on it for you. Gotta run, call you later."

"Great!" I grumbled. "That's the middle of rush hour. I can't wait...." I continued my tirade as I fought peak traffic, weaving in and out of the lanes in a vain attempt to make good time, all the way trying to figure out what could possibly be in that box. All I knew was, whatever it contained, it was not going to solve my immediate problems.

Somehow the snail-paced traffic moved and we made it to our destination, where I squeezed into a "no loading" space and dashed into the baggage section. My frustration mounted as the conveyer belt went round and round with luggage of every size, shape, and description and not one box in sight. One minute became five, then five became ten until finally, at long last, seventeen long minutes of unfruitful scrutiny paid off. I spotted the box.

As I fought through the crowd to claim my box, I saw three more identical boxes following the first one. There were four of them, all labeled in Melanie's precise handwriting. Instead of being thankful for the additional boxes, I was enraged. How did she think I could fit four huge boxes into my car? I continued mumbling and complaining with each trip from the carousel to the car. After repositioning the boxes umpteen times, I was ready to explode.

We began the arduous journey home. I listened in growing annoyance to the children's pleas to open the box, interspersed with their demands to stop at McDonald's, for the entire trip. We were all tired and hungry and I had not a clue what to do for dinner.

The boys tumbled out of the car and each struggled to carry

in a box. Then, using the sharpest implement I could find in a drawer full of dull kitchen utensils, I opened the first box. I stared as the children whooped with joy. Cereal. Boxes and boxes of cereal. After lugging the remaining boxes into the house, I gazed in growing consternation at what seemed to be the contents of a small convenience store on my living room floor. I listened to the squeals of delight emanating from the children and wondered what on earth had prompted Melanie to send all this stuff. Half of this stuff was sugar laden. Why not take an IV needle and just shoot sugar into their veins? How was I going to store all this in Hawaii's humid climate? Where was I going to get the money to buy milk for the cereal?

Continuing to mutter under my breath, I frantically tried to stop the boys from opening all the cereal as they looked for hidden prizes. Yes, I realized that with cereal so expensive in Hawaii it was probably worth a mint. But it did not solve my dinner predicament.

I was at my wit's end when the phone rang and Melanie explained that triple coupon days had allowed her to buy all of this for less than ten dollars. I thanked her as enthusiastically as I could while silently I begged God to explain Himself. Just how did this solve my dinner problems?

Just then I heard a car braking outside, looked out and saw my friend Barbara.

"I can't stay," she said. "I'm in a hurry. I just went to the Foodbank and am on my way home. My boys are allergic to this and I thought maybe you could use it."

She opened the door and there, displayed on the car seat, were four gallons of milk. As I gaped at the milk, I began to laugh.

I realized God had answered my prayers and did know my every need! As a bonus, the box was filled with other packaged foods previously on the "I'm sorry, it's too expensive" list. I thought about what a whiner I'd been the entire day; how miserable I'd made everyone as I ruminated on my own disappointments and trials. Despite that, He was still providing for me. Barbara does not get milk every time she goes to the Foodbank. God guided both her and Melanie to be a part of His plan for my life.

I don't think I adequately said "thank you" to either one of those dear friends. God can, and does use people and things all around us to show His provision. Who would think that something as simple as cereal and milk would make such a difference in my life? He never comes through with half a plan; it is always complete. Sometimes we just need to wait on Him. I took the time to explain the significance of the cereal and milk to the children. I don't know whether or not they understood then, but either way, I am convinced they will in the future.

"No one is useless in this world who lightens the burden of it for anyone else." —Charles Dickens

Cake Walk

MARGIE BERRY

My neighbor of sixteen years—more like a sister than a neighbor—picked me up every Wednesday night so we could ride together to our weekly prayer meeting at church. We used this time as "our time" together, because though she lived next door, we both had full-time jobs and little time to visit. We confided things to each other during those rides that we told no one else.

On July 8, 1987, she picked me up and we attended our weekly prayer meeting as usual. Afterward, we sat in her car in my driveway and chatted awhile. When our visit was over, I got out, exiting the right front passenger seat and crossing in front of her car, parked directly behind mine. She started her car just as I stepped between them. Out of the corner of my eye, I saw her car reverse about a foot, then suddenly shoot forward, and then it slammed into me. In fact, it pushed my Ford LTD seventeen feet, with me caught between the bumpers of the cars. I was pinned by my legs.

I remember the sound of her engine, revved up in full throttle.

I felt no pain, no panic. But I do remember calling out to her, "Stop! Stop!" My friend was terribly distressed. She helped me lay down on the driveway before calling an ambulance and another neighbor of ours. I knew my left leg was broken but I had no idea of the extent of my injuries. I learned later that the bone was crushed just below the knee. My physical therapist at Bulloch Memorial Hospital in Statesboro, Georgia, told me the bone looked like a bowl of corn flakes.

I was taken by ambulance to Screven County Hospital in Sylvania, Georgia, where my leg was stabilized and put into a temporary support. That was when I felt the first pain. My screams could be heard out in the hall. I was then taken to Bulloch Memorial, about twenty-three miles away. I remember an EMT named Gary (God bless him!) who sat in the ambulance with me to comfort me and give me moral support.

Immediately, they took me into surgery, where large, open wounds in both legs were sutured. It was a miracle of miracles that there was so little bleeding from those huge lacerations. The right leg had to be sutured almost completely around, except for about two inches—but the bone was not even fractured... another miracle! The left leg was, of course, put into a cast.

The next day, the pain in my left leg was awful, and I was sick from the anesthesia. My neighbor sat with me all night and most of the next day.

On Monday, July 13th, my oldest son's birthday, my orthopedic doctor, Dr. Loveless, decided I needed to return to surgery so that a rod could be placed inside the crushed bone to stabilize it while it healed. So, back to surgery I went. It was there that I had a stroke; a stroke no one was aware of until much later. I have no memory of the next four days, but my dear friend Betty tells me that I would beg her, "Pray, Betty! Pray!" My subconscious was apparently working. When I finally regained total consciousness, even I did not realize anything was wrong. I suppose this was because there had already been so much trauma, one more catastrophe went unnoticed—for a while. It was my family and friends who began to realize that I was not using my left side, that something was terribly wrong. Surprisingly, the hospital staff said I was just having difficulty coming out of the anesthesia!

Finally, they admitted that something wasn't quite right, and tests revealed that I had suffered a stroke. It was determined that I had no use of my left hand and, of course, my left leg was in a heavy cast. They also realized that the left side of my face drooped slightly. For the next five weeks, I remained at BMH and therapy was started. After that, I was transferred to Candler General Hospital's stroke re-hab unit in Savannah, where I spent six weeks undergoing intense therapy. I learned to get around in a wheelchair. I learned to bathe and dress myself. All the things I'd taken for granted I had to re-learn, but this time using only one hand. I found many friends among the patients and staff; some in much worse condition than I. We lost several to death during my stay there. The memories are mostly unpleasant; adjusting to a new and different lifestyle after a stroke is not easy.

One of my greatest needs was clothes that I could manage, and I found that skirts and blouses were the easiest. When Bobbie Joyner, a long-time friend of mine from school days, heard that I needed more skirts and blouses, she went to one of our town's better boutiques and purchased several for me. She would take nothing but a "thank you" in return.

After my stay in Candler, I returned home and waited another three weeks before my cast could be removed, which was another miracle; originally I was told I would have to wear it for nine months. After it was removed, I went back to the rehab unit for three additional weeks to complete my therapy. I was released only after I was able to do well enough at home and to manage with the help of family members. My youngest son, the only one living at home with me, really came through for me then and is still doing so now. More people than I could mention supported me. For instance, my friend Nell came to visit me in BMH during those long five weeks with a vase of fresh, multi-colored roses from her garden. I remember how beautiful they were and how they always lifted my spirit. And in spite of caring for a handicapped husband and working a full-time job, Bobbie came over to assist me with my baths after I was released from the hospital. She even mopped my kitchen floor!

The Wednesday of my accident, I had unknowingly worked my last day at Torrington. This posed another problem; not being able to ever go back to work meant no income. As a single mother, I had a house to run and bills to pay. That's when Charlie Lee, who also worked at Torrington and is a great cake baker, together with his wife, Linda, organized a bake sale at Torrington to raise money for me. They asked the employees to bake or buy a cake or to donate money if they preferred. They raised $1,500.00 for me and kept a list of what everyone had done to help. I've been told that Charlie baked twenty cakes for the sale. They will always be in my heart for their unselfish generosity, and my prayer is that God richly blesses them!

I am a firm believer that nothing happens by chance if you are God's child. He allowed this to happen to me for my good, and there has been a lot of good, and for His glory.* I give Him all the glory and credit for all the lessons I've learned through this, and for my greater dependence on Him. This alone has been worth all the trauma, pain, and despair I've experienced.

*Romans 8:28

"For memory has painted this perfect day with colors that never fade, and at the end of the day we find the soul of a friend we have made." —Carrie Jacobs Bond

The Most Special

CINDY SAILING

There are certain friends who, in their quiet ways, are the most special of all friends. I have had such friends in my life, and still have several. One came to the funeral home when my husband died. She was there every morning when I arrived and stayed until I left. She sat the entire time with my son, Jonathon, and occupied him so that I would be free to talk and visit with friends and family.

I'm not sure I ever told her how much that meant to me. Some people just know the right things to do in a difficult situation. They do them and don't even think twice about it. Maybe they are our angels here on earth that God sends to help us—just when we need them most.

"In prosperity, our friends know us; in adversity, we know our friends." —John Churton Collins

An Unexpected Reaction

CARMEN LEAL

I hated my parent's divorce. This was just one more reason why. My mom could no longer afford Catholic school, and now everything was ruined. Instead of graduating from eighth grade with the friends I'd had since I was six, this year I had to go to public school with strangers. It wasn't fair, and I was determined to hate the new school and everybody there.

My vow of loneliness dissolved when, on the first day, I met Eileen.* She was pretty and dressed with the understated confidence of someone accustomed to having money. I, on the other hand, made do with much less, and besides, we'd all worn uniforms at my other school. But the disparity in our backgrounds never made a difference. Eileen and I had many common interests; we even sang in the school choir together. We giggled and talked together in such a way that it was like I'd known her even longer than my old friends. Eileen's popularity helped open doors that might have remained firmly shut to me in the adolescent world of cliques. Before I had time to think about it, I felt as if I'd always attended this junior high.

One day, Eileen announced she was having a slumber birthday party. Being invited to this party, given by such a popular girl, was exciting and signaled acceptance. Besides the snacks, I needed a sleeping bag, a pillow, and a multitude of other teenage "musts," including make-up. I can still see the pristine white cotton lace ruffle around the neck of the most beautiful pajamas ever; brand new, petal pink baby dolls.

Finally, the momentous Friday evening arrived. I chattered nonstop as we drove the few blocks to her house. I bounced out of the old car and scrambled up the long walkway to ring the bell, then waited impatiently, clutching my worn, shiny blue sleeping bag to my chest, for what I was sure was going to be a great party.

When Eileen's mom opened the door, she radiated perfection. The pleats in her dress were flawless, and every hair was in place. But the smile on her lips did not quite reach her eyes. I was surprised by her lack of warmth, because at our school concert she had smiled and even commented on my lovely voice. Tonight, however, something was different.

With a quizzical coolness, she glanced at my bright, shining face. "Eileen can't come out this evening. She and her friends are having a birthday sleepover."

"I know about the party," I interrupted. "Eileen invited me." I held out the wrapped present as evidence, an admission ticket of sorts.

A sickening silence descended as the pinched smile faded from her lips. In its place was a cold, questioning look. She insisted I could come tomorrow, but not tonight. Had I imagined the friendship and the invitation? A queasy stomach followed my unstoppable tears.

"Mom, hurry up," Eileen impatiently called as her mother delayed. Before her mother answered, Eileen rounded the corner and stood in the doorway. She had only to look at my tear-ful expression to see there was a problem.

"Mom, what's wrong?" she questioned. Her exasperated sigh and the gripping of her fists told me this was not the first time there had been a run-in between mother and daughter. My defeated posture and downcast expression made her mother's answer redundant.

"Carmen is here to visit," she explained. "I told her to come back tomorrow because you're having a party."

An embarrassed crimson flooded Eileen's face as she nervously glanced at me. "I invited Carmen to my party, Mom. She's my friend, and I want her here." I stood mortified as the discussion continued.

"This is a sleepover," replied her mother in hushed tones. "I can't have a colored girl sleep in our home." I could not believe what I was hearing. A colored girl!

Why did the color of my skin matter? I had excellent manners, I wasn't going to do anything wrong, and besides, Eileen was my best friend.

In an act of ultimate defiance and unparalleled friendship, Eileen firmly stood her ground. "Carmen is my friend. If she can't stay, no one stays. I won't have my party without her."

I couldn't believe what I was hearing. She was willing to cancel her birthday party on my behalf! A look of consternation passed over her mother's face and I saw it harden into a set mask. "All right. If that's want you want, go tell the girls."

There are times when words are pointless. I choked with gratitude at this display of friendship. One by one, the girls quietly assembled under the cold, moonless sky to await their parents. I was suddenly nervous that the blame for the catastrophic end to the planned festivities would fall on my fragile shoulders. As Eileen and her mother argued inside the upper middle class home, I sat alone, while the other girls spoke in whispers, glancing my way from time to time. One by one, we left the wide porch, burdened with our thoughts as well as our gear, and slipped quietly into the waiting cars.

By Monday, the aborted birthday party and the reason for its occurrence, were the main topics of conversation. Most of my so-called friends looked through me and acted as though I didn't exist.

The intense hurt took a long time to heal. Whenever I saw Eileen's mother, a mix of emotions stirred confusion within. As junior high ended and we continued our educational journey, Eileen and I remained close, despite, or perhaps because of, her mother. Eileen's behavior exhibited a maturity far beyond her age. And her living example of true friendship taught me, as probably nothing else could, the value of "a friend." I hope I learned my lesson well, that I have returned her friendship in kind, and that I have been a friend of such quality to others. After all, wasn't it Emerson who said, "The only way to have a friend is to be one"?

*Name changed

"A true friend unbosoms freely, advises justly, assists readily, adventures boldly, takes all patiently, defends courageously, and continues a friend unchangeably." —William Penn

The Gift

CARMEN LEAL

Susan is from a small town close to London, England. I began writing to Susan when we were thirteen. She was one of over fifty pen pals I corresponded with while in school. Somehow, over the years I have lost track of my international cadre of friends. Demands of marriage, children, and careers have caused us to drift apart. My relationship with Susan, though, has endured all of the changes in my life and has enriched it in incredible ways.

For over thirty years we have shared successes and tragedies alike. We have giggled through our first boyfriend stage and cried with each other over the injustices of relationships. Susan has been my sounding board on every issue imaginable. She knows more about me than anyone else. We have traded viewpoints on politics, culture, music, movies, and life in general.

She has walked with me through my marriage and divorce, reentering the dating world, and has experienced my second marriage. Now she is with me as I watch my second husband decline and look into the future as a widow. She has gone with me through my pregnancies and childbirths and parenting. She has seen foreign countries through my eyes as I have through hers, and she has rejoiced in my victories and wept in despair at my disappointments. She has seen me at my highest and my lowest. She has truly been a special friend to me, and I hope I have been the same to her.

Susan has also witnessed my life-altering transformations from passive believer in God to non-believer to a woman on fire for God. When my first marriage ended, she saw God as my husband. She has seen Him as my father, and has also vicariously experienced my intense friendship with Him. She has come to understand that though the longevity of our relationship far outweighs that of my relationship with God, our friendship can never bring me the joy and security that I experience with God.

A few years ago, when little by little I began to share this spiritual relationship with Susan, I could tell from the questions and answers that sped through the mail that the interest was there. As letters became phone calls, I felt a growing frustration at not being able to share my faith with my dear friend, face to face.

Susan and I had spoken over the years of her coming to Hawaii to visit. Months turned into years and still she never came. We had met each other on three separate occasions, but it was sixteen years since the last of those trips.

My husband, David, has never travelled to another country. Our dream was to spend our fifth wedding anniversary enjoying the beauty and history of Europe while seeing friends from my past. With David's diagnosis, I decided what to do with the free mileage being stockpiled at the airlines we frequented. I realized that if I wanted Susan to accept Jesus as her personal Savior, I could not depend on a faceless person in England to make the introduction. I knew that Susan lived in a Godless void, and I knew that only by talking with her face to face could I introduce her to my Best Friend.

Susan was overwhelmed by my offer of an airline ticket to Hawaii. She could not believe such generosity. She knew I had many uses for those 40,000 miles and yet, there I was, offering them to her.

The days crawled by as I waited for her arrival. The interminable wait for Susan added to the pain as David was diagnosed with Huntington's on our third anniversary, and I went through the motions of working and taking care of the financial and household details. Somehow, the days crept along until, finally, I was at the airport gate awaiting her flight.

The years disappeared as I saw her alight from the gateway; she was just as I remembered with her sweet smile and gentle spirit. My heart was elated to have her with me at this precise time. Susan had shared my entire life as a teenager and adult thousands of miles away. Now, during my greatest challenge, when I was at my lowest, she was here. I knew I could cry and speak my unspoken thoughts to Susan. God had truly given me the most wonderful gift imaginable in having Susan come within weeks of learning of David's disease.

When she arrived in Hawaii, she had no idea how much having her there would mean to me. To this day, the hours of conversation as we lay sprawled across her bed in the bed & breakfast are a highlight of her trip. The laughter and tears are a poignant remembrance. Helping her to discover and enjoy Hawaii, along with my family, was truly special. Susan became an even more important part of my life than ever as she experienced my family and friends, my church, Bible study, and various ministries I was involved in.

At my church, Susan saw freshness, a concept she wasn't used to, in a group of Christians committed to helping each other. She witnessed first hand the many people who gave of their time and money to support David and me, showing God's love and caring through His people. The Bible was made alive for her through the teachings of the pastor. I was especially delighted when Susan got to hear me share a message at a small hotel service and listened to me sing on Waikiki Beach with hundreds of other tourists. She began to understand that for me, God is not something kept in a box for Sunday, but He is my constant companion. She saw how every situation is a precious opportunity to share my faith with others.

When friends found out that I had given her the ticket, they could not understand why I would give away something of such value. I explained to Susan and others that nothing on this earth has any lasting value. Only where we will spend eternity really matters. I knew that I had to give Susan a gift that would last a lifetime, a blueprint for a church once she returned to England. I wanted so many things for this visit; I wanted her to hear messages of substance; I wanted to answer every question she had, and I wanted to pray for her while she was here.

Our three weeks flew by too quickly, and all too soon I was again airport bound. I knew we would return to our old ways of communicating as the weeks turned into years. But I also knew the cords that bound us together had been strengthened. And best of all, I knew that she had seen a Jesus that really lives inside me. She constantly commented on my strength and bravery in dealing with David. I assured her it was only through Christ in me that I could be brave and strong.

I wish I could say that I led her to Christ; that when she stepped on the plane she was assured of where she would spend eternity. I do know that I gave her the greatest gift ever—I gave her the knowledge of a God who loves her so much He sent His Son to die for her. In return, she gave me the gift of her friendship. I pray for her that she will, if she has not already, accept the gift. I am selfish enough to know that, having spent the past thirty years as her friend, I want to be her friend forever. So does God.

> *"If you judge people, you have no time to love them."*
> —Mother Teresa of Calcutta

In His Eyes

ROBERT DIACHEYSN, JR.

There are moments of catharsis in every life. Fortunately for us, God's grace exists to afford us the opportunity to learn... to accept our faults and, in humility, to change.

I was a wild and rowdy twenty-year-old, much more like a teenager than a young man. I spent the majority of my time doing plays and socializing with a youth theater troupe associated with our local church. They were a great bunch of kids, mostly well mannered, church going, "good Catholics." It was in this troupe that I met my friend Donald, a talented actor and one of the funniest people I know. We became quite a comedy team on stage as well as at parties.

I was sitting on top of my little world, starring in and directing excellent plays with a bunch of guys I loved. I was popular, considered funny and cool, a natural leader. It was at a cast party that I was to learn just where it was I was "leading" people.

Sally was a young, impressionable girl of sixteen. Nobody was quite sure how she had heard about us, she just sort of showed up one day. Theater, like the church, has a tendency to attract the outcasts of society. It's a place where differences are accepted, sometimes even applauded. Sally was a little slow developmentally. She had a hard time making friends, and so, she decided that we would be her new group of friends. We had made no such decision.

At first, we tried to avoid her, to convince her that there was no job for her, to give her false rehearsal dates. Next, we took to teasing her, calling her names like, "Gum on the shoe," because you couldn't shake her off. But, no matter what we did, she just kept coming back. So, we put her to work as a script girl and eventually accepted her as part of the group. She did, however, continue to occupy the role of "group joke." We teased her endlessly behind her back or directly to her face, and the poor girl was either so dense or so desperate to fit in that she laughed along with us.

At the time of the cast party, she had recently been saddled with the nickname: "Jello." This was a cruel stab at her weight problem. I and several others had convinced one of the moms to make a large Jell-o mold to serve as a joke. When the dessert was served, we were all in hysterics and Sally was in the dark, obviously confused. Being the ring leader, I stood up and tried to convince her to have some. She said she didn't like Jell-o. I don't know if she was telling the truth or if she had sensed the ridicule. I continued to prod her and shoot out one-liners to the raucous delight of my peers. I felt like the funniest guy alive.

I looked around for my friend Donald who usually shared with me in these moments. Don had recently become a Christian, and although he still had his sense of humor, he had turned, at times, strangely pensive. I scanned the room and spotted him sitting quietly in the corner, a look of tremendous hurt on his face.

He lifted his head and looked directly into my eyes. In that moment, I knew how Peter must have felt when he looked into Jesus' eyes after denying him three times. In his eyes, I saw sorrow and disappointment, suffering and compassion, not just for Sally... but for me as well. In Donald's eyes, I saw into His eyes and I understood....

I grew quiet and very pale. I sat down shamefully and did not joke for the rest of that night. Not a word had passed and yet the loudest lesson I had ever learned had been spoken. In my heart, the truth had been heard. Something in me changed that night. Oh, I still have a sense of humor, I still laugh and joke, even tease a little (playfully) now and then, but... I had to give my humor to God for I did not have the compassion to use it properly. Without compassion, humor can be a dangerous thing.

Do you want to hear something funny? Sally and I became great friends. We even gave our lives to the Lord together a few months later—walked up to the altar hand in hand. I don't think I'd have had the courage to go up without her. She's a very brave soul, Sally. We're still friends. She got married last year and she and her husband came to visit us on their honeymoon.

And Donald? He's a pastor up in New Jersey, quite a humorous one I hear.

As for the rest of the people at that party, the ones I was so desperate to entertain and be accepted by, I couldn't tell you where one of them is right now. Life's kind of funny that way... isn't it?

*"If we had no winter, the spring would not be so pleasant:
if we did not sometimes taste of adversity, prosperity would not
be so welcome."* —Anne Bradstreet

Grasshopper

Eva Marie Everson

The grasshopper rested on the outside window ledge, basking in the warm sunshine. Periodically, his wings quivered in the gentle breeze. I intently watched him from my office chair throughout the morning.

Near noon, as the January wind began to increase, the grasshopper was stirred from his resting place. As he inched his way up the tempered glass, I noticed that one of his back legs was missing.

His antenna worked furiously, guiding him. Inch by inch, push by push, with only five legs and the wind force against him, he reached his goal. A while later, satisfied with his victory, he returned to the ledge.

I was immediately reminded of a time, six years earlier, in the lives of my husband, our children, and myself. We had moved to Florida eight months previously to take advantage of a business opportunity for my husband. At the time of the move, it seemed like a most wonderful gift from God. Eight months later, it seemed like a curse from the enemy.

On August 2, 1993, my husband and I stared at a letter that informed us that everything we'd put our "faith" in had been a farce. In a moment that is difficult to describe, our lives changed forever, as did our social position. We went from feeling as though we had the world by the tail, to realizing that everything we had worked so hard for would soon slip through our fingers.

In all honesty, I don't think we truly realized the full impact of the situation. Within months, we saw our savings drained, we cashed in our life insurance policies and IRAs, we sold some of our possessions, and moved into a small, two-bedroom apartment with space a fraction of where we had been living a year earlier. We filed for bankruptcy, hoping that doing so would be sufficient until we could get back on our feet. And finally, in our darkest hour, we requested governmental assistance—welfare and food stamps.

The minutes of every day stretched out like hot, listless summer afternoons. I was keenly aware of every breath I took. Though today I ask God to keep me from ever going through another experience like that again, this was the time of my life when incredible miracles took place.

My husband and I had always been the "givers." I am not speaking just in terms of tithing, but in giving to those we saw who were in need. Previously, I assumed that receiving a gift was easy. It's not. It's uncomfortably humbling. There were many days when I would walk to our mailbox, praying to God, asking Him how we were going to make rent, or pay our electric bill. I would nearly collapse to my knees when I found an unexpected check given to help us meet our needs. There were times when I stood before the open refrigerator, staring into its white vacantness. "Lord," I prayed. "Exactly what are the plans for dinner tonight? We have no food. Yet, You said Your seed would never be forsaken or beg for bread. What would you have me do here?" Before I could close the door and turn to leave the narrow kitchen, the phone would ring. "Just wanted to see if you were free for dinner tonight. We're buying," said the caller. It happened time and again.

One afternoon, a friend called and asked if she could come over. I sensed by the tone of her voice that she had an agenda.

"Certainly," I answered.

When she arrived, we sat side by side on the sofa. She shared with me that she had recently been "blessed" financially. "I wanted to share part of it with you," she continued as she slipped a sealed envelope toward me. I was speechless, but words weren't necessary.

With all the miracles—too numerous to list in this limited space—there is one that stands above them all: the miracle that took place inside my heart. Never had I clung to the Word of God as I did during that trial. Never had I felt His comforting hand on my shoulder as I felt it then. I felt His wisdom growing inside me, forming me to be what He had always desired of me.

The defining moment came one brisk, winter's morning. Weeks earlier I had seen an outfit in a boutique window that just had my name all over it. Oh, how I wanted it! It was me! A year earlier, I'd have just bought it and thought nothing of it. But at this time, I didn't have enough to shop at a thrift store, much less an upscale boutique. That morning I saw the wife of my husband's nemesis wearing the outfit. I cried all the way home, begging God to explain this to me.

"Isn't it enough that I'm down on my knees? Does life have to kick me in the gut, too?" I cried in my agony.

I nearly ran into our apartment. As I bolted the door behind me, the phone rang. It was my dear, dear friend Donald. "Hey, honey," he greeted me in his usual way. "Listen, I don't know why, but God has impressed on me to tell you this. It doesn't matter what you drive, where you live, how much money you have, or *what clothes you wear*. What matters is that you trust Him."

This was more than just a moment of truth for me. It was the ultimate act of salt and light in my life. Donald received a message meant for him to give to me, and he followed through with what God told him to do. It was the message I needed to change my heart. From that moment, wounded and battered like the grasshopper, I turned my faith upward and began the road toward perfection.

No, no. I won't achieve it in this lifetime. But I'm on the road. I'm going toward my destination. With my face to the wind, I can see the prize.

Now I know, I really know, what this "salt and light" thing is all about. And, by the way, the move was a most wonderful gift of God. I lost a lot. But, oh! Look what I gained!

Salt and Light In Life

"For this reason... we have not stopped praying for you and asking God to fill you with the knowledge of His will through spiritual wisdom and understanding. And we pray this in order that you may live a life worthy of the Lord and may please Him in every way: bearing fruit in every good work...."

—Colossians 1:9-10

*"Loving a child doesn't mean giving in to all his whims;
to love him is to bring out the best in him, to teach him to love
what is difficult."* —Nadia Boulanger

ᴐ Can

EVA MARIE EVERSON

I was the quintessential "I can't" child; the poster child for the advancement of the word, "can't." Whatever my mother told or asked me to do was immediately followed by my whining, "I caaaaan't." Consequently, very few tasks or goals that I set out to accomplish were ever completed.

"I want you to read this article," Mother began. "It's about Marlo Thomas. She tells how a simple poem that she was forced to learn by her father changed her life. She went from saying, 'I can't,' to 'I can!' According to this article, she was able to restructure her life, and eventually her career, by learning the principles in the poem."

Sensing a conspiracy between Marlo Thomas and my mother, I took the small magazine from Mother and looked down at the glossy pages. There was Marlo, looking perky and adorable. Her smile was radiant and her trademark shoulder-flip hair was styled to perfection. I thought it must be grand to be Marlo! Beside her photo was the poem my mother had spoken of; a simple poem entitled, "I Can."

"I want you to memorize that poem," Mother said firmly.

"Mamaaaaa," I belly-ached. "I can't learn that poem. It's too loooong."

"It's not too long, and yes, you can learn it. I want you to know it perfectly by this time tomorrow."

One does not say "no" to my mother. She coined the phrase,

"When I tell you to jump you ask how high." She was the Queen of Dogwood Drive. I adored her, but this was going too far!

I slumped my shoulders, turned, and trudged my way back to my bedroom with the magazine loosely held in my small right hand. With a heavy heart, I plopped on my bed, fell back against the cotton spread, and began my task. "Can't is a word that is foe to ambition," I began. I repeated the line. I repeated it again and again until it held firm in my heart. "An enemy ambush to shatter your will...." I continued the process until the following evening, when I proudly recited the poem that has continued to be my motto.

Ms. Thomas did not know me, but her story forever changed my life. Saying, "I can," helped me to survive the worst moments of my life. Saying, "I can," encouraged me to accomplish things I would have otherwise seen as out of my reach. A simple poem learned at seven is a poem that will sustain me to seventy-seven. Maybe even longer.

I Can

Can't is the word that is foe to ambition,
An enemy ambushed to shatter your will;
Its prey is forever the man with a mission
And bows but to courage and patience and skill.
Hate it, with hatred that's deep and undying,
For once it is welcomed 'twill break any man;
Whatever the goal you are seeking, keep trying
And answer this demon by saying: "I *can*."

—From a poem by Edgar A. Guest

"The best use of life is to spend it for something that outlasts life."
—William James

Miss Mary, A Life Well Lived

MABEL WILKINSON

On May 5, 1898, in Fredonia, Kentucky, Mrs. Alexander (Rosa) Hamilton gave birth to a baby girl whom she named Mary. Rosa's frail health caused doctors to advise against having other children, so Mary was therefore reared as the only child of a happy couple. Mr. Hamilton was the owner of three hundred acres of farm land, growing an abundance of apples. The small but complete family attended New Bethel Baptist Church, a rural church near their home in Fredonia.

Mary's mother taught her in her early years. She attended high school in Fredonia, and was persuaded by a cousin to attend college with her at Tennessee College for Girls in Murphreesboro. She traveled to the college by train and began her pursuit of a music degree.

Photographs in an old, worn album attest to her "fun" years. She fondly remembers her music teacher, Mr. John Nash, and a class trip taken by train to Washington, D.C., for the inauguration of Woodrow Wilson in 1913. Mary says that these were the happiest days of her life.

One of Mary's roommates was Mattilee Craig, from Louisburg, Tennessee. Mattilee's mother, a seamstress, sometimes sewed identical dresses for the girls, one of which Mary remembers as being especially dear. It was an ankle length, blue satin dress.

Mary completed college in 1919 and returned to Fredonia, to the home of her parents. A short time later, she received a letter from a college roommate, Tyra Stanley, of Collins, Georgia, telling her of the need for a music teacher in nearby Glennville. When Mary applied for the job and was hired, sight unseen, she promptly packed her trunk, boarded the train alone, and made the long ride to Glennville.

Once there, she looked for a place to board. She soon found a room in the home of Joseph and Lena Grice, a young lawyer and his wife. The Grices attended the Glennville Baptist Church and, as was proper, the young Mary continued in her church attendance with the Grices every week.

It was there that she met Mr. Prentice Kicklighter, a tall young teacher with a quick smile and a gleam of mischief in his blue eyes. They fell in love, and in less than a year, he asked for the hand of the beautiful young music teacher.

They married December 10, 1920, in the Grice home. At first, the newlyweds lived with Samuel and Eva Kicklighter, but they soon moved to their own place, a tin "shack," where they almost froze to death during their first winter. A year later, they built a two-bedroom house across the street.

In 1921, when "The Christian Church" was organized, Prentice became interested right away. Mary, firm in her Baptist faith, eventually joined her husband, and there they remained faithful members.

Mary's first pregnancy, in 1921, ended with a stillborn child. But before long, a second child was on the way. After much discussion, Prentice and Mary decided that she should go to Kentucky for the birth of the baby, where she would have the help of her mother. The child was born a healthy, beautiful baby girl and was named Millicent. Mary and Milly, as the baby was called, arrived back in Glennville to resume their lives. Other children blessed the home—Edward, Mary Anne, Kerry, and Lindy. Lindy died in 1944 at the age of twelve, and another son, named Alexander, was stillborn.

Mary was a devoted wife and mother, a peacekeeper, and a good sport who "went along with most everything." Prentice, who inherited a large tract of land, built a spacious two-story house in 1935-36, on property that they called Playland, covering approximately twenty acres. The grounds contained a 9-hole golf course, a baseball field, a pool, horseshoe pits, volleyball, tennis and basketball courts, and a gym.

Playland was for residents of Glennville; a virtual open-house of recreation. There were rules, of course. Those who attended The First Christian Church could play anything free, provided they had attended Sunday School. Others, not from the church, had to pay the small amount of five to ten cents. One resident remembers being picked up from school to be taken to Playland, skating on Friday nights in the gym, and reciting Playland's motto: God first, others second, and I am third.

Prentice and Mary purchased a bus to carry young people to various places, most usually to the campgrounds. Their favorite stop was on Shellman's Bluff, on the coast near Darien, Georgia. In 1939, they carried a busload of children to the World's Fair in New York.

In spite of his retirement from teaching school, Prentice continued to teach the young, and Mary played the piano for church services until her eyesight declined and she could no longer read the music. Then, after her husband's death in 1976, Mary sold her home, and Playland, and built a smaller home with a tennis court to be enjoyed by others. She lived alone as long as she could, eventually becoming a resident of Glennvue Nursing Home in Glennville. Today, the chair she sits in is well worn from years of use. Along the sides and back are several small pillows of various colors, adjusted so as to accommodate her 95-pound figure. A hand-crocheted afghan is casually draped across the arm of the chair so it can be easily pulled around her shoulders should she become chilled. Her sight is growing more dim, her hearing not as sharp, and her memory has begun fading. Old and worn books adorn bookcases, their patina serving as proof of the many times they have been read and loved.

Her Bible lays on a table beside her chair, with a bookmark holding the place she had last read. Also on the table is a book entitled *Women of the Bible*. "Miss Mary," as she is affectionately called, has crowded more in a lifetime of one hundred years than most. She, as the women featured in the nearby book, leaves a legacy difficult to compete with, to follow, or to forget.

EDITOR'S NOTE: The day after this essay was prepared for publication, "Miss Mary" went home to be with her Lord.

"I love to think of nature as an unlimited broadcasting station, through which God speaks to us every hour, if we only will tune in."
—George Washington Carver

Blessings

PHIL PIATT

A morning walk in loveliness—
In woods, in winter cold,
Where trunk and trunk there stood in random rank
'Til they could not be seen;

But covered by the multitude
Of branch and bough, profuse, extravagant,
That seemed to fill the sight.
A clamoring stream there danced and laughed
Across the shallow stones,
Then calmed and rested, deep and quiet,
'Neath a rim of ice along the rooted bank;
And all below, the wood's and sky's reflection
In unreal, surreal detail,
In dimpled flow.
A heart at rest, a common scene—
Complex, artistic,
Far above man's art.
I walked in wonder, saw God's hand,
And I was blessed.

"*A teacher affects eternity; he can never tell where his influence stops.*" —Henry Brooks Adams

King and I

EVA MARIE EVERSON

About six months ago, I returned to my home town to visit my family. That Saturday morning when my mother and I went to the grocery store, I was met with a familiar scene from my childhood—Reverend King I. Evans, now over ninety years old, walking up and down the aisles. He greeted the young children who walked alongside their mothers or rode inside the shopping cart as he had done for so many years,

"Well, hello there, young lady," he said to a fair-haired girl. "How are you today?"

"Fine," came the shy answer. But her eyes danced because she knew what followed.

"Can you say a Bible verse for me?"

"Uh-huh," she nodded. Then she recited a verse she'd learned.

"Very good." He reached into his suit's coat pocket and retrieved a stick of gum. The little girl accepted it and King I. moved on.

"Well, hello there, young man," he said to the next child in his path. "How are you today?"

"Fine."

"Can you recite a Bible verse for me?"

"No," came the reluctant reply.

"Are you going to get Mama and Daddy to take you to Sunday School tomorrow?"

"Yes, sir," the child answered happily.

"Very good," King I. said as he reached into his pocket.

I folded my arms and inhaled deeply, remembering the countless times I had been the recipient of one of King I.'s pieces of gum. What an ingenious idea! I now thought. What a superb way to encourage children to go to church and learn the Word of God!

Months later, in preparation for this story, I spoke with King's son, George, and daughter, Carolyn.

"How did this ministry get started?" I asked.

"Daddy always enjoyed children," Carolyn reported. "He began his ministry as the Middle Baptist Association missionary. In 1943, he was the first pastor in the association to have Vacation Bible School. He wrote songs for the children, as well as little word games to help them remember spiritual principles.

What is faith? Forsaking All I Take Him. It wasn't until after my brother, sister, and I were grown and Daddy retired that he began concentrating on his grocery store ministry. But whether he's in a grocery store or not, he always keeps gum in his pockets. Even to this day, at ninety-five years of age, he never misses the opportunity to minister to a child!"

As we finished talking, I recalled my husband's favorite Bible verse: [Jesus said], "See that you do not look down on one of these little ones. For I tell you that their angels in heaven always see the face of my Father in heaven" (Matthew 18:10).

"If there be any truer measure of a man than by what he does, it must be by what he gives." —Robert South

A Generous Heart

NATALIE NICOLE GILBERT

The ad was short and sweet, but had all the signs of a good find. The man was looking for an instrument that would hold up for a while and be easy enough for him to play. He called the number provided and made arrangements to stop in later that night, after taking his grandson to baseball practice.

The apartment was situated on a busy highway, squeezed between a gas station and a department store, and the old Cadillac found its way with ease. Before he even had a chance to knock, the door was opened by a young man with a warm, welcoming smile.

"Hi, I'm John, the one you spoke to on the phone." He

extended his hand, which was shaken firmly. "I think you'll like what you see."

John led him through the rather sparse living room to a back room. There it sat, in an open case—a beautiful acoustic guitar. This was just what the older man was looking for.

"Would you like to play it to see how it feels?" John asked.

"Me? Play? I don't know that I could just yet. I'm hoping to learn, but right now I'm not even sure how to hold a pick, son."

"Well, if you like, I could play something to give you an idea of its potential. I spent a few years taking lessons, and used this guitar for a number of concerts and campfire retreats."

The look of joy on John's face was unmistakable as he picked up his old friend and began to play a medley. It was obvious that he knew the guitar well, his fingers flowed with ease over every chord he held. As John journeyed through his short solo, the older man smiled at his enthusiasm and zeal for the instrument. The music found its end, and the visitor breathed a sigh of appreciation.

"May I ask a question, John?"

"Certainly!" he smiled. "I'll tell you anything I know."

"Why would someone with your talent be selling a guitar? Did someone give you an instrument nicer than this one?"

John's smile deflated. "Well, sir, fact is my wife and I need the money that selling this guitar will give us. You see, we're expecting a child soon, and what we make just won't provide for the added expenses just now. Truth is, I hate to see this beauty go." John looked to the floor, acknowledging his longing to see a different answer to the current need. "But I have another little beauty coming," John said with a smile. "She's worth the sacrifice."

The prospective buyer gave the matter just a moment's consideration before making his offer. "Well, son, I'm ready to write you a check."

"That's great! I sure appreciate your coming by tonight. Your timing couldn't be better. Little Sara is due in just a matter of weeks now. I have some guitar books I used when I first took some lessons. Would you like me to toss those in?"

"I don't think they'd do me much good," the older man said as he scribbled his signature on the check.

John was puzzled. "I can tell you they're pretty easy to work with. I didn't know much about guitars when I used them, and I think they helped me a good bit."

"I'm sure the books are good, but I won't have a guitar to practice on, so they wouldn't help me much."

Confused, John stumbled over his words. "You're not... you don't want... but, you're giving me a check for the guitar? I don't understand."

The old man grinned. "I'm paying you to keep the guitar. It belongs in your hands, young man. No one else knows that guitar the way you do. No one else would play it as well as you do. But I do believe the good Lord had in mind for me to give you this check to help you." The man handed him the check. "I was once in your shoes, and I know your need. I've seen a piece of your heart today, knowing that you'd be willing to give up your most prized possession for your family's needs. I admire that, and I'm happy to reward you for your willingness to sacrifice."

John was silent. Humbled, he asked, "But can't I offer you something?"

With evident contentment, the old man said, "Just love that little girl, and never let your wife wonder about where your affections are."

With that said, the older man turned to make his way to the door. John took a quick moment to reflect on this man's generosity as he walked with him. "I don't know how to thank you for what you've just done."

"You already have, son."

The man got into his car and drove off without glancing back. John watched him as far as he could from his front door. As he pushed the door closed, he took a look at the check the man had written him, and his eyes began to water as he looked at the amount. The day had started with a hope, and his hope had been answered with a gift even greater than he could have imagined.

"Light is the symbol of truth." —James Russell Lowell

Night-Light Security

JO HUDDLESTON

As a youngster, I needed a light left on at bedtime. Its small beam relieved my fears of the dark and helped me to sleep peacefully. Now I depend on the comforting glow of God's protection whenever I'm in the dark. In turn, I can reflect His brilliance to those around me. I strive not to let temptations or evil habits spoil my witness for God. Only then can my light shine so that He will be glorified (Matthew 5:16).

I cherish the memory of that childhood night-light's security. It encourages me to leave a spiritual light on for others. A light to brighten their way to God while struggling through Satan's concealing darkness.

"Therefore I tell you, whatever you ask for in prayer, believe that you have received it, and it will be yours." —Mark 11:24

When Lightning Strikes

CARMEN LEAL

"Mom, my bike's been stolen."

From the tone of my twelve-year-old son's voice, I knew he was genuinely dismayed. Hoping against hope, I took a deep breath and said, "You're kidding, right?"

"No, Mom," he croaked dejectedly, "it's really gone."

Justin had picked out his first new bicycle just a few weeks before and purchased it with his own savings, plus some help from my mom and myself. The bicycle was one that could easily take him through high school.

But that first bike was stolen after less than one week. His dad had replaced it with a bicycle of similar quality. Now it seemed the second bike was gone as well. "Can I take my bike to Dad's house this summer?" he had pleaded. I knew Waikiki was not the safest place for bicycles, but since his dad doesn't have a car, I'd relented. Now my worst fears were realized.

I could hear the unasked question in his voice, and I knew the answer had to be, "No." There was no way that my limited resources could be stretched to cover the cost of a new bicycle. I carefully explained to him that we would have to pray about it and see how God would provide. At twelve, a bicycle is like a car to an adult. Transportation to school, self-image, and just being a carefree kid were all wrapped up in the bike. My sons would be staying with their dad for a few more weeks and that would give me the time to think things through.

During the next few weeks, I traveled to a convention on

the east coast and was able to stop in Kansas to see my parents. "You'll never believe what happened this summer," my mom exclaimed. "Lightning struck my house, and look what happened."

She showed me the new television and VCR that were purchased to replace those that had been ruined. Even the fuse box was new, and the roof damage had been completed. We took a moment to praise God that no one was hurt and that everything had been replaced or repaired.

"By the way, Mom, Justin's new bicycle you helped to buy was stolen."

With great sincerity, she said, "I'm sorry that happened. I wish I could help to replace it, but I just can't right now."

"I know, Mom. And I really don't expect you to. Somehow I know God is going to replace that bicycle. I just hope He does it by the time school begins next month."

No sooner had I returned home, Justin called and said, "Mom, Dad says if you pay for the rest, he'll give me $100.00 for my bike. And I have $24.00."

One hundred twenty-four dollars! That's nothing! *The bicycle was stolen while he was the responsible parent. Let him pay for the whole bike*, I thought to myself. In my mind, I angrily summed up all of my responsibilities as the custodial parent. It just was not fair that I should have to find the extra money.

In the midst of my silent tantrum, I heard God say, "I have a plan. Do you really doubt I can get a new bicycle?" It wasn't that I didn't trust God. I knew God could easily provide for all of my needs. But somehow the mortgage and food, not to mention school supplies and clothing, seemed much more important. Besides, the bicycle that their dad had purchased cost $424.00. Where would I find the money?

My sons returned home for the balance of the summer and we proceeded to look for the replacement bicycle. We went to garage sales and combed the classified ads. The calendar sped by, and still Justin had no bicycle. I continued to fret over the situation even as I assured Justin that God knew of his need and had a plan. "Will God make me ride a rusty old bike, Mom?" I could tell from the quiver in his voice that he was worried he would have to ride to his first day of Junior High on an eyesore.

One day, late in August, my mom's voice fairly sang with excitement over the phone. "You'll never believe what happened!"

"Did lightning strike again?" I joked.

"In a way," she said, smugly. "I thought the insurance company had already paid all they planned on paying for the damages. Everything was repaired and I was happy with the results. I just got a letter that informed me the balance of my payment would be sent within ten days. Since everything is repaired, I thought you could use the money for Justin's bike."

Convinced that she was talking about maybe $50.00 or so, and since that was $50.00 more than I had in the bicycle fund, I told her, "Of course I can use the money."

I opened the mailbox a few days later to find a check for $300.00. With the $100.00 from their dad, and Justin's $24.00, adding up to $424.00, it was exactly what was needed to purchase not the rusty bicycle of Justin's nightmare, but the shiny new one of his dreams. I could hardly wait to tell Justin the news.

Bubbling over enthusiastically, I related the details of lightning striking twice and the insurance company paying more than was expected. As I got to the part of the story about the amount of the check that had arrived, Justin's face broke into a smile.

"Mom, I can get my bike!" he shouted.

Since they spend their weekends with their dad, my sons don't often get to attend church. He is a confirmed atheist and does his best to share his lack of faith with them. I couldn't help but wonder in awe how great God is. Not only did He find a creative way for us to afford the new bicycle, but He did it in such a way that I could show my children that God really does care.

From the disaster of lightning striking over 4,000 miles away, God provided the best for my son. I was able to explain that we need to come to Him in prayer with our needs and be patient as He provides. It is a lesson I am constantly learning in my life and I am glad that this time, we all learned it together.

"Where we love is home—home that our feet may leave, but not our hearts." —Oliver Wendall Holmes, Sr.

Found Within an Essay

JULIA ARRANTS

There is a warmth and a light
that reminds me of the rest of who I am,
a memory of pinto beans and biscuits big as pancakes,
my first taste of sin (collards with fatback),
an aluminum ladle from which I could drink
with no mention of germs.
And melted cheese eaten with a spoon.
Houses full of chemistry sets, trumpets, paints,
Bibles and toy race cars,
instant coffee, sandwich cookies out of the wrapper
and dunked to my heart's content.
Houses warm and small,

nowhere to be lost or lonely,
always plenty more.
Percolator coffee on the burner,
the last of last night's cake.
There is a warmth that beckons me in,
the warmth of genuine words,
of easy embraces and gently scented hair,
of suppers anticipated and coffeepots full.
Always plenty more, and more than meets the eye,
more than simply coming home.

"The best things you can give children, next to good habits, are good memories." —Sydney J. Harrie

Jarrod's First "Almost" Catch

MARY VON PLESS

The air smelled clean that Saturday afternoon, and the ready-to-set sun threw splashes of orange, pink, and red onto cotton candy clouds, sailing across the sky. According to my seven-year-old grandson, Jarrod Talbott Whittaker or Mr. Lump (as in my sugar lump), one of the clouds was shaped like a funny looking dog.

Jarrod was glad his dad was going fishing with him. So, as their dogs watched with interest just inside the chain-link fence, they walked across their backyard, through the gate, and down to where the Indian River meets their land. Ruby, a Golden Retriever, lay down, watching with intelligent eyes, and

Sonic, a black lab, stood with tail pointed, his ebony coat shining in the morning's glow. He was ready to follow the instincts that would lead him into the water after something—anything! But the closed gate restrained him, and he whined in frustration.

That morning at the breakfast table, Jarrod had asked his dad, Craig, to go fishing. Craig agreed and said they would try out the larger blue and black fishing rod he'd bought at K-Mart the week before. Jarrod's first rod was now too small for him, and this new one had a lure with two hooks. "Poor fish," said Jarrod. "Two hooks is too many."

Jarrod and Craig arrived at the river bank, threw their lines in the water and stood silently.

"We have to be patient," Craig said quietly.

Suddenly, Jarrod had a hit on his line. It was a big fish and it was strong; at least twenty inches long. Its body was gray, the tail and fins silvery.

"It's a snook," shouted Craig.

Jarrod's rod bent as he pulled as hard as he could, trying to wind the reel.

"Dad," he shouted. "I can't hold it!"

Craig hastily threw down his rod and took his son's. My daughter, Jarrod's mom, came running down the river bank yelling to Craig, "Pull it this way! This way!"

In the clamor, Jarrod's friend, Kyle, ran over from next door hollering encouragement, and everyone leaped about excitedly, shouting, and finally laughing.

Craig fought hard, but even he couldn't bring in the fish. The line tangled itself in the mangroves, and after a while, it broke. Jarrod's fish swam away.

"I wonder about those hooks," Jarrod later told his dad. They pondered this together in silence.

That evening, Jarrod called to tell me of his adventure. "It was so exciting!" he exclaimed. "It would have been cool to bring the fish to shore, for my first catch and all—but I was happy that I almost caught one. Next time I'll know more about how to catch a fish and if I really want to catch one, I'll be experienced."

"Did anyone catch anything, Jarrod?" I asked him.

"Nobody but me had a nibble!" he said proudly. "But it doesn't matter. We had a good time together, and my mom was proud of me, even if the fish got away. I can always count on her to be proud."

Jarrod will always remember that special afternoon and his first "almost" catch. But, more importantly, as he later said, "Most of all, I'll remember that my dad went fishing with me."

"A Gentleman... one who never hurts anyone's feelings intentionally." —Oliver Herford

A Southern Gentleman

MARION H. ROBBINS, JR.

"Are you going home?" asked Mrs. Ennis, the school principal. The year was 1925, and we were on the Gilgal School grounds. My uncle Obie had me firmly by the hand and was leading me away from a very embarrassing situation.

"Yes'um," he replied. By this time we were past her and she needed no further explanation.

School was out for lunch and I had been on my way to the boys privy, which was in the branch across the side road from the school house. I was running and yelling, as five-year-olds will do, and as I passed the older boys sitting on the ditch bank eating their lunches, I yelled, "Going fifty miles an hour! Going fifty miles an hour!"

When I got there, I concealed myself behind some gallberry bushes. But I had trouble with the buttons of my short pants. The call of nature would not be denied, however, and as I passed by the boys on the ditch bank again, they easily saw why my speed was now reduced from "fifty miles an hour" to a slow crawl.

My uncle, Lee Attys Robbins (Obie), who was about fifteen at the time, walked with me the two miles back home, where I could be properly tended to. Our home in the early years was with my grandmother and her youngest son, Obie, who was more like a brother to me than an uncle. We were a typical southern farm family, living and working as our neighbors did at that time.

In the '20s and '30s, our fields were plowed and cultivated by mule power. My dad and my uncle, along with the field hands, did the plowing and cultivating. We kids and the help's kids worked and played together; chopped and hoed cotton and peanuts in the summertime, and in the fall, we picked cotton and broke corn. I couldn't pick much cotton. My brother, Ray, once picked over two hundred pounds in a day. That might seem like a lot, but it was not unusual for some of the field hands to pick four hundred pounds in a day.

Uncle Obie was always a hard worker. When he finished high school, he plowed with a mule from "sun up till sunset," five days a week. He worked in the Minkovitz department store on Saturdays. His pay was used to pay the hired hand who helped during the week on the "two horse farm."

After he was married, Uncle Obie operated a country store for several years. I worked for him as a clerk while I was in high school. I worked from noon to midnight for fifty cents. Later, Uncle Obie was employed as a rural mail carrier, which was his occupation until his retirement. He was a very quiet, steady, and religious family man, president of our church brotherhood, and chairman of the board of deacons in our small, struggling rural church. His wife, Wynette, was church pianist for many years. They were both positive influences in my life.

Uncle Obie had a dog named Sport. He was a yard dog of undetermined ancestry who would bark to let you know if a stranger came up or that something unusual was happening.

My aunt also had a dog, a pet that stayed inside the house; a poodle that she bought dog food for. Old Sport ate whatever he could... scraps thrown out the kitchen door, etc.

My aunt and uncle kept up a continuous but good-natured argument about the relative worth of the two dogs. He determined Sport to be the best of watch dogs and said he was worth his keep. She countered that her poodle was a pedigree and could not be compared to a lowly mongrel dog.

One day, a furniture delivery truck came by and stopped to ask directions. Old Sport had the bad habit of chasing cars and this time he got too close and was run over. His back seemed to be broken. The truck driver was very apologetic and offered to put Old Sport out of his misery. Aunt Wynette hurried to fetch the .22 rifle, and the driver shot Sport in the head, loaded him in his truck, and later discarded his body about two miles away in the creek.

Several days after the accident, my uncle heard a dog barking outside. When he opened the door, he found Old Sport standing at the kitchen door, begging for food. After feeding him, Uncle Obie examined him and found that the bullet from the .22 had only grazed his head and not gone through his skull. Only temporarily paralyzed from the accident, he had recovered in the creek and come home.

Uncle Obie and Aunt Wynette are both gone now. He left us when he had a heart attack at the age of sixty-four, and she died later at the age of seventy-eight. They are sadly missed by those of us who knew and loved them. Lee Attys and Wynette were fortunate to have two great children, Carlton and Ann, who gave them grandchildren they lived long enough to know, love, and appreciate. Our church family has suffered a great loss with their going. Their legacy to us is the will and determination to continue onward with our efforts and prayer for our church and to our God.

"Christianity does not remove you from the world and its problems; it makes you fit to live in it, triumphantly and usefully."
—Charles Templeton

The Manure at the Foot of the Cross

BECKY RUSSELL

One evening, after a particularly stressful week, I found myself in a church yard waiting for my granddaughter's preschool program to begin. Noticing an area with three large crosses and benches, I decided to sit there quietly for a few minutes and to pray for peace and less stress in my life. It was after I had finished my prayers that something behind one of the crosses caught my eye.

Closer inspection showed that it was a bag of manure. It did not belong in the well kept, manicured setting with its beautiful flowers, shrubs, and palm trees. I thought, "That is just like life at times. It is just manure!" That manure could be smelly and unsightly, but it was used to fertilize the plants so they could flourish.

Even though my life seemed like manure at that moment, I realized that I could use the circumstances that I was going through to help others flourish. I could become more compassionate and understanding because of what I had experienced. The crosses helped me remember that Jesus died for me and asked me to bring the manure of my life to the foot of the cross.

It was amazing how that lowly bag of manure could enable me to gain a needed perspective on my problems. Couldn't I reach out to others to do the same?

Salt and Light In Work

"Whatever you do, work at it with all your heart, as working for the Lord, not for men"

—Colossians 3:23

"Work is love made visible." —Kahlil Gibran

Peter's Ministry

EVA MARIE EVERSON

His name was Peter. After retirement, he worked as a school crossing guard at the corner of Gillionville Road and Magnolia Street; a fairly simple job with an unquestionable level of importance.

Peter did his job as unto the Lord. He did more than merely walk to the center of the crosswalk and extend the hand held "STOP" sign. Peter practically danced! He laughed with the children, stroking their small heads like a loving grandfather. He stood on the street corners and waved jovially to those of us in our automobiles, and the children hung their heads out of car windows to call out a greeting that was always eagerly received and returned. For my young daughter, who's school was down the street from Peter's post, waving to Peter was a highlight of her day. My daughter was only one of many.

One morning, as Peter skipped across Gillionville like the Pied Piper with a handful of children at his heels, he suddenly collapsed. Someone called 911 as spectators worked to escort frightened children away from the scene and to their schools. An ambulance arrived and whisked Peter away to the hospital. That afternoon, bunches of flowers lay at the corner of Peter's post, in memory of a great man.

His name was Peter. He was a school crossing guard, who did his job as unto the Lord. There is no greater ministry.

*"Constant kindness can accomplish much.
As the sun makes ice melt, kindness causes misunderstanding,
mistrust, and hostility to evaporate."* —Albert Schweitzer

Just Me & Mutsy

CARLA TRETHAWAY

It was six o'clock Monday morning. My twelve-hour shift in the emergency room of a county hospital was about to come to a close, and I moved through the sterile rooms, silently grateful that the weekend was over. These nights are the busiest of my work-week, when we see more accidents, more drunks, and more stab and gunshot wounds. But, I thought, in one hour I can go home and climb into the security and comfort of my bed. It was an inviting thought.

Unexpectedly, the emergency room front door buzzer sounded. Glancing around, I realized that I was alone in the ward. This was unusual, and it made me uncomfortable. I moved hesitantly toward the half-glass door that led to an outside ramp. In the pale light that dawned just over the horizon and split through the tall pine trees around the hospital, I could make out the figures of two young black men. They were dressed in grunge; their heads wrapped in do-rags. Neither of them appeared to be in distress, and I felt a chill run through me. If they were part of a gang, I surmised, they may be here to rob the narcotic cabinet. At ninety-five pounds, I'd be no match for them.

"I'm back here alone," I reminded myself. Still, I unlocked the door and pushed it open.

"Can I help you?" The question sounded meek, even to me.

"We've got a man out here we think is having a heart attack," one of the young men answered.

That's when I noticed an elderly white man leaning over the cab of an old pick-up truck. My nursing instincts took over. I immediately called for help. The maintenance man, who happened to be close by, aided me in getting the man into a wheelchair as the two men rattled off their story.

"The old man drove up to the service station. Said he was having chest pains and could we tell him where the nearest hospital is. That's when we said, 'We'll take ya, man.'"

I marveled that, with their appearance, the old man had given them his keys.

We got the man into an examination room, leaving the two young men behind. As we began triage, the patient began to panic. "My dog's in the truck!"

"That's okay, sir," I soothed. "We'll have someone take care of your dog."

"You don't understand," he continued. "Mutsy's over twenty years old. She can't take the heat."

An orderly was immediately sent to the truck to open the windows for the dog.

"All I have is Mutsy," the old man said. "It's just me and Mutsy, traveling around the states."

The orderly returned with a pill box he'd found on the front seat of the truck, and I was stunned to see that none of the bottles had labels. One was filled with aspirin, a common prescription for heart patients.

"Sir, can you tell me how much aspirin you take a day?" I asked.

Kind, watered-down, old eyes focused on the bottle in my hand. "Oh, that's not mine," he informed me. "That's Mutsy's!"

The Respiratory Therapist came in. "Carla, you've gotta see this dog! He's Benji with an over-bite!"

Once our patient was stabilized, the doctor on duty told him that he would need to be kept for observation.

"What about Mutsy?" he asked.

"Don't worry about Mutsy," the R.T. said. "She's going home with me."

He thanked us. "By the way," he added. "Do you know who those two young men are?"

In the efficiency of my work, I'd been unaware that they had left. "No, sir. I don't."

"They sure were nice."

I quickly chastised myself when I recalled my initial reaction upon seeing them standing on the other side of the ER door. One hears so much about racial unrest, it felt good to see fellow human beings working together. I wish I'd taken their names so that we could thank them. But in my heart, I know that they didn't come to the aid of the man for a pat on the back. They came because, underneath their gang-style clothing, pure hearts are beating.

"After silence that which comes nearest to expressing the inexpressible is music." —Aldous Huxley

Upon This Rock

CARMEN LEAL

"You've got a beautiful voice. We'd love it if you would sing a special one Sunday."

I enjoyed the obvious warmth in the pastor's words, but the style of music was foreign to me. This was a Presbyterian church with music so different from what I'd known in my Catholic

113

childhood.

Even though I'd only gone back to church to get a free hour of babysitting for my two toddlers each week, I enjoyed the people. If I was going to continue with this church, I should get involved. My brothers had all begun attending Assemblies of God churches, and my youngest brother was even a pastor. Maybe he would have some suggestions.

"Merrill, I need to sing a song at church, and I don't know any of this kind of music. Where do I start?"

Merrill's counsel led me to a small Christian bookstore. I'd never been to a store devoted to Christian books and music, but on a lunch hour from work, I climbed the steps and entered the small store. Even with every shelf filled, there was an overflow of products making it hard to navigate through the narrow aisles.

The owner, Peter, obviously busy, took the time to help me select songs that might fit my voice. He patiently listened as I mentioned various pop artists and songs I enjoyed. From that list, he was able to send me to a tape player and headset with accompaniment tracks from well-known Christian artists.

For years I sat in that hard pew at Holy Name Church, whispering with my siblings, making fun of the ritual, and being bored. I was only there because I had no choice, and as soon as I left home, I left the church. Even though I thought I retained nothing from my youth, the music made me realize I not only remembered words from the past, but now understood them. What had been like Greek to me, seemingly going in one ear and flowing at lightning speed out the other, had simply been waiting. Like a flickering flame needing only the slightest breeze, the words set to music fanned the embers of belief already in my heart. The songs I listened to that day had portions of Scripture in them, just waiting to be remembered. My lunch hour passed all too quickly and I dashed back to the office.

For the rest of the week, I quietly slipped up the stairs, into the overcrowded shop, and grabbed some cassettes and a player. Artist after artist sang of a God I wanted to know. He seemed more real to me after those few days, than He ever had growing up.

The Presbyterian church I was attending was filled with pleasant people, but they never had an invitation or explained what it was to be a Christian. I could have gone months, or even years, and never known about a personal relationship with Christ.

On the last day of that fateful week, I listened to Sandi Patti singing a song called *Upon This Rock*. My eyes filled with tears, and I knew, without really knowing how, that I had to invite Christ into my heart, to become a follower of His.

God is perfect in His choice of timing and location. With strangers surrounding me, and tears cascading, I gave my life to Him. I also knew I wanted to use my gift of music for Him, since it was music that had opened my heart.

I never told Peter what his shop did in my life. Rhema Bookstore was a struggling business, and I'm sure there were times Peter wanted to give up the dream of using his abilities to win souls for Christ. Fourteen years later, Rhema Bookstore is still in business and Peter is still doing what God called him to do. I'm sure Peter must sometimes wonder if his work really matters.

Yes, Peter. It does.

"Without humility there can be no humanity." —John Buchan

Blind Leading

BETTY K. PURVIS

The year 1978 was not one of my better years. Recently separated from my husband, I went back into full-time employment for the first time in twenty-two years. In our separation agreement, I kept the house while my husband kept our new car and purchased an older one for me.

One afternoon, a dear friend of mine, also named Betty, called and asked if I could drive her and her mother to Augusta on my afternoon off for Mrs. Jones' eye appointment. Betty could not drive her mother because she is blind, and Mrs. Jones is both blind and deaf. Naturally, I said that I would.

So, on a hot, steamy day in July, we arrived in Augusta, about an hour's drive from our hometown. Turning onto a congested, divided highway, we proceeded on our way until, at the base of a hill, my old car sputtered, choked, and died. Luckily, I was able to pull over to the side of the road and out of the flow of traffic.

I left Betty and her mother and began to trudge up the hill in the heat, uttering one silent prayer after another. For one thing, I prayed for God to send me Christian help. I finally walked into the coolness of a store and I told the manager my dilemma.

"No problem," he said. "I know a man to call. He's a fair man... Christian... doesn't take advantage of women with car problems. I can call him for you."

"Please do," I said. "I'm at the bottom of the hill."

I walked back down the hill to my waiting passengers.

When I got into the car and told them the news, Betty was fine but Mrs. Jones was a bit frightened.

About fifteen minutes later, I watched as a tow truck pull up in front of me. I got out of my car, intending to speak with the driver, but stopped short. Standing before me was a bear of a man. He wore his wiry, red hair long, sported a long beard, and was sloppily dressed. He was completely unkempt. This was the Christian man who wouldn't cheat me?

Swallowing my fear and frustration, I said, "I need to get these women to the eye doctor." He nodded, but said nothing, merely walked to the back of the truck and began to connect the towing apparatus to the bumper of my car.

I returned to the car and cheerfully explained to the ladies that I would help them into the cab of the truck and we'd be on our way. Silently, though, I prayed that my voice didn't convey my anxiety. Without a word, he drove us to the doctor's office. After I had helped the ladies inside, got them settled, then re-joined my brother in the Lord, I prayed, "Dear God, I'm all alone with this man. All alone, except for You...."

Still without speaking a word, the man drove me to his service station where, within minutes, my alternator was replaced. True to the convenience store manager's word, I was not taken advantage of financially. I thanked the rather taciturn, burly man, returned to my car and drove to the doctor's office before Mrs. Jones was done with her appointment.

Over the past twenty years, I have thought a lot about that quiet giant. He was obviously a man of few words who performed his task in humility, as unto the Lord. I have never completely understood why he never spoke, not even a word, but I am grateful that he quietly came and saved me from what could have been a disaster. Whenever I think of salt and light, he is the first person that comes to mind.

"All that is worth cherishing in this world begins in the heart, not the head." —Suzanne Chazin

My Job Is To Say, "I Love You"

CARMEN LEAL

I am a caregiver. My forty-seven-year-old husband, David, has a little-known genetic disease called "Huntington's Disease," and can do almost nothing for himself. As a caregiver, I can tell you that we experience a wide range of emotions which largely depends upon the person we are caring for. Lately, I have felt there is really no reward for what I am doing.

David has difficulty feeding himself, and swallowing is only accomplished with a great deal of effort. One day, with more food landing on his shirt than in his mouth, David and I were going through the usual "change the shirt" game.

"David, lift up your arms," I pleaded. "If you do, we can go and have ice cream."

David's garbled speech made his response to my urging impossible to comprehend. I did, however, figure out that he had no intention of lifting his arms or cooperating as I changed the shirt.

I felt myself tense, and sighed in frustration. I didn't need this today. Try as I would, I simply couldn't understand what he was saying, and anyway, we weren't moving any nearer our goal—a clean shirt.

"David, my job is to feed you, make sure you take your medications, and help your doctors and nurses. Your job is to help me to help you. You need to lift your arms, please."

With an endearing smile so like that of the man I married before the ravages of Huntington's Disease, David said, "No. My job is to say 'I love you,' in as clear a voice as possible."

Caregiving is not something I would ever choose to do. I imagine most people would not choose what is usually an almost thankless job. Especially without pay. But though there may not be pay, there are rewards. Remembering David's smile and his "job" is a nice memory I can pull out on days when things get really tough. We all have our jobs, and David's job is to say, "I love you."

I love you, too, David.

"Measure not men by Sundays, without regarding what they do all the week after." —Thomas Fuller

Use Me, Lord

SUSANNA VELASQUEZ

Most people think modeling is a glamorous profession filled with nonstop excitement. While it certainly has its moments, modeling, and acting too, have many more moments of sitting around, waiting to work.

This was the case back in 1996, when I participated in a commercial shoot one day at Universal Studios Florida. While many of the actors I work with have anything *but* a Christian lifestyle, I am often blessed to have Christians on the set, and sometimes, those I've even worked with in the past. This was one such time.

There must have been about twenty-five actors working on the set that day. While we waited to do our job, I noticed my friend Linzey talking with Monica, a girl I had met that day. Monica, a believer, was in the midst of marital problems. I decided to join their conversation, but just as I walked over, Linzey began praying with Monica. I didn't want to interrupt, so I sat, waiting, while Monica quietly cried.

At the close of the prayer, Linzey explained that he'd been praying for Monica's husband. As we talked, we shared how God was working in our lives, and as Linzey always has his Bible on commercial shoots, we started to look up Scriptures. That was when another Christian actress, Katie, joined our little group and asked what was going on.

"We're having some church!" Linzey exclaimed, and invited Katie to stay. A few minutes later, Karen approached the growing group. Karen was not born-again, but was a church-going person, and she listened to the conversation. Eventually, there were seven of us in fellowship as we felt the presence of the Holy Spirit right on that set.

Other actors passed by and heard us talking, but they wouldn't stay, until it was finally time to shoot the scene and we got into our positions. As we waited for the director and crew to finish setting up the shot, a couple of actors started asking Linzey and me questions about our faith. We planted many seeds that day by answering their questions between takes.

Instead of just waiting to go on, we got to witness on the set of a commercial. I haven't seen those actors that we witnessed to since then, but I have prayed for them. Sometimes I wonder if they ever did become believers. I may never know this side of heaven what our impact was on our fellow actors, but God does.

"While they were saying among themselves it cannot be done, it was done." —Helen Keller

Let Your Light So Shine

KATHY SEVEN WILLIAMS

"Hello, little lollypop!"

We were met by a smiling voice every morning as we came to class. We were all blind to one degree or another, but right then, first thing in the morning, the important thing was that someone was glad to see us at school. Because one of us couldn't say his "l's," we all practiced so he didn't feel singled out. She cared about us all, this "Resource Teacher in the Resource Room."

The state had a residential blind school where families sent their blind children. Mom didn't want to send me there. The story goes that she said I wasn't dangerous, just blind, and so there was no reason I needed to be institutionalized. There was provision in the law for a Resource Room if a district had enough blind children. The district didn't come looking for us though, so when it was time for me to start first grade, Mom had to search for other blind kids. From four or maybe five cities they came to go to public school with the assistance of our Resource Teacher, who was hired by the district when Mom showed them they did, indeed, have a need.

Mrs. Crocker was her name. She'd been a math teacher, so I knew she was smart. She was pretty and really nice to us all. But most of all, she didn't hold our being blind against us. She never told us we couldn't do things like the other kids. But when we tried to get out of something by saying we couldn't see so we couldn't do, there she was, right by our side, guiding us to

121

find a way to do it right along with everyone else. She didn't let us hide or leave class and go off to the resource room to get out of work. She didn't solve our problems for us, either. She would ask us all questions until we figured out the answers that showed us the way.

I remember one time in second grade, we were all drawing these big Easter bunnies. We'd pass a pattern down the rows and each kid would trace the bunny on a new piece of paper, and then we'd color it. I couldn't see the faint pattern through my drawing paper and I started to cry because I really wanted to draw a bunny, too. The next thing I knew Mrs. Crocker was standing there next to me, asking what was wrong.

"I can't draw a bunny," I blubbered.

"Why not?" she demanded, without much sympathy in her voice at all.

"Because I'm blind!" I shouted at her.

"But what is the problem right now with the rabbit?" she asked calmly.

"I can't see it through my paper to trace it so I can color it." I sniffled, analyzing the problem as I'd been taught with so many other problems I'd encountered already in school.

"Is there anything you can do to make it better?" she prompted. "What would help you see it through your paper?"

"If I put the picture up on the window, the light will shine through the back and I can see it then."

And that was what I did. She had gone back to the resource room before I'd finished tracing my project. Not knowing the other kids did colors differently, I then read the big print color names on my jumbo Crayons and colored the bunny just like all the other kids.

A child doesn't know what they can and cannot do, whether they are physically challenged or not. A child will try as long as they can unless they are told otherwise. If I said, "I can't!" my mother would respond, "Can't died a long time ago. Find a way that you can." Between her and Mrs. Crocker, I didn't have a chance to grow up disabled.

The little boy who couldn't say his "l's" had gone on to get his driver's license in high school. That news confused me until I learned that there was a huge difference between being partially sighted and legally blind. I had been put in the class with the partially sighted children because my dad didn't want me to be blind. But really, I was legally blind and couldn't see nearly as much as all the others. I had to work hard to do what the others could do with their so-much better vision.

Our state required successful completion of Driver's Education to graduate from high school. I took the class between tenth and eleventh grade in summer school with all my friends. When we finished the Driver's Ed part of the class, everyone went out on the parking lot to divide into Driver's Training groups. The instructor told me to go home, that I wasn't going to be able to take that part of the class. I knew I couldn't see well enough to drive. I knew it intellectually, but it wasn't until that instant that I knew it in my heart. I realized I really was different and that there really was something I couldn't do.

Reluctantly, I determined I wouldn't drive and I wouldn't ski, but I'd do everything else. I sailed, rode bicycles, skated, sewed all my own clothes, cooked, made pottery, ran lighting for stage performances, and did anything else that came my way. In college, I jumped horses, helped build a radio station, taught primary school, programmed computers, and moved forward without pause. At the ripe old age of thirty-five, shortly after my second child was born, I decided I had gravity on my side and went skiing. After all, blind people were doing that all over the country. Having found the different ways to do it wasn't that hard to figure out, after all. I laughed when I realized I'd avoided skiing all my life because of my blindness, only to discover my hips dislocate when I snow plow, so it wasn't the sport for me.

The final "can't" was driving. Watching the rest of the world do it, I must admit I don't mind not being out there with them. While finding transportation to be a real challenge, driving is a menace to life and sanity. Still, there was that special something inside me that said, "Find a way." And I did. The local bus company has an annual bus rodeo, including what they called "Rookie at the Wheel," where anyone who liked could take a turn driving a city bus. I walked up to the table guided by Karat, my German Shepherd Guide dog, and signed up for my turn with the help of a friend guiding my signature to the line.

When I boarded the bus and tied Karat's leash around a railing, the driver instructor in charge said, "You can see well enough to do this, can't you?"

"I don't think so," I answered truthfully.

"Don't worry. We'll manage." With him instructing, "Right, Left and *REALLY NOW! TURN RIGHT!*" I successfully drove the bus around the parking lot and back to the starting point. I had driven. I don't need to drive again. Mrs. Crocker had been right. I could do anything—I just had to find the way for me to do it, too.

When I was a college student, I visited her. Then, after I graduated from college and had children of my own, my very special teacher stopped by my home in Utah to visit and meet my family. We were sitting, talking on the couch in my living room, when she told me that she was a Christian. I was surprised. Keeping the mandatory separation of Church and State, she'd never said a single word about God or church. She just lived what she believed and shared it with me, showing me that I could live what I believed as well. No matter how blind any of us kids were, she let her light shine so we could follow. What a blessing to have known her! She still keeps track of her students when she can. I think most, if not all of that starting class,

124

actually graduated from our home high schools with no special help or resource room at all.

I know I did.

"When you meet a man, you judge him by his clothes; when you leave, you judge him by his heart." —Russian Proverb

My Airborne Driver

SKYLLA MOON

My husband and I own a home business, selling a database to businesses that we ship nationwide on diskettes. We do business with FedEx, C.O.D. or Airborne. The drivers are born-again, and we have enjoyed our fellowship with them... it's great to share a quick *Praise the Lord* with a brother in Christ!

During the UPS strike last year, Airborne was overloaded and the drivers were working many long hours. Overtime pay was apparently not an option. After unsuccessful attempts at working it out, many drivers, including ours, quit. The new driver just wasn't the same! He was unshaved, had some missing teeth in the front and wore mirrored sunglasses all the time. Scared me! I would quickly get things done with him and scurry back into the house.

One morning, I told my husband that I just couldn't deal with the driver that day and asked him to do it. Airborne came to pick up several packages, and my husband and the new driver were out front signing the papers and doing the routine when a telephone call came in for my husband. I had to call him in to get the call. When I stuck my head out the door, my husband said, "Sky, I'd like you to meet Jerry. Jerry got saved last week. He got saved on the 11th, baptized on the 13th and married on the 15th." Jerry grinned and piped up, "Yeah, and I prayed for a new job and got it the next day!"

So there we stood, me and the new, scraggly Airborne driver, praising God together. We discussed how he came to know the Lord and he told me about God's wonderful grace and goodness. He told me about getting saved in a little Baptist church, and then he raised his right hand high in the air and said, "See, all I have to do is this and I can feel the presence of the Lord. 'Course, they don't do that much at this Baptist church, but I went to a revival and they're on fire for the Lord over there! My father-in-law anointed me with oil just last night and prayed over me for healing in my neck and back, and God healed me!"

All I could say was, "Hallelujah!"

I noticed he had what appeared to be a cocaine vial hanging around his neck. "What is that?" I asked him rather accusingly.

Grabbing the vial tenderly, he said, "Oh, that's my anointing oil. When the enemy, Satan, comes at me, I just grab this oil and pray. I have my Bible in the truck and read it all day long between stops. The enemy is after me, but he can't have me now!"

I grabbed him and hugged him and exclaimed, "Welcome to the family of God, brother in Christ." And when I embraced him, I realized that this is why Jesus came... for those who are unlovely, for the unkempt, for a lost and hurting world... you, me, all.

I went into the house and fell to my knees in confession. I was so convicted of my lack of love, my judgemental and superior attitude because of his appearance. I wept deeply and praised God for His everlasting mercy and grace unto me, who is unworthy.

We are all "under God's construction." There is none perfect, except the One who came to rescue and redeem and revitalize, Jesus Christ. We all have to grow up in the Lord. "Instead, speaking the truth in love, we will in all things grow up into Him who is the Head, that is, Christ. From Him the whole body, joined and held together by every supporting ligament, grows and builds itself up in love, as each part does its work" (Ephesians. 4:15-16). Nowhere in the Scripture does it say that we are to be critical of each other, but rather we are to love one another as Jesus repeatedly commanded us. We are each a work in progress. We never know what any particular person is going through, we just cannot judge lives nor can we judge hearts.

We prayed together that day. I couldn't stop weeping during the afternoon... couldn't shake the realization of God's infinite goodness. About an hour later, I was on the phone with a friend and began to testify about what occurred. This friend said the most precious thing after we told him our story. He said, "That Airborne driver is now really, truly HEIRborne."

Even now, all I can say is, "Hallelujah!"

Salt and Light In Death and Dying

"He will wipe every tear from their eyes. There will be no more death or mourning or crying or pain, for the old order of things has passed away."

—Revelation 21:4

"From the salt of the earth,
From the light of the world,
From the hearts you've redeemed...
One voice we raise, Lord." —Eleanor Tracey

A Rabbi's Story

(EDITOR'S NOTE: The following is an excerpt from a sermon given by RABBI ED BORAZ)

I grew up in an all Jewish neighborhood. There, I learned the values of Jewish community. A Jewish neighborhood must have a Kosher butcher shop down the street. The public school system should close because of lack of attendance on High Holy Days. The school teachers must speak with foreign accents, either European or Israeli.

I learned that Jews should live together. We should not "mix" too much with the non-Jewish community. I grew up with words like "goyim," "shicksehs," and "shagetzes." Most probably, these words grew out of the antisemitic experiences of my European ancestors. Until Israel, words were the Jewish response to these attacks. Like genetic traits, we carried these words with us when we settled in this country.

In my community, there was an air of superiority toward the non-Jewish world. In my home, as in many households at that time, even the dating of a non-Jew would cause the kind of anguish associated with divorce, or worst yet, some type of disease.

In the summer of 1994, my boyhood friend Danny died of cancer. He had been ill for six months. Danny saved my life when I was a little boy. My parents divorced when I was ten, though they later remarried. While I was floundering, Danny extended his ten-year-old hand to mine. We lived next door to each other and were lifelong friends.

Though we stayed in touch, we went our separate ways. From childhood until now, I remained involved in Jewish synagogue life. Though Danny's father, Samuel, came from a distinguished line of rabbis, Danny went to college, attended an Ivy League Law School, and met and married Margaret, who was not Jewish. They had two boys, Noah and William. Aside from teaching Noah, the older one, to read Hebrew letters, Danny taught his sons no Hebrew. Their observance of Judaism consisted largely of having a Sedar once a year for Passover.

Danny's work was with the Legal Services Corporation (Legal Aid) in Columbia, Kentucky, a town of three thousand non-Jewish people. Driving through its main street, you'll find churches of varying denominations, but no synagogue or other Jewish institution.

Danny knew he was dying of cancer. None of the treatments he received had worked. The week before his death, I received the telephone call from Margaret. I should come and see him. Danny wanted to talk.

I arrived late that evening. As I entered the town, I said aloud to no one, "What in the world is he doing here? Why did he choose to spend his life in this God-forsaken town? There are no Jews here." I was angry that Danny had chosen such a place to spend his life.

I drove to Danny's farmhouse, one mile out of "downtown" Columbia and in the middle of nowhere. Danny lay catherized on the sofa. Cancer had spread through his body and he could not move without the support of a walker and his wife. He was heavily medicated for pain.

He smiled. I asked, "How are you doing with all this?" He smiled again and with great effort explained that he wanted a traditional Jewish funeral in Columbia, Kentucky. Would I help make this possible? This was his last request of me.

The next day, Margaret invited Steve, a local Gentile carpenter, to their home to discuss building a casket. We sat in the dining room and I explained to Steve that according to Jewish law, a casket should not be made of metal, if possible, and pine should be used. There should be little ornamentation. I explained the Jewish belief that one's life arises from the dust and returns to the dust. Therefore, materials which decompose in the earth over time were required.

He responded, "I've never done this before. I don't know whether I can go in and see Danny [who was in the next room]. I'll do my best." He rose to go to Danny's room, turned, and said, "Can I use honey oak instead of pine and carve a six-pointed star on top?"

"Of course," I answered.

Steve stayed while we drove to the funeral home. I told the funeral director that he needed to remove all symbols of Christianity. I explained about the shrouds, the traditional white burial garments that are worn by the deceased. He said if I would obtain them, they would do their best to prepare Danny's body.

He then explained that they had never had a Jewish funeral before; in fact, as people in this community had never been to a Jewish funeral, I might have to take it slow and keep it simple. He was very kind.

When we returned to the house, Danny and Steve were talking and laughing.

Danny died five days later. Steve telephoned me in Bloomington, Indiana. He needed Danny's Hebrew name to carve on the casket. I took out a Jewish Bible, made a photostat of Danny's Hebrew name, "Dahyniel ben Sh'muel," cut and pasted the words together and faxed them to Danny's law office.

I arrived late Wednesday with the traditional burial garments: fifty kippot (yalmulkes, or skull caps), a few funeral booklets, and a Shiva candle. Driving past church after church, I wondered, "Could Danny's last wish to me be fulfilled?"

Later, at the funeral home, the director warned me that a large turnout was expected and repeated his advice to slowly explain the service. In the room where the service would be held, Danny lay in the casket, the lid in place as I had requested. The casket was beautiful. It was stained, with a Magen David, a Jewish star, on top. Underneath the star was Danny's Hebrew name, carved perfectly in Hebrew characters. When I saw Steve, I could not help but think that this great mitzvah (commandment) that he performed was also an act of "t'shuvah," repentance.

The only Jews there were Danny's mother, myself, his brother and sister, a nephew and cousins, and Danny's supervisor, John Rosenberg.

That night, Danny's death was the lead story on the six o'clock news. To get away from the grief-laden atmosphere and to review for the following day, William, Noah, and I went out for a "walk on the town." They were worried about the service and their obligation to recite the Kaddish, the prayer for those who suffer the loss of a family member, for their father.

None of what occurred that day prepared me for what was to come.

Two hundred people attended Danny's funeral. Though there were only eight Jews in the audience, all fifty kippot were used. The service began. From beginning to end, there was a stillness that is difficult to describe. I explained each step, from "k'riah," the traditional tearing of the garment to symbolize the beginning of the mourning period, to the "El Mahleh Rachamim," the prayer seeking God's compassion for Danny's soul. I did not omit any Hebrew. When we came to the twenty-third Psalm, "The Lord Is My Shepherd," everyone recited it softly. I began to take comfort. With fifty kippot clearly visible, a town mourning the loss of its sole Jew was becoming Jewish.

When John spoke, I learned why so many people had come. Danny made a difference in the life of that community. From protecting parental rights to civil rights cases involving sexual and racial discriminations, Danny's list of accomplishments in this small, conservative community, was formidable. Yet, Danny seldom talked about them whenever we saw each other. It was clear that the principle of "tzedek, tzedek, tirdoph" (justice, justice, you shall vigorously pursue, Deuteronomy 16:20) was Danny's life. He lived his life fulfilling one of the highest Jewish precepts found in the Torah (the Law) and thus carried the mantel of his ancestry at its very essence.

When the pallbearers moved the casket to the hearse, everyone rose as if given a cue. I asked those who were going to the burial site, a small stretch of land situated thirty miles from the funeral home, to remain while I explained the rituals that we would perform. All two hundred people sat and the room was as quiet as when the service began. I explained the tradition. Each person may choose to throw a shovel full of dirt onto the casket at the end of the burial service. Then they would form an aisle for Danny's family to walk through to their cars while the observers recited the Hebrew phrase, "Hamakom y'nachem m'avlei tziyon," meaning "May God comfort you among the mourners of Zion."

Fifty cars drove in procession the thirty miles. The casket was lowered. During the Kaddish, I looked over at Noah and William. John had his arms around one boy, Margaret's arms were around the other, and the boys lips moved to the traditional words of Kaddish. An indescribable feeling grew ever so deep in my soul. The universe was responding as it should. Though Danny was dead, the essence of his wish was being fulfilled; William and Noah—his sons—were saying the Kaddish.

Margaret began to shovel the dirt, followed by her family. Everyone present fulfilled the commandment of helping Danny return to the earth from which he had come. Immediately, the Christian people of Columbia, Kentucky, formed an aisle, and Danny's family walked between them as they repeated the traditional words of comfort to those who mourn; the first Hebrew words they had ever recited. They performed "g'milat hesed," a righteous act. For that moment, an entire town became a part of "k'lai yisrael," a Jewish community, granting Danny's desire for a traditional Jewish funeral.

Stories have an infinite number of interpretations. Everyone hears them and understands them from different vantage points. Here are three lessons I learned from Danny's life and death.

1. The mysteries of life are for us to engage in and to wonder. I was foolish to judge Danny's life with my question, "What is Danny doing in this God-forsaken town?" One can only marvel at the sense of meaning his life took as he took the Jewish principle of "tzedek" (justice) and injected the Jewish ideal into his world of Columbia, Kentucky. From this narrow-minded question I learned an important lesson. When a life seems to contradict the normal path, understanding and love is the human response.

2. People can become Jewish, even if for a moment in time. People other than Jews can do "mitzvot" (commandments). A whole town can become Jewish, if only for a few hours. For me, the "air of religious superiority" that I experienced and perceived and chose to incorporate into my personality at an early age was shameful in light of all that I have seen.

3. The human response to death is Torah and the doing of mitzvot. On the surface, it is easy. Underneath, it becomes harder in a world full of colorful choices of how Torah and mitzvot (the Law and commandments) are to operate. Nevertheless, a

mitzvah, an entire Torah, can be done at each moment in the unfolding of human history, by anyone, Jew and non-Jew alike.

And when one does mitzvah, he or she stands not only for the moment in time, but for the legacy of Sinai. Our tradition teaches that God gave the Torah in the wilderness, a place that has no private ownership. The reason is to teach that everyone may lay claim to it, to possess it and to live it. This is the lesson that Danny, Margaret, William, Noah, John, Steve, and the good people of Columbia, Kentucky, taught me in the summer of 1994.

"Great men are the guideposts and landmarks in the state."
—Edmund Burke

My Father's Gift

TANDY CHILES BARRETT

EDITOR'S NOTE: The following is from the spoken eulogy message delivered by Tandy Chiles Barrett at the celebration service for her father, the late Governor Lawton Chiles, on December 16, 1998.

I think I heard Daddy say today—as we were sitting here and [listening to] all the things that have been said, "It's gettin' a little thick in here!" And one of the things I wanted to say—that I think he would have said, too—is to give a disclaimer. He knew he wasn't perfect; he knew he wasn't anything but a man struggling with the flesh and with, what he called, "the old man." But I've been reading some of the lessons he wrote in a Bible study he was teaching at the Mansion, and I read one on the law and grace. And as I read his lesson, [I saw that] he summed it up in two words at the end: flesh and Spirit.

I believe that my father *used* the anointing that the Lord gave him during his public service to undo yokes and to lift burdens. I believe he *loved* the people of this state, and he *loved* the privilege that he had been given a chance to serve the state. And I believe he showed us how to *give*, not grudgingly or out of necessity, but *cheerfully*.

People have told me, "I'm sorry you lost your father."

I believe [today] we've *found* Lawton Chiles.

"Only a life lived for others is the life worthwhile."
—Albert Einstein

Nieces and Nephews

Eva Marie Everson

The essence of being an example is commitment, a willingness to step out of our comfort zones. Doing whatever it takes to lead others to righteousness requires a walk down paths that others might find restraining. Christ did it. He stepped down from gold-covered streets to walk among the thorns and thistles. He left a crystal throne to sit in sand and upon hard stone. He turned his back on unimaginable riches for rarely understood poverty.

He told us to be salt and light.

I have known many examples of this teaching, but two remain at the forefront of my heart. The first is my mother. In 1990, her eighty-one-year-old aunt, no longer able to care for herself, moved in with Mother. By 1991, Mother realized that full-time care was necessary. Her aunt was a love, but basically cantankerous in nature. Aunt Della either liked you or she didn't. If she didn't, there was no changing her mind. Consequently, hiring someone to stay with her while mother worked was an effort in futility. In obedience to God and family, my mother quit her job and became a full-time caregiver to a woman she loved dearly, but from time to time, had to merely tolerate.

The days grew long and difficult. As Aunt Della neared her death in July of 1992, the nights became endless hours of screaming and moaning. Friends and family suggested a nursing home, but mother refused. This woman had been like a mother to her since her own mother's death in 1956; she would never think of putting Aunt Della in a facility.

I was stunned by my mother's appearance when I arrived home for the funeral. She had aged ten years in six months. I was appalled at the bruises on her arms, inflicted by her aunt in unknowing abuse. There was a tinge of bitterness about Mother that I couldn't quite understand. But Aunt Della's care had been exceptional.

"If I ever get sick," the doctor told my mother after he'd pronounced Aunt Della dead, "I want you to be my nurse." Mother was a testimony, not only to her family but to friends and neighbors.

My dear friend, Donald Harris, is the second example of humble salt and light. I use the word humble because salt does not know that it must retain its saltiness in order to bring praise. Light does not shine to bring attention to itself, but brings light to that which falls within the light. Mother and Donald humbly shine a light on the One who falls within its circle.

Donald's paternal Aunt Lois ("WoWo") had become dependent on him in these past couple of years. As Donald and his nearly ninety-year-old aunt lived in the same city, he visited her three or four times weekly to sit with her. He took care of her shopping, performed her housekeeping chores on weekends, and then, two years ago, he purchased next door homes for them. A year later, as her condition worsened, he took a leave of absence from his job and began to care for her full-time. I have watched him gently bathe her with the aide of a nurse. He calmly fed her small spoonfuls of baby food, changed her adult diapers, washed her hair, and sat next to her bed, held her withered, old hand, and prayed with her. He listened helplessly to her calling out to those who had gone on to glory before her.

One evening, as he sat on one side of her bed and I stood on the other, "WoWo" moaned, "Sing to me that pretty song."

"What song?" I asked. "Jesus Loves Me?"

"No."

"The Lord's Prayer?"

"No."

"Then which song?"

"C-r-o-double-s."

I looked over to the tear-stained face of my dear friend. We began, "On a hill far away...."

I have sung this song more times than I can count over the years, but I had never truly listened to the words. When we sang the last lines, something caught in my heart. The final reward for being salt and light—the prize that we all strive for—can be found there.

"I will sing to the old rugged cross, till my trophies at last I lay down. I will cling to the old rugged cross, and exchange it someday for a crown."

Thank you, Mother and Donald. Thank you for being salt and light to someone else, and for being salt and light to me.

"Do all the good you can,
By all the means you can,
In all the ways you can,
In all the places you can,
At all the times you can,
To all the people you can,
As long as you can." —John Wesley

All That We Ask

SAMANTHA MARCHANT

EDITOR'S NOTE: On March 23, 1983, Amanda Dale and Samantha Gale Marchant, age fifteen months, perished in a house fire. A few weeks later, the following letter to the editor was published in the hometown newspaper of their parents.

To the Editor, Friends, and Neighbors:

In our time of bereavement, it has been hard for us to find the sufficient words to express our gratitude to each of you. We want to thank you for the prayers, love, and gifts you were so kind to share. The tragic deaths of our daughters, Amanda Dale and Samantha Gale, have touched the lives of many both far and near in different ways. No one knows why their lives had to end at this time, but we do believe that God has a plan and a reason for these things happening. We do not blame God for their deaths. We are just thankful they did not suffer. We cannot change what has happened to Amanda Dale and Samantha Gale, but we can control how it affects us. With God's love and yours, we can grow more loving, more compassionate, and more Christ-like people.

The only other thing we ask from each of you is to love God; be thankful for what you have and enjoy life to its fullest each day. Just look around and you will find that there are others less fortunate than you. Love your family and friends more each day and share your time with them, because we can never be sure when the time will come for one of them to leave this life.

Once again, thank you very, very much and may God bless each of you in a very special way.

With deep love, Samantha and Roger Marchant

"It was pride that changed angels into devils; it is humility that makes men as angels." —Saint Augustine

Dave's Goofy Day

CARMEN LEAL

Tuesday, February 24, 1998, is more glorious than I could have anticipated. In the aftermath of the terrible Central Florida storms, the picture perfect day is a gift. Not only is it welcome respite for those who have lost their homes in the devastating level four tornadoes, but it is an answer to prayer for Dave.

My husband, Dave, loves Goofy. No, let me replace "loves" with the word, "obsesses." What Dave feels for Goofy is definitely bordering on obsession. For Christmas I gave him his heart's desire, two Goofy shirts, that he wears almost exclusively. It is no surprise that the last thing on Dave's "to do" list is going to Disney World.

Dave is dying. He has Huntington's Disease, a rare, devastating, degenerative brain disorder for which, right now, there is no cure. At forty-six years of age, Dave shuffles through his days like an old man of eighty. As his appetite and ability to swallow continue to decrease, so does his weight. Sometimes I am not sure who lives in his body; the three-year-old child, or the old man who sits and stares into space. On this day, there is no question; it is the three-year-old, dressed in his purple Goofy shirt, eager to go to Disney World.

I could never afford Disney tickets for my family of four, but I want to give Dave a special day. In the last stage of Huntington's, I know time is running out. Thanks to the generosity of the wonderful Disney Compassion Program, we are going to make a memory.

As excited as Dave is about the excursion, I have a nagging concern. What if we get to the park and Goofy can't be found? But no need to worry! Look! There's Goofy, right inside the front gate, holding court to dozens of young fans clutching their autograph books, faces glowing as they excitedly wait to greet their favorite character. I wheel Dave's chair up the ramp and wait behind the children, none of them older than five. I alternate between feeling happy for Dave, embarrassed because of his obvious age and disability, and unbearably sad for myself at the loss of my dreams. Before Huntington's Disease ravaged his brain, Dave earned a Masters of Business Administration degree. Dave is himself a parent, yet now, the crowning achievement in his life is to spend time with Goofy.

It's Dave's turn. His face is one incredibly ecstatic smile and Goofy seems to know he's special. Instead of the brief time spent with the kids, Dave gets a hug, a caress on the arm with the floppy ear, a kiss on the cheek, posing for pictures, and another hug.

A lady with a Polaroid camera takes a picture for Dave to carry around all day, since our photos will need developing. I am trying hard to smile, but it's difficult to breathe as I watch Dave's childlike delight through a veil of tears.

A turquoise Goofy shirt and colorful Goofy doll are a necessity, and every few minutes Goofy comes out of the bag and Dave talks to him and beams. Dave's wheelchair gets the royal treatment, and there are no lines for us as we breeze through the park. Dave and Goofy enjoy every ride, even the scary ones. It is truly a perfect day.

Tonight, Dave sleeps with Goofy and wakes me to find the doll whenever it gets tangled in the covers, or falls to the floor. I know when the Hospice workers come tomorrow, he will trip over his words as he excitedly relates the story of his day and Goofy to them.

He told me this morning that now, since he got to meet Goofy, God can call him home so he can see the angels in heaven. I think Dave has already seen some angels. I am convinced Donna with Disney Compassion Program and the employee in the Goofy suit are angels. Only an angel would have treated Dave with such dignity and joy on his extraordinary day. The caring lady, conveniently standing nearby with a Polaroid, just has to reside in heaven.

Part of me is happy to give Dave his Goofy day, and the other half is in mourning for the husband I thought I had already said goodbye to years ago. I feel a loss as I have not felt since he was first diagnosed. Sometimes I wonder how I can ever survive, but I know God will continue to bring angels alongside me whenever I really need them. He always does.

"Mature love that lasts involves growing from a state of receiving much and giving little toward a state of cheerfully giving everything and demanding nothing in return." —Dr. Richard Strauss

On the Twenty-Sixth Day of May

LYNNE MIXSON

On the 26th day of May they were wed,
young love just beginning to bloom.
Through raindrops they ran,
past spaces left vacant
by a disapproving family.

A cottage by the ocean,
first one boy, then another by her knee.
The curls of a girl followed
and old dreams went floating out to the sea.

Years went by, holidays passed,
gifts were given... no jewelry.
Few words were spoken, cheeks turned to meet lips...
little emotion.
No flowers, no dancing, no romantic vacations.
But, in the silence, grew devotion.

Tender is the night that is shared by two,
wretched is the illness
that separates two in the night;
that locks one's mind far away, unknowing, but still living;
offering only a brief smile, the opening of eyes,
the flicker of a light.

144

His love lives not in flowers or passion or emotion.
His love lives in patience, in perseverance,
in holding crippled hands, in paying beauticians,
and keeping after floor nurses,
His love lives, in devotion...

On this 26th day of May.

"I don't think of all the misery but of all the beauty that still remains." —Anne Frank

God In a Paper Bag

CHUCK BATES

The streets where we lived, in Geneva, Illinois, were lined with maple, oak, and elm trees, all at their peak in living fall colors. Part of Geneva's charm is its well-preserved older homes, and ours, built in 1906, was one of them. It was a big two-story family home with stairs that creaked, a large brick fireplace, and five bedrooms, which our six children filled with ease.

It was four o'clock on a lovely autumn day. Our twelve-year-old boy, Chucky, hopped on his bicycle on his way to deliver neighborhood newspapers for his best friend who was out of town.

"Bye, Mom! See you later!" The door slammed.

But the neighborhood missed their newspapers that evening. Instead, papers wound up strewn over an intersection two blocks from our home.

It was a study in "instants." One instant he was an enthusiastic, innocent twelve-year-old boy riding a bicycle. The next instant, a car crashed into the side of his bicycle, tossing him thirty feet into the air. The next instant, he slammed back to earth onto the unyielding cement pavement. He lay motionless. He was, perhaps mercifully, unconscious.

In a sense, that night never ended. There are not enough back issues of *Newsweek* and *Outdoor Life* magazines in any hospital waiting room to ease the anxiety, the near-madness brought on by a six, almost seven-hour wait during neurosurgery.

Finally, in perspiration soaked "greens," three doctors appeared. The neurosurgeon in charge said, "Everything has been done that we know to do. Your boy has suffered severe brain damage. He may die soon. Or, he may not."

He did not "die soon." He suffered seizures and further neurosurgery, yet lived on for months in hospitals and rehab centers. For nine months we nursed him in our own home. We were so happy to have him home again, though we, as his family, and he, as our patient, faced an uphill battle. Day after day after day we worked with him. He simply could not open his eyes. He could not talk. We were never sure how much he heard or comprehended, but at times we detected a faint smile and squeezing of our fingers.

He remained comatose for two years and three months. Then, quite suddenly, on New Year's Day morning, he died. Have you ever prayed and wondered why God, in His silence, appeared to be sleeping on the job? I have. God was not sleeping, but it took a special wake-up call for me to believe that; a call that came in the form of a plain, brown paper bag.

Every fourth or fifth day after the accident, we found a paper bag of fresh fruit left on our front door step. No note, no card, no name. Sometimes there would be a few bananas, an orange or two, and a couple of apples. Other times it would be pears and peaches and maybe grapefruit. Those paper bags kept coming.

That was my wake-up call: fruit in a plain, brown paper bag with no name tag. For some reason—maybe because of that anonymous brown paper bag—I began to pay attention to what was happening all around us. Family, friends, even strangers rallied to lift and carry us through those trying months, each in their own manner, and in a variety of ways.

It took awhile, but it dawned on me that God was not silent, nor was He sleeping. He was revealing Himself, offering His love and strength, through all those people.

But what about Chucky? Was God, through people or in any other way helping him? Yes. He was loved. He had good medical and nursing care. Doctors assured us that though he still had the capacity to feel physical pain, he was not in pain. But he didn't wake up. He died. Yes, he died, but he was not alone. We were not alone. I know that now.

We did learn the identity of the fruit bearer. He was a man we hardly knew, the kind of man you wouldn't notice in a room full of people, if for no other reason than I'm sure he avoided rooms full of people. He was quiet, a man of few words, sort of a loner.

When I thanked him for all the wonderful fresh fruit, I don't remember that he said anything. He just looked at me, smiled, and put out his hand, which I grasped in mine and shook soundly.

*"You will find as you look back upon your life that the moments
when you have really lived, are the moments you have done things
in a spirit of love."* —Henry Drummond

Sixty-Six Poinsettias

EVA MARIE EVERSON

"Sixty-six," my neighbor Maryse said. I'd just entered
her front door to find her standing, emotionless, staring at the
red, pink, and white poinsettias crowding the foyer and lining
the hallway. I shivered in the chill that permeated the home;
not so much from the December air, but from the events of the
past week. On December 2, 1987, Maryse's daughter Laura had
been killed in an auto accident.

Neighbors for nearly a decade, we'd raised our six children
together. Mine were as much a part of her home as hers were of
mine. We even had special nicknames for the kids; I called
twenty-year-old Laura, "Laura Sue."

"Sixty-six," she repeated. "Sixty-six poinsettias. Sixty-six
reminders that my daughter is dead."

I'd never thought of the traditional flower-giving at funerals
in such a way. I also couldn't imagine, nor begin to imagine, the
agony my friend was experiencing, but I saw that the flowers
only seemed to add to the grief.

"Do you want me to take them somewhere?" I said softly. "I
can do that. I will do that."

"No," she said with a sudden jerk of her head. "I'll think of
something."

A few hours later, she called. "I know what I want to do. I
want to do what Laura would have done. She loved the elderly.
Remember how she used to bake cookies and take them to the

nursing home?"

I remembered.

"I want to do what Laura would have done," she said again. "Are you and Jessie available Friday night?"

"Sure," I said. Jessica, my six-year-old, and Maryse's son, Hayes, (Haysie-Bean) were best friends.

Then she filled me in on the plan.

Friday evening, Maryse was armed with the poinsettias. Hayes and Jessica, dressed like Santa's elves, carried candy canes donated by Bob's Candy Company, a friend of Maryse's husband came dressed as Santa, and I toted a camcorder on my shoulder to record the evening. We entered the warm, antiseptic hallway of a nearby nursing home with a "Ho! Ho! Ho!" and a "Merry Christmas!" Tired, age-lined faces broke into childlike amusement and wonder, their old, watered-down eyes beamed with excitement.

Santa's joyful, "Ho! Ho! Ho!" proclaimed our presence mirthfully at each room's doorway.

"Oh, little darlings! *Little darlings!*" The residents extended their arms, welcoming our little elves.

Greeting each resident by name (their names were on the doors), Maryse said, "Merry Christmas," and placed a poinsettia on the nearby bedside tables.

"Merry Christmas," they said. "You're so sweet! So sweet!"

I steadied the camera and peered in the lens through tears. This was the single, most selfless act of love I had ever witnessed. My friend gave out of her grief. She took flowers commemorating her daughter's death and turned them into gifts of the season of hope, joy, and the ultimate gift of love.

I have no doubt that Laura stood next to her Lord and smiled at the five of us. It was exactly what she would have done.

I wrote this poem a few days later:

On the first day
God made sunshine,
He knew just what to do.
He sent to earth a little girl;
I called her "Laura Sue."

"Hope is not the conviction that something will turn out well but the certainty that something makes sense, regardless of how it turns out." —Vaclav Havel

Candle Bearers in Common Places

VICTORIA GAINES

The phone slipped from my ear. It was like someone had shut the blinds in my life. No way to see. Just the word cancer spinning around in my head. This dark, insidious disease had invaded all my father's vital organs. He was beyond chemo, radiation, and hope itself. The doctors canceled his hip surgery, summoned the family—and the daughter in me went completely numb.

That next morning, a weight, unmovable, lay tightly across my chest. Fear pressed in; it stifled my prayers. It reminded me that my father and I were estranged, that no one can really "go home again," and the time for reconciliation had passed. My heart grieved. Weighty, eternal issues haunted me. Someone needed to break the silence. Someone needed to make things right. Who would speak to my father about God? As I packed and prayed, so much seemed to depend on me. Such is the plight of the firstborn child.

God knew my plight. He knew my limits. Only He can take the darkness of affliction, weave a heavenly tapestry, then send earthly "Candle Bearers" to make some sense of it all. I prayed for the tiniest shred of a miracle—evidence of Providence in a family shattered by pain.

My first Candle Bearer was a friend well-acquainted with grief: "Even in the darkest times of our souls He can bring light, Vicki, but never in the way we expect it or want it." I couldn't imagine good coming from cancer. My friends prayed for healing. With or without the shadow of Death lurking over my father's bed, our reunion would be painful. Tearfully, I listened to my friend's words: "Praise God in the darkness and He will bring His light, in His way, which is always best." From there, my journey began.

During the long drive home, my teenage daughter became my Jesus-with-skin-on. When I took a wrong turn, she set me back on course. When a tear trickled down my cheek, she hummed or sang a quiet tune. She didn't always know what to say. Sometimes she even fell asleep. But she was there for me. She comforted me.

Finally, I stood behind my father's hospital door, my heart racing. I wanted to leave and never return. I managed a deep breath, hugged my sisters, and pushed the door open. A frail, gray man turned his head and looked up with tired eyes. I ran to hug him. No words, just tears—lots of tears. I was unprepared for his gracious acceptance of me. Oh, how God was in that room! My family cried. Maybe the angels needed hankies, too. Surely they rejoiced, for this prodigal father and daughter reunited after nearly ten years.

A decision for Daddy's care was urgent. With no treatment options, the hospital planned a speedy discharge. Medicare wouldn't justify more room charges, and our backs were against the wall with decision-making. The thought of a nursing home angered my brother, but we weren't convinced that Mama could take care of Daddy all alone. God, I prayed, where do we go from here?

"Hospice care," a staff nurse said. "Think about it."

Soon, someone from Hospice of Georgia greeted us and led us to a quiet room. Linda's gentleness soothed our broken spirits. She encouraged Mama to recount the events leading to Daddy's fall, and Mama cried. Eventually, we all poured out our fears to her. As Linda explained hospice care, I sensed God's hand and prayed for confirmation. That's when Linda asked if she could pray for us. When she did, I wept. But I didn't cry for Daddy; I cried because the presence of the Lord was so heavy in that room.

We made swift arrangements to move Daddy home. With hospice care, Daddy could rest in familiar surroundings and stay fairly comfortable with pain medicine around the clock. Although Mama became his chief caregiver, Hospice was right there, providing physical, emotional, and spiritual support. I watched Daddy move through the stages of grief. Finally, he accepted his illness. The more he talked with Linda, the more peaceful he became. Her compassion blessed him, and soon he nicknamed her, "my guardian angel."

I wish I could explain the last six weeks of my father's life. God lavished His love through complete strangers who pointed my family to Christ. Daddy was thankful for Linda, her pastor, the hospice chaplain, and numerous other humble folk who gave their time freely. But see? God didn't need me to be my father's nurse, pastor, conscience, or guide. He had a plan. Clearly, He manifests His own love in the midst of our suffering. "The light shines in the darkness..." (John 1:5).

My father drifted in and out of consciousness those last few weeks, but I believe he received Christ in his spirit. He credited God for healing our family after years of separation—and through the ministry of Hospice of Georgia, he tasted the fruit of redemption. In my own search for Light on this painful journey, I found it on the lips of my own father: "I tell you, my child... I love you. Be kind and forgiving like your Heavenly Father. He'll always take care of you."

One morning after that, a single red gladioli bloomed in front of Daddy's window. It fell to the ground as he took his last breath. At his side was Linda, our sweet hospice nurse. She knew his earthly end had come. Linda had spent the night with my mother, helping change sheets, praying, and reading Scripture. Maybe Daddy was right. Maybe Linda *was his* guardian angel. Surely her prayers ushered him into the presence of God.

When darkness comes, Candle Bearers shine a path to God. When we've misplaced our hope, they lend us theirs. But above all, they embody the mercy, love, and peace of God Himself—in common places.

"You don't get to choose how you're going to die. Or when. You can only decide how you're going to live. Now." —Joan Baez

The Treasure Box

CARMEN LEAL

My brother died on January 8, 1998. Merrill, a pastor, passionate about his ministry, was thirty-six. Far too young, most would say.

Merrill was buried on January 12, his birthday and his twin's. At his funeral, a celebration really, my oldest brother,

Kevin, spoke of a dream he'd had a few days before Merrill entered the hospital for the last time. In his dream, he saw a box in heaven, engraved with Merrill's name and filled to the brim with gold coins. And on these coins were engraved the names of people he had led to the Lord, deeds he had done in the name of Jesus, people he had helped, and songs he had written.

As Kevin stepped closer and peered inside, he saw that the box was not just filled with coins, it was filled to the point that not one more coin could be placed inside. Kevin awoke, knowing with certainty that Merrill, who had been ill off and on for four years, would be going home soon. You see, his treasure box was filled, and God wanted him home. At thirty-six years of age, he had done all God required of him.

Merrill did more for God in the twenty or so years since he began living for Jesus than most of us do in our entire lives. At the funeral, people stood and rejoiced at what he had meant to them, telegrams from around the world bespoke of his goodness, and over a thousand people crowded into the sanctuary of the borrowed church to honor this man. His own church, started five years previously, was too small. Churches throughout the city hosted meals for the family and congregation.

Yes, there were tears shed freely as we all realized we would never again hear his laughter, or his music, or one of his messages. But tears of joy flowed just as freely, as the stream of people who were saved because of his ministry came forward to tell their stories.

It was Benjamin Franklin who said, "Work as if you were to live one hundred years; pray as if you were to die tomorrow." That is exactly the way Merrill lived his life. He prayed, and he lived, as if he were to die tomorrow.

"One cannot get through life without pain.
What we can do is choose how to use the pain life presents to us."
—Bernie S. Siegel, M.D.

Kathi

MARGARET JOHNSON, Author of 18, No Time to Waste

Sometimes it's hard to look at her picture. Her long raven-colored hair, her tilted head, her lips curved into a half-smile, and her luminous brown eyes looking straight into mine bring bittersweet memories and flowing tears.

The day she raced into the house to show me the picture, she proudly handed it to me with a wide smile. Someone had placed it on a cardboard with a printed note. "Kathi Johnson for Homecoming Queen." Posed next to an oak tree, a classmate had clicked his camera and caught the sun on her glistening hair and a winsome expression in her large brown eyes.

"How beautiful, Kathi." I looked at the photo for long moments until she reached for it and, with a flashing smile, called, "See you later," and ran out the door.

In looking back on that very ordinary day, I never could have dreamed that picture of my just turned eighteen-year-old daughter would grace the cover of a bestselling book telling of her brief, yet eventful life.

If only I had known. I would have treasured each moment, speaking less, listening more, and gently expressing my love with words too often left unspoken. But life topples our dreams, forcing us onto unexpected curves, bumpy roads, and sharp turns.

As I held each of my five babies in my arms, I had two projected expectations. One, that they would have a heart after

God, and two, that they would experience the American Dream. Through the years, I have come to realize that God did not initiate the American Dream, nor does He necessarily sanction it. But then, my hopeful expectations were intact for our two daughters and three sons, and for many years they were precisely on course.

That is, until Kathi, our second daughter, reached adolescence. At first, an uneasy breeze drifted through our home, but as Kathi became a teenager, that breeze blew into a blustering hurricane.

Kathi and I conflicted on everything; her clothes, her hairstyles, the messy state of her room, and her choice of friends. Especially her best friend Felicia.

Kathi was a strong-willed child. And I was a strong-willed mother. Our conversations usually became a battle of our wills.

During Kathi's senior year in high school, she approached me one day.

"Mom," she said, "there is something I want to talk to you about, now don't say no, until you hear me out."

I waited for what I suspected would follow. She and Felicia planned to get an apartment together after they graduated the following June. My adamant opposition to their plans sent Kathi slamming out the door, clothes over her arm. Tears sprang to my eyes and I paced the floor, confessing what I knew was true. I was much to blame for frequently comparing my outgoing, vivacious, often irresponsible Kathi to her demure, acquiescent older sister Cindy.

Kathi was gone and I had to leave soon for the hospital for scheduled minor surgery. With a saddened heart, I lay on my hospital bed and begged God to please change Kathi and resolve the conflict between us.

"I want to change you," He tenderly whispered to my inner spirit. I couldn't believe what I'd heard. I was the mother, wasn't

I? I knew what was best for my daughter, didn't I? I continued to argue with God, explaining to Him the consequences of Kathi moving out of our home and away from our influence.

But God knew His glorious plan for my daughter, and gently, so tenderly, He spoke again. "Let go of her, she belongs to Me, release her to Me."

"Letting go" has now become a catch phrase, but on that long ago night, God Himself tutored me in the art of releasing my children to Him, a lesson I would need again and again as we raised three sons to adulthood.

During that midnight hour on my hospital bed, I literally opened my hands, and surrendered my daughter into His loving care.

When I returned from the hospital, I heard the piano. Kathi was home. I walked to the piano bench, took her face in my hands, and with flowing tears, I asked her to forgive me for not accepting her as she was, for comparing her to her sister. She asked my forgiveness too, and as we wept together, the walls between us came tumbling down.

In my wildest imagination, I couldn't have dreamed that Kathi had less than three months to live! But, in those three months, the communication between us was warm and sweet, the kind I wish had been there throughout her eighteen years.

She did move in with Felicia. However, the washer and dryer were home, and food was readily available in our refrigerator, thus home became a revolving door.

By surrendering to God and asking Kathi's forgiveness, He changed both of our hearts and speedily worked in Kathi's life in the few short months she had left on this earth.

She'd not been active in church for the past year, but with our conflicts healed, she attended the youth group one Sunday and met John Wallis, the son of missionaries to Brazil.

Excitedly, she told us that John had invited her to attend a youth camp with him, his brother Dave, and a friend named Mike. And she was going, and had promised to drive the new red Mustang her dad had purchased for her.

During their fantastic week at Camp Hammer in Northern California, the four teenagers met veteran missionaries and other young people from around the country, and more importantly, they renewed their commitment to Christ. At a campfire service, they each gave their testimonies.

Mike: "For me to live is Christ and to die is gain."

Dave: "I'm going to Brazil and help my parents as missionaries."

John: "I want Christ to be glorified in my body."

Kathi: "I want to tell everyone, everywhere about Jesus."

On the drive home, the four happy teenagers shared their goals. They were young, healthy, and excited about their future plans.

But, in a moment, their plans, their hopes, and their futures were shattered by a head-on collision on a curving mountain road home.

Kathi, Mike, and John were instantly in the presence of the Lord. Dave was spared.

On her last day at camp, Kathi wrote a letter to Felicia, pleading with her to turn her life over to God. Her touching letter became the inspiration for me to tell Kathi's story, to write openly and honestly of our mother-daughter conflicts, and to convey the message of accepting our children as they are, to ask forgiveness when necessary, and to ultimately release them to God.

I wrote *18, No Time To Waste* as a memorial to Kathi, as a gift to her friends, with the hope that it might fulfill her dream of "telling everyone, everywhere about Jesus."

Since the book was published, letters have arrived from around the world, from bereaved parents pouring out their grief and from mothers who have experienced similar conflicts with their own teenagers. My own grief softened as I grew to understand that "God's ways are perfect" and "He causes all things to work together for good to those who love Him."

Kathi has been physically absent from our family for many years now, yet our memories remain vivid... memories of her racing through the house, rushing out the door, waving her last goodbye with a vibrant smile, and roaring down the street in her red Mustang.

"I had an angel and didn't know it.
She hurried through life in a breathless sort of way,
She touched this one and that one in her short life span,
Like a candle burning wildly and then flickering out too soon.
For one brief, shining hour she warmed so many with that glow."

Time heals fresh grief and tender wounds, and gives a wider perspective that proves the promises of God again and again. No matter how deep the pain, this truth remains clear; God's grace is greater than all our hurts, greater than all our failures, greater than our painfully aching hearts. If we relax in His promises, if we relinquish our anxieties, if we allow our faith to rise to believe His Word, He will generously reward us with the wondrous gift of "beauty for ashes; joy instead of mourning; praise instead of heaviness."

I know that coming years will bring other pleasures, other heartaches, and other losses, and as the years pass, the memory of Kathi will fade a little as it must. But whatever the future holds, Kathi will always have been the one who taught me the most about being a mother, about being a Christian, about being a friend.

Thank you, Kathi.

Unto the Least of These

RUBY G. SLATER

When the roll is called up yonder,
And I lay upon my bed,
Thinking out the weary hours,
My Master's voice, it softly said;
"Fret not my weary traveler,
Never toss your fevered brow,
For within my gentle bosom
You will soon be resting now.
Many years ago I left you
When I suffered, bled, and died.
When I from the cross was taken
Where I had been crucified.
And when from you I departed
To prepare for you a place
Here, your cornerstone in Glory
Stands with dignity and grace.
Here it waits for you in Glory
And is growing day by day,
For the things that it is built of
Will never, ever pass away.
Patience, love, and all the kindness
Went to grow your family tree,
So while all these seeds were growing,
These were done as unto me.

Salt and Light To the Unlovely

[Jesus said], "But when you give a banquet, invite the poor, the crippled, the lame, the blind, and you will be blessed. Although they cannot repay you, you will be repaid at the resurrection of the righteous."

—Luke 14:13,14

"Be kind and compassionate to one another, forgiving each other, just as in Christ God forgave you." —Ephesians 4:32

King Brutus

CARMEN LEAL

He was an engaging puppy. His big, brown puppy eyes just begged us to keep him. His champagne-colored fur, the color women pay fortunes for, was soft and silky.

"Can we keep him, Mom? We'll never be bad again. We'll take care of him ourselves. You won't even know he's here!"

My two little ones spouted every excuse that a little boy can dream of in the space of three minutes. For years, their father and I had succeeded as a united front against becoming "Pet Owners."

Now Dad no longer lived at home. Divorce rent the very fabric of my children's lives, a jagged tear that threatened to last forever. Time had passed and I was ready to begin anew. Whereas the children were still upset, I had healed sufficiently and had even gone through the excitement of falling in love again. David was the perfect man who would make the perfect husband. He had only one flaw—he loved dogs.

For each reason given by the two boys, David echoed it and added one of his own. These sons of mine had not been too sure about Dave. They'd been acting as a united hedge around Mom to protect her from this interloper. But now there was a crack in their defenses, and the three banded together to persuade Mom to keep the dog.

Under the weight of their pleas, I finally crumbled. I said yes. The boys, spurred on by the thrill of ownership, rocketed to get their puppy.

Brutus had a peaceful first night. We didn't even hear a peep from him. Half standard poodle and half golden retriever, he was 100% adorable.

It began with Brutus eating my mother's white shoes, purchased especially for my wedding. A rush to the hardware store for white paint, along with a "Bad dog, bad dog!" took care of both problems.

The fun really started after the wedding. It seemed no matter what we tried, we simply could not train him. To conquer the problem, the boys and David eagerly trotted Brutus off to obedience training each Wednesday.

As bright as this bundle of joy was, the minute he walked into our home it became his territory. Brutus quickly discovered that during the day the house was his kingdom, and he was King Brutus. As we worked and studied, Brutus frolicked through his castle, ate shoes and other delectable belongings, devoured any food left in his sight, and generally wreaked havoc of his surroundings.

No matter what we tried, this was a dog out of our control. The glass-topped coffee table near the window became his throne where he sunned himself each day.

His throne crashed one day—because of his ever increasing weight—leaving shards of glass strewn around the floor. Brutus sat cowering, waiting for the phrase he'd so often heard. "Bad dog! Bad dog!"

There was the day the wind slammed the door shut and trapped him in our bedroom. He clawed his way out of the hollow core door, creating a two-foot high jagged hole in his wake.

Brutus, relentless in his quest for food, discovered an ability to open the refrigerator door. Oh, the glories of food that were his! As if he was doing something wonderful for me, Brutus carted his prizes to my side of the bed. He then proceeded to deposit chunks of food, doggie slobber, and other less-than-delightful presents on my bedspread.

Each time I determined to call the pound, the children cried. They would do anything to keep their dog—pay for the damage, train him—please Mom, please! They even tried using guilt to make their point. First it was Dad, now it's Brutus.

As my guilt increased, so did the pressure to keep the dog. Meanwhile, the damage to my home continued and I despaired of ever reclaiming domestic peace and tranquility. When the broken door through which he escaped to roam the neighborhood was fixed, Brutus the Wonderdog discovered the window as an alternative route despite the glass and screen. Off he went on another exploration.

Finally, there came The Day. The lines had been drawn and Brutus had crossed them all. The damage, the dirt, the incessant barking all contributed to the ultimatum. This dog must go. The tears coursed down their faces as my sons wailed in protest. I was the worst mother in the world. And all the time, as the battle raged, my husband silently sat with an accusing stare. Finally, exhausted, I promised I'd sleep on it and have a decision by morning.

The house grew quiet, and I turned to God to help with my dilemma. As if He were not fully aware of the situation, I pleaded my cause, stressing just how bad the situation had become with this eighty-pound terror. I justified my actions, convinced He would agree. But the peace I expected to have once I'd made a decision simply would not come. I tossed and turned until, finally, I went into the living room to sit on the residue of the sofa Brutus had ravaged.

As I sat close to tears, I peered under the kitchen table— and there was Brutus. His soft snores whistled through the silent house. I weighed my options as the indecision mounted. I cried out my anguish. I knew my sons would survive the loss of Brutus, but would I survive their anger and hurt?

I realized that my experience with Brutus was a mirror image of how God must feel about me so often. Whenever Brutus disobeyed, it was just like each time I sinned. The sofa being shredded was no different than the untruths I continued to tell. Crashing through the window and eating the door were like me losing my temper unjustly with my family, or failing to be the woman that God expects me to be. No, I hadn't murdered anyone or been unfaithful to my husband, but I was a sinner.

My sons cleaned up after Brutus each time he made a mess. They offered up their allowance to pay for the damages, endured rainy nights to walk him, and listened to endless hours of complaints from neighbors after each barking rampage. Brutus could do no wrong grave enough for them to give him to the pound. They were even willing to plead his case to their mean-spirited, heartless mother. They had an unconditional love at which I marvelled.

The love my boys showed for their dog was not dissimilar to the love God has for me. I continue to sin. I try to do better and yet I fail. The pain I have caused God over the years is so much greater than the pain Brutus caused me. The lessons Brutus needed to learn seemed so easy, as are the lessons I should learn from God. Brutus should have known he would be fed and protected. And I should trust God's Word. Yet, my nemesis and I were alike in our lack of trust.

Just as my children paid the price daily for their dog's indiscretions, so did Jesus pay the price for my sins. Before I was born, God knew exactly every weakness of mine and how often I would fall. Yet, loving me as He does, He made provisions for me. Knowing I would be the sinner I am, He sent Jesus to die on the cross for me.

As these truths set in, I was filled with love and thankfulness for my Father. That He would accept someone no better than a dog still fills me with amazement. I saw Brutus in a new light.

I realized that if God had the patience and understanding for me, I could show those qualities to Brutus. Brutus lived at our house until we moved to a new state five thousand miles away. As he matured, he learned more and made fewer mistakes. Hopefully, as I grow older in the Lord, I, too, will learn more. There were still ups and downs with Brutus as God continues to have ups and downs with me. I was never as forgiving with Brutus as God is with me. But every so often, as I tread upon the path of sin, I remember Brutus and think twice about my destination.

Thanks, Brutus.

"Kind words can be short and easy to speak, but their echoes are truly endless." —Mother Teresa of Calcutta

Hero

CAROLYNN J. SCULLY

A hero is a person
    Exposing his heart to another in need,
    Touching a heart full of
        Loneliness,
          Pain,
            Fear,
              Embarrassment,
                Anger, and the
                  Hopelessness
                    Of one he may not know.

Responding, not to what he feels
Or sees on the outside,
But what he knows to be true:
    A heart is calling for someone's touch.

"Success in life has nothing to do with what you gain in life
or accomplish for yourself. It's what you do for others."
—Danny Thomas

Missionary Sunday

LINDA D. SCHOONOVER

I don't know about you, but as a child, I never considered Missionary Sunday one of the more exciting parts of church. That changed for me last summer. I had become one of a fifteen-member team flying to Brasov, Romania, to minister to street children. These children are typically homeless and without parents.

Upon our arrival in Romania, the missionaries prepared us for our first visit with the street children. They were going to be dirty, perhaps with lice in their hair or scurvy. Some of us hesitated a bit. Should we touch them?

The missionaries assured us that we would be all right—just take a good bath afterwards, they warned. At Brasov train station, we first noticed lines of dusty cars and taxis. There was no sign of any street children.

Then, as our taxis pulled into the alcove, thirty to forty children suddenly erupted from behind the bushes and ran toward the cars. They gawked to see whom the missionaries that they'd grown to love and trust had brought for them to meet. At first glimpse, they looked like ordinary children. As they approached, though, you could see that they weren't. The girls—mostly from eight to eighteen—had cut their hair to look like boys. The streets and sewers where they live offer them no protection from physical and sexual abusers, so the girls mimic the boys' gestures and grooming in self-protection.

Despite the heat, the children wear all the clothes they own; they have no other place to keep them safely. So they wear their winter caps, sweaters, and everything else, to keep them from being stolen. They have no showers and no beds. These children live in the sewers, in the train station, and in nearby bushes. This little section of the parking lot was the only "home" they knew.

These children live in deplorable conditions, and their histories are almost unbelievable. Some didn't know their names, their birth dates, or their ages. Their parents had made them go out begging on the streets, and when they failed to bring in enough money, they kicked their own children out, and abandoned them. Some of their parents had even broken their bones and tied them to heal improperly, so they would be better beggars.

But one characteristic was more noticeable than any other in these street children. They were starved for hugs, love, and affection. They desperately wanted someone to tell them that they were special—and loved.

With the help of missionaries and others who spoke both Romanian and English, I was able to communicate with the children. There was twelve-year-old Ana Maria, whose hair was cropped so short she looked like a boy. She immediately approached me and, after looking for approval from the missionaries, allowed me to give her a hug. She wanted another, then another. She was like a gas tank that couldn't be filled.

I looked down and into the face of another little girl, Sorena. In Sorena, I saw myself as a little girl, and I remembered how it felt to be abandoned by your parents.

My being here was not accidental, but carefully orchestrated by God. I knew that God wanted me to be here for Sorena and the others because I could relate to them.

As I hugged her, she asked me to take her picture. Despite her self-cropped haircut and the black spots of cavities dotting her front teeth, nothing could darken the golden personality within. Hugging herself, she smiled gleefully into the camera.

Katena was eighteen. Her dark hair was also cropped like a boy's, and her arms, scored like a tic-tac-toe board, displayed years of self-mutilation. Where is her hope? She'd been on the street most of her life. She and the others didn't know about Jesus, the One who loved and cared for them, the One who comforted them in their loneliness. These children knew only the streets, the harsh brutality of minus fifty degree winters, and fights for their lives over warm pipes. They hadn't known love other than that of these missionaries, who came every afternoon with outstretched arms and juice and sandwiches.

There I was, in the middle of Brasov, Romania, far away from the fifteen-hour days my law practice had become, and the courtrooms where people argued over the "principal" of things. I suddenly wondered whether I'd really helped anyone with toiling all those long, fifteen-hour-days.

The children swarmed around us like bees near a beehive. In an instant, my life was changed. "Oh, God," I thought, "what have I done for you? All my striving, all my education, all my work—have they served the purpose you have for me? Has my life glorified You?"

I recalled the eighty-hour weeks, in the middle of federal lawsuits and clients who used me to litigate for them because of the "principal of the matter." Whose principles was I fighting and spending my life for? Whose "feelings" had drawn me away from my Lord? Whose "mission" had drawn my time away from God's plans, and my attention from what God needed me to do?

Far from the courts, the law books, and my office—yet I was exactly where God wanted me to be. This was exactly where He had prepared me to be, it was all part of His plan. God was shaking me and saying, "Hello! Are you listening? Are you watching? Isn't it time you were sensitive to why you are here? Your days are numbered and I have plans for you. Are you listening?"

Our last day in Romania, we went back to the train station to catch a bus. As we waited to board, a little hand grasped mine. It was Anna Maria. She didn't let go; she boarded the bus and sat down in the seat next to me. I worried that she would not find her way back; maybe she thought I could take her home. But no, she sat there quietly, just glad to be near me. I hugged her before she got off. As we departed, I waved goodbye, wondering whether I would ever see Ana Maria again. Would she be able to endure another winter of below-zero temperatures? Would she have food and avoid the evils that steal away the lives of the street children?

As the winter progressed, I wondered if she thought that the tourist that had come to visit her on those few occasions had forgotten her and the others. Had I listened to what God wanted me to do? Had I imparted any hope to these children?

Missionary Sunday at church would never be the same for me again. You see, someday soon, I want to be a missionary too.

"Those who bring sunshine to the lives of others cannot keep it from themselves." —James M. Barrie

Happy Holidays

CARMEN LEAL

My first Christmas season as a single mother was incredibly difficult. Happy couples were everywhere; they surrounded me at church, shopping malls, and at every party I attended. But as the holidays loomed ever nearer, I faced the thought of being alone—of my children spending Christmas without Daddy—with increasing dread.

I recognized my need of help, and I prayed to God to make me more accepting of my situation. That's when I realized there is always someone else in a similar or worse situation. My solution was to reach out to other single parent families and invite them to my home for an open house. Families were invited to stop by between one and five o'clock on Christmas Day and to bring something to share.

What a great day! People came early and stayed late. With the many children and all the laughter, music, and conversation, it was one of my most memorable Christmases ever. The day was transformed from an opportunity to dwell on myself and my sad situation to a day I didn't want to end.

Everyone wants to be a part of a group, and that is never more true than during the holidays. I have created precious memories by hosting a holiday open house. Adopting a family for holidays and birthdays is another way I've shown that I care. When I purchase gifts for the children, I make their Christmas happier, and when I involve my own children in selecting the perfect presents for others in need, they learn an invaluable lesson, too.

Like everyone else, single parents need support throughout the entire year, but they need an extra amount of TLC during the holidays. And guess who got the biggest blessing by reaching out and caring? I did!

"The highest exercise of charity is charity towards the uncharitable."
—J.S. Buckminster

All Being Well

CAROLYN JONES

I could tell you about Elizabeth, the child of a British diplomat born in the Uruguay, or about the war bride who married an American GI and came to live in a rural backwoods home in south Georgia. Or I could tell you about Elizabeth, the single mother who reared three red-haired daughters after her marriage broke up because of her husband's alcoholism. But what I really want to tell you about is Elizabeth, a compassionate, accommodating, generous woman who gives herself to caring for people in crisis.

If you meet her on the street or at church, her British accent is quite attractively evident. When she takes on a job, she intends to do it or have it done. And when she makes plans, the conclusion is, "all being well." This is her way, though she does not appear "religious" in any sanctimonious sense, of expressing the old phrase, "God willing." And the faith this phrase reveals portrays who she is.

After her retirement from banking, I became aware that she

spent a lot of time looking after Hilda, who lived next door. Hilda, a retired schoolteacher in her eighties, had a negative attitude about everything. This was not only Elizabeth's opinion, but also that of others who knew the elderly woman.

As Hilda's health deteriorated, Elizabeth gradually began to do her shopping, write her checks, and manage other household necessities. Once, Elizabeth was changing a light bulb in Hilda's kitchen and fell off the ladder, severely injuring her shoulder and fracturing her knee. Hilda's response was complaint that Elizabeth couldn't do things for her for a while. But Elizabeth returned home after therapy and continued to look after the older woman until she couldn't live alone any longer.

Hilda had no family except for a half sister in California and a nephew in Atlanta, but she had alienated them both. So, Elizabeth did what was necessary to get her into a retirement home and visited her there for a year. When Hilda fell and went to the hospital, then through rehabilitation for a month, Elizabeth was there for her. Her condition meant that she could not go back into the retirement home, and it was left to Elizabeth to arrange for a nursing home. Later, Hilda suffered congestive heart failure and spent another three weeks in the hospital, after which it was necessary to find a home that would take patients needing complete nursing care. During all this time, Elizabeth managed Hilda's affairs, from medical care to insurance. Thus it was that after Hilda was transferred to the complete-care nursing home, and died there the following day at the age of eighty-nine, Elizabeth again handled the necessary arrangements.

Elizabeth, always so unpretentious, turns others' attention away from herself and on to the people in crises and to what could or should be done for them. Her ministry to Hilda is only one of many examples. Not only does she express, in her delightful English accent, her heart's sentiments about "all being well," her life says it loud and clear.

"Charity sees the need, not the cause." —German Proverb

Intersections of Hope

CHARLES AND SANDRA POCK

God did not intend homelessness nor hunger to be a part of this world when He created it. These appalling realities of life exist only because of sinful choices we, God's creation, make. Now, that isn't to say that the tiny child with distended stomach, screaming in the agony that accompanies hunger, is at fault for her problems. Of course not. But the sins of mankind have made us all—young and old, rich and poor, white and black and every shade between—reapers of sin's consequences.

Have you ever been *truly* hungry? That's when the memory of the last full meal you had is faded into oblivion. Have you ever been forced to sleep in a cardboard box on a night when the freezing air penetrates the very marrow of your bones? Probably not. But these are facts of life for the transient homeless everywhere, people living in a state of desolation. These are the facts of life for the transients who converge at the crossroads of the sunbelt in San Antonio, Texas.

Here, the two great Interstate Highways 10 and 35 intersect, as do the Santa Fe and Union Pacific railroads. More precisely, they meet near Kirby, a suburb of San Antonio.

Kirby, bounded by these biways, is basically a nice, middle-class, single-family community. It is the original railroad town for Bexar County.

The residents of Kirby don't usually see the homeless needy within their town, but most who commute to and from work within the city can't help but meet them on their way. These travelers inevitably congregate at the intersections; it's where they eventually find rides to wherever their going. Almost every day we pass them, faces gaunt, eyes pleading, holding up signs, usually lettered in crayon on cardboard. Often, you'll recognize a sign because once it's made, it's left behind for others to use. The placards are sometimes printed with their destination; many times, they are silent pleas for help, and for food. They can say anything from, "Need Help God Bless," to the more original, heart-rending one once held by a woman, saying, "Will Trade Toys For Food." One time, a pair of women, one younger and one older, held up a sign pleading, "Pregnant—Please Help." These are people from everywhere. For instance, a couple from Oregon were traveling by car with their children and had a transmission breakdown. They were stranded, penniless and frightened. Evidently seeing others in their same predicament with signs, they made one for themselves, too.

To see the homeless, the hungry people on America's roads, belies all reports of our "booming" United States economy. Truly, we are experiencing both the best of times and the worst of times. The media has television viewers throughout the world believing that all Americans are carefree, rich jet-setters—but the people of Kirby, Texas, know better. They know, as do city dwellers across our great country, that a third-world co-exists with American affluence.

San Antonio, like most other American cities, has its share of programs, both local and federal, to feed and cloth its poverty-stricken citizens. But the majority of the homeless transients who frequent Bexar County's major intersections are out of their reach; they are on their ways to "greener pastures" for one reason or another, and the inner-city is for other, more permanent denizens. The regular programs are useless to the homeless and hungry who populate those byways.

Yes, it's true that many of our nation's homeless are drug abusers, indolent and deeply troubled souls. It's also true that these conditions are often self-induced. Does that mean it's okay to see them hungry? In a country that clamors for nation-wide self-confidence, these people are reduced to the lowest status on our self-declared rule of societal tolerance. Are we supposed to thumb our noses at them and say, "Well, it's their own fault!" and walk away as though they were invisible?

Some residents of St. Joan d'Arc Catholic Parish in Kirby are not walking away. Individuals who drive through the intersections daily have started carrying a number of brown-bag lunches in their cars. These bags contain non-perishable, individually packed foods such as grocery shelves abound with: canned Vienna sausages, chips, dates, raisins and canned fruit juice, to name a few. One family goes to Sam's Club to buy family-size boxes of twenty-four single pack items for this specific purpose. They put a package from each box into sacks that are then tied and ready to put on the floor of the family car, within reach of the driver. Whenever the car is stopped by a traffic light and a hungry person asks for food, they reach for a bagged meal from behind the seat and offer it with a blessing.

As to be expected, there are critics of this program who argue that this *ad hoc* approach to the problem simply encourages indolence and dependency. Proponents contend that hunger under any name is still hunger. Just *why* someone is hungry doesn't matter; what matters is that someone is hungry.

Even within the parish, there are those who favor spending their charitable resources in a more traditional manner, to help families who "try to help themselves" instead of "begging."

Jesus fed the masses, five thousand and more at a time, without asking credentials, or drilling them on just why they didn't come prepared like the boy with his loaves and fishes. He went about healing, and feeding the hungry, and He asked us to do the same. It wasn't His intention that the needy meet certain requirements in order to be helped. The *reasons* for their neediness don't come into question. In fact, He says, as part of an acceptable fast to Him, "...to share your bread with the hungry..." (Isa. 58:7a). God deals with their judgements and their souls; it's our business simply to obey Him. Giving a lunch to a hungry traveler—whatever reason they're traveling—is to "share your bread with the hungry."

These hungry transients may not ever come to know our Lord. They may never really stop to wonder just why somebody helped them when they needed help without even knowing them. But maybe, just maybe, even *one* of them will remember the blessing, and be curious about a Lord who loves them, and feeds them through helping hands, while they are yet in their sins. Just *maybe* one soul will come to Him—because they saw His love in us.

Wouldn't that be wonderful?

"Love means to love that which is unloveable; or it is no virtue at all." —G.K. Chesterton

Carnies

EVA MARIE EVERSON

I went to the fair
And saw them there;
Those people who
Run the rides and
Attend the booths.

So easily recognized,
The men dressed in
Old jeans and tee shirts,
Grease and dirt in their nails.
The girls with too much
Make-up, hair out of place;
So obviously young
And yet so learned.

"Low life," I thought,
Society would call them.
"Carnies, white trash,
Scum of the earth."
Did I view them the same way, too?

"My children," I thought,
God would call them.
"Precious and important.
Part of My creation."
Mustn't I view them
The same way, too?

"The miracle is this—the more we share, the more we have."
—Leonard Nimoy

Big Brown Eyes

PHIL PIATT

Many years ago—depression days—a little lad was underfoot in his mother's kitchen when there came a rap at the back door. "It's tramps," she said, then greeted two rough men with hats in hand.

"Ma'am, could you spare some supper? Do you have some jobs that we could do?"

The smell of chicken frying may have led them there!

"Pick up the limbs and sticks and clean the yard, and I'll have something for you in a little while."

Time to open more canned peas and fix more mashed potatoes, make the gravy. Big brown eyes of a four-year-old peered through the bulging, rusted screen door, and saw life as it was in those days. Widowed mother with young children; regular men, very polite and mannerly, but down on their luck, like many of that time.

"Delicious ma'am. Yes, thank you, ma'am. So very nice. God bless you, ma'am." They went away well fed. Big brown eyes were watching three of the least of God's children doing what they could. Eyes that took it in, and could not forget.

179

"Be such a man, and live such a life, that if every man were such as you, and every life like yours, this earth would be God's Paradise." —Phillip Brooks

Running the Race

LAURA SHERWOOD

I have been a runner for ten years. My running partner, Linda, is to blame for getting me hooked on this crazy sport. We are comfortable running together and know each other's habits and hang-ups. As Christians, we enjoy "solving" the world's problems in our hour-and-a-half run. Then, last December, Linda threw a wrench into our training.

We have run two Disney Marathons together. Every December we run a half-marathon to get ready for the "real thing" the following month. It's great training and helps us prepare mentally.

The day of the race, Linda brought in a rookie—her neighbor, who I didn't know—to run with us. Normally, being the warm person that I am, I wouldn't have minded. But we had never run with this person. I couldn't begin to imagine what lay ahead!

Let's talk baggage! This gal, I'll call her Freida, had all sorts of paraphernalia she planned to run with: headphones and music, a fanny-pack strapped to her narrow waist, a water bottle....

We started our thirteen-mile run, which in and of itself is no stroll in the park. Freida, headphones blasting and singing along as though we could hear the music, too, shouted to us periodically over the music, interrupting our conversation. All in all, she was annoying. It's hard enough to run thirteen miles without that!

After five or six miles of hearing, "Why in the world did I bring along this heavy fanny-pack?" Linda did the unthinkable: she decided to carry Freida's burden. Perhaps it was only to shut her up, yet I couldn't help but see the similarities of Jesus carrying our burdens even when we're unlovable. Linda didn't mind... but that's Linda. Me? I was ready to take the pack and give it the old heave-ho!

When we neared the finish line (yes, we did finish the race), we saw the real reason for Freida's pack: she pulled out a comb and a tube of bright, pink lipstick. She knew photos would be taken. Rain had soaked us, and we were all sweaty, yet she was primping as if she'd be modeling for the cover of *Runner's World*! I was ready to pull my hair out!

Thinking back on this day, I can't help but laugh. But I also compare my attitude to Linda's. I allowed myself to be miserable the two-and-a-half hours, while Linda had treated this woman with love by lightening her load. Would Jesus do anything less? Linda displayed Jesus, while I was... well, you know, a horse's pa-toot!

I learned my lesson. In the future, I will try to display Christ-like behavior. It's hard when the unlovable need love, but these are the tests God gives. I flunked the exam that rainy December day, but I look forward to future tests.

"Therefore, since we are surrounded by such a great cloud of witnesses, let us throw off everything that hinders and the sin that so easily entangles, and let us run with perseverance the race marked out for us. Let us fix our eyes on Jesus, the author and perfecter of our faith, who for the joy set before Him endured the cross, scorning its shame, and sat down at the right hand of the throne of God. Consider Him who endured such opposition from sinful men, so that you will not grow weary and lose heart." —Hebrews 12:1-3

"Only eyes washed by tears can see clearly." —Louis L. Mann

To See With the Heart

ESTHER PHELPS

Driving to South Florida to visit Uncle Tony, I found myself remembering him before Parkinson's disease started to rob him of his life. Tony was my second cousin, but out of respect for his age, my sons and I had always called him "Uncle Tony."

My son, Garry, was with me, and I hoped the nursing home wouldn't be too boring for a five-year-old. As we walked down the bare, dimly lit halls, the smells of decay and disinfectant hit me; I wished there was a way to hold my breath until I got back outside. I heard the familiar sound of "Jeopardy" around the corner and walked toward it, hoping I would find someone to direct me to Uncle Tony's room.

There were perhaps thirty-five or forty elderly people, all in wheelchairs, staring at a television in the large room at the end of the hall. At first they appeared to be watching TV, but when I walked in the room I could see that the black-and-white screen was in a permanent horizontal roll. No one moved or even looked our way as we entered the room, and I saw that many of them were semi-comatose; slumped in their wheelchairs, staring blankly into nothingness. A room full of has-beens, zombies, forgotten souls, I thought.

"Please, God, don't let him be here in this awful place," I prayed.

I pulled Garry close to me and scanned the room, looking for the kind, distinguished gentleman who had always looked out for me. Relief washed over me as I realized that Uncle Tony was not there. I started to back out of the room, pulling Garry with me.

"Mom, no, wait!" Garry refused to budge. Instead, he pulled me back into the room with him.

"Garry, come with me and we'll find Uncle Tony. He's not here," I said.

I saw the anguish on Garry's face, and tears in his eyes. "Garry, what's the matter?" I asked concerned.

"Mom, they're crying."

I took another look around the cold, dismal room. "No, Garry, they're not crying, they're just resting."

He shook his head adamantly, insisting, "No, they're crying!"

I tried reasoning with Garry, but there was no persuading him to leave. "Garry, what do you want to do?"

"I want to give 'em a hug."

I nodded and watched him trot off to the first chair, never expecting what I was about to witness. As his arms circled the woman's pale, thin frame, her vacant eyes came alive, and she reached her arms out to hug Garry. She was revived! Garry patted her bloodless cheek and tenderly kissed it, then moved to the next chair.

The old man slumped over the arm of the chair, drooling, his eyes closed. Both legs were amputated above the knee. Garry didn't seem to notice the drool or the missing legs, as he leaned down to give the same tender hug and kiss. The old man jerked to attention. When he realized he was being hugged, he started crying and saying, "That's the first hug I've had since I got here; this little boy really loves me!"

Garry clapped his hands and cheered! He moved on to the next person, and then the next, and soon the room was a hubbub of laughter and tears.

I sank into an empty chair, tears streaming down my face as

Garry hugged every person in the room, taking care not to miss anyone. He was as delighted to hug and kiss the last one as he was the first.

Finally, he stood at the front of the room, grinning and waving both hands as the old men and women waved back and called, "Hi, Garry!" and, "Can I have another hug?"

Then I realized that Garry had been right; they *were* crying; although there were no tears, inside they were crying out of loneliness. When we look beyond the obvious, we may find what's real. Gary had done that; he found what's real.

You see, Garry has Down's Syndrome, and most people who meet him might think he doesn't understand much. It is true that Garry's development is not "normal." His speech, skills, and his growth are delayed. But when it comes to seeing with the heart, Garry is beyond his years. He has brought unconditional love to me and everyone he touches. I often wish I could be more like Garry.

His spirit, unencumbered by fear, greed, jealousy, envy, or competition, is free to feel what the eyes can't see and the words try to hide.

Garry's gift is to see with the heart.

Salt and Light In Travel

"Now that same day two of them were going to a village called Emmaus, about seven miles from Jerusalem. They were talking with each other about everything that had happened. As they talked and discussed these things with each other, Jesus Himself came up and walked along with them…."

—Luke 24:13-15

"Blessed is the influence of one true, loving human soul on another."
—George Eliot

Night Train To Madrid

G.W. FRANCIS CHADWICK

Vacations, especially those taken in Europe, are not generally used for going on the typical missionary field. But for me, it was during such a trip that a turning point in my life occurred. I was twenty-one years old and traveling through Europe during a university year-abroad program. Until that time, I thought I was a Christian.

Backpackers, as I was, tend to convene at the train stations, town squares, or youth hostels. At the Calais train station, shortly after the ferry ride across the Channel, I met Steve Knots, a youth minister from Berkley, California. He was on his way to L'Abri, a retreat in Switzerland run by Francis Schaefer. As we seemed to click, and partly because I spoke French, he decided to change his travel plans and join me in mine.

We were joined in Barcelona by another young man, Tony, who also was on his way to L'Abri. Though none of us knew it, the Lord in His infinite wisdom had set the wheels in motion for the beginnings of my relationship with Him. It began on the night train to Madrid, when Steve and Tony began to fellowship. Looking back, I think it was the fact that they were not talking directly to me, but at me, that had the greatest impact. It was amazing, because they spoke to my deep-seated, wrongheaded convictions about what it meant to become "born again."

Until that time, my main exposure to "active" Christianity had been the bizarre missionary types in Jamaica, where I was raised. My concept of being "saved" meant missionaries going to the Third World and harassing people for contributions, as were my parents and family. Steve and Tony really shattered that image for me. They were so human and so at peace with themselves and the world. Steve talked about his experiences with the many young people he worked with, and about how Jesus is viewed by so many as a religion, which totally obscures the relationship aspect. As humans, we are "naturally" religious, but God hates religion, and proved it by sending his Son, who lived His life as a lowly carpenter, to die a humiliating death. Any attempts at religiosity, such as by Peter saying, "Let us build three tabernacles," were spurned by Christ. He was prophesied as this type of Savior hundreds of years earlier, but the majority of His people totally missed it, largely because of their religious and political expectations. In Steve's message, the lowliness of Christ really touched me, as well as what he said about how people's concept today of what and who Christ is, is still totally off the mark. Because my heart was fertile and well tilled, I was exceedingly touched.

By the time we got to Madrid, I was very tired. I slept twelve hours, waking only once to remove my T-shirt. It was oddly drenched with sweat—yet the weather was not hot, nor did I have a fever! I later realized that the joy ineffable of the Holy Spirit had changed my life forever. Steve and Tony had been complete strangers on a European vacation, yet they were the messengers of the Gospel to me.

I tried without success to contact Steve when I returned to the States, wanting to tell him just how much his willingness to yield to the Spirit meant to me. It's a lesson for us all. God calls us to His work in unexpected places. Are we willing to be used, even while on vacation? This is one soul, forever saved, who cries, "Yes!"

"Kindness is never wasted. If it has no effect on the recipient, at least it benefits the bestower." —S.H. Simmons

Everyday Heroes

CHRISTY TURNER

Spring Break. For many, those two words conjure images of scantily clad females romping on the current popular beach. Or of all-night parties and drunken brawls that too often resulting in damaged property, injuries, and even death.

For one group of students, however, those words recall memories of an entirely different sort. My name is Christy Turner. I am a junior at Central Michigan University, and vice-president of Alternative Spring Break, a program where students volunteer their spring break to help others along the east coast.

Last year, I was a site leader for a Habitat for Humanity project in Battle Creek, Michigan. When I got my assignment, I was at first disappointed because it meant I would be staying in Michigan instead of working in a different state. Although I soon grew excited, people kept expressing sympathy because I was just going to Battle Creek. But I am not to be pitied.

Our group was small; six people, only one male. We stayed in a church and worked at building Habitat houses. We learned useful skills, made new friends, and met amazing people. For instance, there was the group of retired men who volunteered tirelessly and helped us learn the harder skills. One family worked with us on their own home. They had several children and even the youngest got his hands dirty. We found easy tasks for those who could only help a little, and more difficult tasks for those up to the challenge. No one was turned away.

Towards the end of the week, an incredible woman came to

lend a hand. She was a single mom with two children, one deaf. She worked full-time, went to school at night, taught herself and her son sign language, tutored him, and had worked on her own Habitat house. She came and volunteered her spare time with her kids! Her strength, dedication, and success helped us understand what we should have seen before. There are everyday heroes who struggle against the odds—and make it. Those people, like the woman we met, truly inspired us.

We received much undeserved recognition that week. The middle school principal across the street from our work site gave us free hot lunches every day, as a way to thank us for our support of the community. Two news vans came and we were interviewed for the nightly news. After the broadcast, people noticed us in town and started thanking us for coming.

But we were the ones who needed to do the thanking. We got so much more from volunteering than we gave. We learned about Habitat, working, and ourselves. We expended little effort and yet we received more thanks than the everyday heroes who deserved recognition. I believe that everyone should do two things—volunteer and give thanks.

Give thanks for volunteering and most of all, give thanks to the everyday heroes you meet.

"Out of clutter, find simplicity. From discord, send harmony. In the middle of difficulty, lies opportunity." —Albert Einstein

Fires of Sorrow

BENNIE MCDONALD, as told to NANETTE THORSEN-SNIPES

It was cold as we headed for Monterey, Kentucky, after the Kentucky River spilled over its banks in early March, 1997. Wearing our yellow disaster relief uniforms, my wife and I gassed up at Interstate 75 in Georgia. How could I have ever known that on my quest to help others, a personal disaster would strike me?

As I pumped gas, a woman approached me. "Where are you people going?" she asked.

"A small town in Kentucky, to help with the floods," I said. I watched compassion grow in her eyes as she pressed $60 into my palm.

"Take this to them," she said, then walked away. Thanking God for small mercies, I tucked the money into my jacket pocket. I knew someone could use that money.

We drove all day. By night time, the rain was pounding the car, slashing across our windshield in sheets. We couldn't even see the car directly in front of us.

Once in Monterey, our headlights lit up mud-covered streets. Both sides of the narrow streets were junked with TVs, sofas, and other debris contaminated by the mud. And the *smell*. Once the stench reached your nose, it stayed with you.

I learned quickly that there's something about a flood that's different from other natural disasters. Floods leave debris permeated with bacteria in their wake, which must be decontaminated. In many cases, houses have to be ripped apart and washed with a Clorox mixture before they're fit to be lived in again.

The next day, the rain quit and the temperature dropped. It was so cold, raindrops froze on the hood of my car. I had trouble breathing as our Communications Unit set up that morning, but believing my problem was due to the cold, I ignored my symptoms and threw myself into the work at hand.

As a ham radio operator, I helped provide timely information about supplies, personnel in the area, equipment, and special assistance. I helped coordinate the units, keeping the operation running smoothly.

Later that day, I watched flood victims Barbara and her young son work well into the night, ripping out a floor in their house. My heart nearly broke. When her husband got off work, the two of them labored until the whole family collapsed into one bed—the only one they'd salvaged. When the flood waters had filled the house several days earlier, the family had fled to a rented motel room.

The morning of our second day, some of us from the Unit offered to help Barbara's family. So I slogged through the mud and began tearing down sheetrock. As I worked, though, it felt as if a vice gripped my lungs. I couldn't breathe in that house. It seemed like the dampness just about shut me down. Again, I shrugged it off, thinking I had a touch of the flu.

While I ripped out a section of wet sheetrock, I remembered the last time I'd worked that hard on a house. It was just before my wife died of cancer in 1986.

Though she was sick, Ann had wanted to build a log home. It took me six months to build the home while holding down a job at the post office and taking care of a sick wife. I was physically and emotionally spent.

Ann died a month after we moved in, before she'd really had time to enjoy the house. I was angry—angry at God for putting me through a trial full of so much pain. I had no idea that within three years, God would put me through another trial. Then, in 1989, my thirty-year-old daughter died at the hands of her husband. I had recently learned of the physical abuse, but had no idea how serious the situation was.

When I got to the mobile home the day my daughter died, I was so enraged I slammed my fist into the side of the structure. That blind anger stayed with me for a long time. I wanted to scream at God. Why is this happening to me? Every day, I felt I was walking through fire born of all my sorrow, and the flames threatened to consume me.

Then in 1996, my present wife and I began to volunteer for a relief ministry that shares the love of God in communities hit by disasters. By this time, I had come to grips with my anger. I felt it was time to help others. So when the flood hit Monterey, Kentucky, I was ready.

Helping Barbara's family tear down the sheetrock and pressure-wash some of the floors with Clorox gave me satisfaction. But every time I took a breath, it was with effort.

We finished the job and returned to Georgia, where my symptoms worsened. On May 1st, I was so ill that I had to leave my job at the post office and go home. My legs were swelling because I was retaining so much fluid.

By mid-June, standing all day at the postal window was unbearable and I finally told my boss about it. That day inside his office, I lifted my pant legs to show him how my legs were swollen from my knees to my feet. My skin was so tight it looked ready to pop if anyone touched me. Also, by this time my breathing had become so difficult, I had to speak quickly while exhaling.

As I faced my boss that day, I'm sure the fear registered in my face. "I'm scared to death," I said. "I don't know what's wrong with me."

My boss just shook his head in disbelief. "You've got to see a doctor, Bennie," he said.

I left work that day and did just that. And for the next few days, I endured a battery of tests including CAT scans, X-rays and biopsies.

Finally, on June 14, I was scheduled for exploratory surgery. In my hospital bed, I winced at the memory of the night before, when the doctor had removed over two liters of fluid from my chest cavity. But that morning, what I'd feared most became reality—the earlier biopsies indicated lung cancer. I knew the gravity of my situation. Choking back tears, I gave the doctor permission to remove anything ominous.

As I lay there, I thought, "This isn't fair, Lord. I've lost my wife to cancer and my daughter was murdered. I've tried to do what you want. I've helped others. What do you want from me?"

A young nurse stepped into my room, and I watched as she checked my IVs. She said, "The doctor is running late for your exploratory."

After she left, I closed my eyes, thankful for a few moments to myself. Briefly, I recalled Barbara in Monterey. Aware that she'd been out of work most of the week, the unit director and I had passed around a disaster relief hat. We all put in some money. Silently, I had thanked God for angels of mercy as I reached into my jacket pocket, and then dropped in the $60 in bills that the woman had given me at the gas station.

When we handed Barbara the money, her eyes filled with tears. "That's exactly what we needed to pay our motel bill," she said. Like many others in Monterey, she asked, "Why are you doing this?"

"Because we want to share God's love," I said.

She was really thankful for the little we'd given her. We knew that her entire lifestyle would change now, and this money was a mere drop in the bucket compared to what she'd be needing later.

Though the flood swept through Barbara's house leaving a monstrous mess, she stuck it out. Now she and her family were well on the way to restoring their home—and their lives. Like Isaiah 43:2 says, "When you pass through the waters, I will be with you; and when you pass through the rivers, they will not sweep over you. When you walk through the fire, you will not be burned; the flames will not set you ablaze." I focused upon the IVs connected to me and my thoughts returned to the present and my own battle. Had God forgotten me? What about the fiery trials that I'd been through? I wondered deep down if I could handle anything else.

I realized then that before I went into surgery, there were things I needed to get straight with God. Like Barbara, bravely facing the aftermath of a flood and doing what had to be done, I had to do the same. I needed to face the possibility of dying.

It was the hardest thing I'd ever done—facing my mortality. I took a deep breath, closed my eyes, and prayed, "Lord, if I have cancer and I'm going to die, then I'll accept it. It's in Your hands. But if it's not my time to go, then I pray Your will be done." Then and there, I made my peace with God. For the first time, I released everything to Him—including my fiery trials.

When I was being wheeled into surgery, it seemed as though the flames that had consumed me for so long were finally extinguished. I had a sweet peace that surpassed my understanding. I went into surgery knowing I was safe in the steady hands of God—no matter what the outcome.

That day, the doctors successfully removed the tumor that had threatened my life. They seemed surprised that the "cancer" was a benign softball-sized tumor attached to the lower lobe of my right lung.

Unlike the doctors, I wasn't surprised at all—because I remembered the other half of that Scripture. When you walk through fiery trials, you will not be burned up—the flames will not consume you.

"Prayer begins where human capacity ends." —Marian Anderson

In Flight

EVA MARIE EVERSON

In the late eighties, I accepted a new job requiring me to attend about four or five seminars a year. With the exception of the seminar scheduled in Nashville, the locations were too far away for travel by car.

I knew my mother's opinion of air travel. She was terrified! In spite of my careful explanations of the ratio of airplane accidents to auto accidents, she continued to prefer that her children stay grounded. Literally. If she knew we were in the air, she worried herself into a frenzy.

So I made one of my more "mature" adult decisions: I would not tell Mother of my departures until just before the fact. In my mind's eye, I could see her hanging up the phone, dropping to her knees, calling out to God, and holding a nonstop conversation with Him until I returned days later. All other communication to Him may as well cease! Put the Vatican on hold, Mother's baby is in the air!

"Watch over her, Lord...."

My first trip was to Boston, accompanied by a coworker. We sat in our departing plane for an hour, waiting for an oil leak to be repaired while we sipped on soft drinks and watched the beginning of a movie. Finally, we were transferred to a safer plane. We arrived at Logan late, but we arrived!

"Watch over her, Lord...."

My next trip was to Los Angeles. Again, I was accompanied by a coworker. We had problems from the beginning. First plane out of Atlanta was delayed. Then when we arrived at the Redondo Beach hotel we learned our reservations had been made, in error, for the following night. That problem was fixed, but the waitress in the hotel restaurant made fun of our southern accents. Next we were awakened around midnight when that same restaurant caught on fire. The remainder of our trip was riddled with sporadic tremblings from beneath the surface of the earth. The locals were calm, but we were not! We had scarcely left Los Angeles International Airport to return to Georgia when an earthquake struck the area.

"Watch over her, Lord...."

My final trip to Los Angeles was made alone. I was so concerned about my mother's learning that choice piece of information, I decided to make a full confession only after I returned. Please understand, telling her would not have been in *her* best interest. Besides, I was a tad nervous about it myself.

When one takes a seat on a plane and does not know their seatmate, there is that awkward moment of introduction. One could be sitting next to the nicest person in the world—or a "nut." Atlanta to Los Angeles by plane would be four miserable hours were it the latter.

But my seatmate was a charming Englishman named Peter. We chatted nonstop, enjoyed a cup of hot tea, and observed the beauty of the landscape below. At some point, I shared with Peter my apprehension about retrieving my luggage and locating the hotel's limousine service.

"Don't worry," he said. "I'll make certain you get your luggage and are in the limo before I leave the airport."

I was so grateful! Ironically enough, Peter sat a few seats from me on my return flight. Again, we enjoyed light conversation and hot tea.

"Watch over her, Lord...."

I think of Peter often. Not so much of him, but of the way God provided someone to watch over me.

In the past decade, I've done my fair share of flying. I guess you could say I'm "seasoned." I'm no longer afraid to travel alone. I deal with parking, luggage, sky caps, crowds, long walks between gates, layovers, and airline food like an old pro! Rather than worrying about my mother's anxieties, I watch at the gate for someone traveling with me who appears anxious. It may be my opportunity to be a caretaker... the answer to another mother's prayers... and I don't want to miss it.

"In the faces of men and women I see God." —Walt Whitman

Jesus Loves You

KATHY COLLARD MILLER

To be salt and light for Jesus, it usually requires our obedience. Some time ago, I was waiting in the airport for my next connecting flight, minding my own business while enjoying my novel. Once, I glanced up and noticed a small food counter nearby where a woman was serving customers. After a bit, I continued reading. Unexpectedly, the Lord's still small voice within my heart whispered, "Go talk to that woman behind the counter about Me."

My reaction was unfortunately one that I usually had: "Oh, Lord, you know I don't like doing things like this. Please! No!"

I could sense Him patiently waiting.

"Oh, all right, Lord. What should I say to her?"

"Tell her I love her."

Well, that wasn't very original! I still wasn't convinced I wanted to go, and I tried reading my book again. But I knew He wouldn't let me rest, so I gathered my things together and got at the end of the line for the counter. I was amazed that by the time all the customers in front of me had been helped, no one had gotten in line behind me. When I faced the woman at the counter, I gulped and shot an arrow prayer, "OK, Lord, here we go."

"Ma'am, I know this will sound strange, but God wanted me to tell you He loves you."

The woman's face seemed to harden for a second. *"Oh, no, Father, what have you gotten me into now?"* I cringed.

Then, suddenly, her face softened and tears welled up in her eyes. She stared at me in surprise and said, "Oh, my husband recently died and I'd begun to believe God didn't love me. Thanks for telling me that."

I ordered my iced tea and she began sharing her hurt and pain with me. As I went to the side of the counter to mix in the sweetener, she followed me over and again thanked me for reaffirming her belief in God's great love. I was amazed that no one came up to the counter; the room was full of people. God had opened a door of opportunity and I was so glad I hadn't refused His prompting to be salt and light.

"The value of compassion cannot be over-emphasized. Anyone can criticize. It takes a true believer to be compassionate.
No greater burden can be borne by an individual than to know no one cares or understands." —Arthur H. Stainback

"Try" Does Not Apply

SHARI LEE BEYNON

"How would you like to go with Joan, Cindy, and me to New York?" came the excited voice of my friend over the telephone. "We have tickets for the Rosie O'Donnell Show. We also want to try and see a play, do some shopping, and Joan's aunt and uncle want to take us out to dinner one night. We'll be gone for four days."

"You don't have to ask me twice," I replied enthusiastically. "When do we leave?"

"The second week of November. Can you really go?"

I told her I could absolutely go, and we began making plans. It was just what I needed.

With only a week to prepare, I immediately started to get my work and packing organized. It had been a long time since I'd done anything like this, and I was looking forward to all the promised excitement. I was ready!

We flew up to New York together, making our trip that much more fun. We'd checked into our hotel, freshened up, and headed out to dinner when, immediately upon entering the street, I couldn't help noticing a homeless man sitting on the pavement against the building. Homeless people are everywhere, but in New York City they are as much a part of the landscape as taxi cabs, tall buildings, and thousands of people hurrying to their destinations.

Every time I go there, I have a hard time passing by human beings so obviously in need. I usually give them money, and sometimes food. Once, I went out and bought a whole bunch of bagel sandwiches and carried them with me that day. Whenever I saw someone who was clearly hungry, I gave them a sandwich. It didn't help the empty feeling I had inside.

That evening we had a nice dinner, and the next morning we were at the Rosie O'Donnell Show early, to insure our seats. I loved being a part of that show. I wanted to get up there with her and be a "real" part of it. I made as much noise as everyone around me, and when the camera came our way, I got as animated as possible—just in case my kids were watching at home.

We had plans to go to dinner with Joan's aunt and uncle, and to see a play that evening, so as soon as we finished dinner we hurried to the theater. None of us had bothered finding out what theater tickets her aunt had purchased for us; it was such late notice, we felt we were lucky to get tickets at all. We arrived at the theater only to find the play lewd and outrageous, so much so that my best friend and I just couldn't sit through it. Joan and Cindy didn't mind our leaving and we arranged to meet back at the hotel.

Outside, it was a very cold, but clear night. But it felt good, so we decided to walk back to our hotel as far as we could. After walking quite a distance, though, we noticed there were fewer people on the streets than before, and as it was getting colder, we decided to start looking for a taxi.

It was at the corner of Madison Avenue and Fifth that we saw someone, apparently another homeless person, sitting on the pavement, seated inside a cardboard box up against the building. The person was still and unmoving. To my horror, I saw, upon closer inspection, that this was a completely naked woman. I called my friend over, and we stared, horrified, at this poor, naked woman, her only "shelter" a cardboard box. She peered upward at our faces, and I will never forget the hopelessness in those eyes. Lowering her head, she sat there, exposed but for the meager box. We were shocked, in a dilemma as to what to do. I took off my scarf and wrapped it about her shoulders, and my friend put some money in her cup, but we were both aware that there was most likely someone hiding in the shadows—someone who had put her there, in that condition, in order to exploit her.

Just then, a man came along and stopped to see what was happening. "Oh, my God!" he exclaimed. "I've lived here all my life and never seen anything like this!" He immediately went to a nearby pay phone to call the police, then told us to go on, that he would wait with the woman until they came.

We left, because we really did not know what else we could do, but neither of us could stop thinking about that poor, naked woman. "What would the Good Samaritan have done?" I wondered. "Our society is not one where you can take a person who is in a drug-induced stupor—cold and naked on the street though she may be—and pay to put her in a hotel, telling them to care for her until she is well. Even if we had the money to do that—what help would she get? You can't pay her bills forever." These thoughts kept running through my mind—along with the Scripture in Matthew 25:36 where Jesus said, "I was naked, and you clothed Me."

All year, our church had been learning how to be salt and light in the world. I felt miserable. "The man who stayed with her until the police came was more salt and light than you were," I told myself.

As I was beating myself up with these thoughts, the Holy Spirit impressed me with another thought; God is the provider. The Lord allowed me to find the woman, have compassion on her, pray for her, and wrap her in my scarf. That was the role He had given me. He gave the man the role of calling the police and waiting with her for them to come. Through this experience, God taught me that He only expects me to do the best I can with what He gives me. He taught me that beating myself up because I did not do what I was not equipped to do is not a productive use of my time, energy, or resources.

There is so much freedom in that. Being salt and light when I have access to a salt shaker and a lantern makes so much more sense than trying to be salt and light when I have neither. God will tell me when. God will tell me where. God will show me how. The word "try" will not apply—I'll just be able to "do" it!

~ & ~

"Some things have to be believed to be seen." —Ralph Hodgson

The Lighted Sign

MARY G. BEASLEY

Ten o'clock at night is early when one is driving near a city, but wheeling into a storm through Georgia swamplands, it's just too risky.

Jagged streaks of lightning chased each other across the sky while resounding thunder told of trouble rolling in from the northwest. Big drops of rain pelted my car and strong gusty winds slapped at trees, cars, and everything in its path.

As I drove over a highway that contained bridge after bridge, I wondered whether to turn around or keep rolling. What shall I do? If I continue to U.S. 301, the storm will soon overtake me with all its fury. Yet, if I go back, my chances of finding a place to stay are negligible. After all, I'd searched four hours and had not found a single spot where I could spend the night.

The next turnaround approached. My mind—and the wind playing with my Volkswagon— made the final decision. I would go back toward Statesboro, Claxton, or Jesup, I argued with myself. Maybe I'd missed a tourist lodge. Maybe it would be a waste of time to backtrack. On the other hand, the storm was getting worse, and the lost miles could be redeemed tomorrow even though I'd get to Winston-Salem, North Carolina, later than planned.

The next fifteen miles were almost traffic-free, but as I neared Statesboro's city limits, both pedestrian and motorist activity increased. At the fifth traffic signal, a lighted sign reflected the message, "Our Home—Mrs. Smith's Tourist Home." Instead of following the highway left, I made a right turn into a side street and found a parking place in front of a large southern home with wide wrap-around porch surrounding three sides of a four-story white house. My attention was immediately directed to the lighted sign and front porch entrance, which welcomed me with its beckoning warmth.

As I waited for someone to answer the doorbell, I thought how much this residence reminded me of Aunt Kate's home in Chattanooga, Tennessee. The wide door swung open, jolting me from my reminiscence, bringing me face-to-face with a smiling, plumpish, middle-aged woman.

"I'd like to rent a room."

"My dear, we're full."

"You say there're no rooms? Oh, I'm so sorry," I said with a half laugh of disbelief.

"I'm always full during tobacco marketing season, so I've not had a vacancy for six weeks. Honey, you're certainly not out alone in this weather, are you?"

It was Mrs. Smith's turn to reflect skepticism as she looked past me toward the empty Volkswagon parked in front of her home.

"Yes. I've tried for four hours to find lodging. I'm not afraid, but I'm getting tired and hungry. I left Orlando, Florida, at noon, then stopped in Jacksonville on business. I left about five p.m. without eating and got into heavy traffic. I want to reach Winston-Salem as early as possible tomorrow."

"Well, honey, if you don't mind sleeping in my room, I'll put my hide-away bed in the kitchen. I've told the men who manage the auction and their wives who stay with me every year that in emergencies, they must share the bathroom facilities. Tonight is just such a time. Yes, we'll make room."

I scurried through the rain to get my bag. When I returned, Mrs. Smith was standing in the doorway with a hall light to her back. She reminded me of a Dresden doll painted as a portrait-in-oil, encased by the doorjamb and lintel. Her blue and white dress hung three inches below her knees. Her salt and pepper hair was braided and pinned to the top of her head. Everything about her appeared motherly, and kind.

As I signed the register, she asked, "There's one thing I'd like to know. Why did you decide to stop here?"

"Well, it was your lighted tourist sign. It had such a welcome glow. I was just sure you had a room."

Mrs. Smith's face showed amazement. "My dear, that sign has not been lit for six weeks!"

And sure enough, when I went to the corner restaurant, I found the sign was dark.

"Your worst humiliation is only someone else's momentary entertainment." —Karen Crockett

Flight to Forgiveness

CARMEN LEAL

It had happened again. I had proof of my husband's infidelity. I knew he was not a Christian, but I had thought he was an honorable man. The first time it happened, I was hurt and wondered what I could do to change his philandering ways. I rationalized that if I could be a better wife, a thinner wife, a more attractive wife, he would have no reason to look elsewhere to satisfy his desires.

This time, however, I was just plain furious. I looked back over all the "I'm sorrys" and the "I'll never do it agains" and realized I could no longer trust him. My resentment grew until it was all encompassing.

My husband's infidelity consumed me as I waited at the airport, on my way to Chicago on business. I was flying standby and nervously waiting for my name to be called for one of the coveted seats. As the crush of people converged on the gate, even as I assessed my odds of getting aboard, I fumed with each thought of my husband. Though I was a Christian, I gave in to the temptation to "get even." Rage got the best of me, and my mind raced while I appeared to sit calmly and wait.

By the time my name was finally called and I took the last seat on the plane, first class no less, I'd devised a fitting plan: have an affair and make sure he found out. It would serve him right to feel the same betrayal and anguish I felt. So I settled into my comfortable seat and buckled in.

Glancing at the passenger next to me, I was thrilled to note what a handsome man he was, and he wasn't wearing a wedding ring. Immediately, I began my campaign to entice him. The first class cabin seemed suitable for this challenge and I plunged right in. I laughed and flirted and thoroughly enjoyed myself. He seemed just as eager to engage me in conversation, and we merrily flirted our way across the Pacific. That I was a married woman only added an edge to the excitement that was building within me minute by minute.

My personal details exhausted, I leaned over and touched his hand.

"Enough about me," I purred. "What do you do for a living?"

"I'm in the army," he replied.

"The army," I gushed. "What rank are you?"

"I'm a Colonel. I'm on my way to Washington, DC, for a conference."

I smiled coquettishly and caught his eye, convinced he was enjoying our close quarters, and that I would be continuing on to Washington instead of deplaning in Chicago. Even as I enjoyed our banter, I gloated, visualizing the stricken look on my husband's face when he learned of my conquest.

Knowing that men can't resist the temptation to talk about themselves, I went in for the kill.

"A Colonel," I exclaimed in my best southern belle imitation. "I never knew a Colonel before. What exactly do you do in the army?"

The gentleman smiled invitingly and replied without missing a beat, "I'm a Catholic priest."

I wanted to die. A priest! I had hit on a priest. I immediately feigned total immersion in my novel and remained speechless for the remainder of the eight-hour flight. For the next seven hours, I was forced to endure the uncomfortable feelings my rage had produced. Instead of enjoying my quiet time on the plane as I normally do, I was reduced to a state of near panic.

Dinner was served, the movie shown, and still I could not even glance at this impostor who dared to lounge next to me. How dare he masquerade as an available, unmarried man! He should have known the effect he had on women. Worse yet, he probably did, and was using his looks and personality in some perverse way. My righteous indignation rose as the miles disappeared. My wrath increased as it blotted out all thoughts of my obvious role in this predicament.

Finally, as the overhead lights were extinguished one by one, I calmed down. I thoughtfully replayed the entire humiliating scene in my head in slow motion. As I did, the man's duplicity disappeared until he became what he was; a seatmate willing to talk to me for eight hours. The horror of what I had tried to do slowly dawned on me as I accepted the blame and focused on my sin.

Then I remembered a Bible verse. Philippians 4:8 says, "Finally, brothers, whatever is true, whatever is honorable, whatever is just, whatever is pure, whatever is lovely, whatever is gracious, if there is any excellence and if there is anything worthy of praise, think about these things." What had been in my heart and my mind was the complete opposite of that verse. My outrage and misery, along with my temper, had turned me into another person.

As we drew near our destination, I was no less mortified but much more contrite. I'd failed the one person in my life that mattered most of all. I could picture the anguish engraved on God's face. I knew this had been a huge crossroads in my relationship with Him, and I had taken a wrong turn. I began to pray for forgiveness, feeling that if I wouldn't forgive myself, why should He?

I forced myself to focus on my sin and on how I had hurt God. I felt His gentle presence and knew that, even if I could not forgive myself, God could forgive me. I realized that God knew, even before I fell, that the temptation would be placed squarely in front of me. This wasn't the first time I'd fallen, nor would it be the last—only one of the more humiliating.

I started to feel better, thankful for a God who loved me despite my actions. Then another thought surfaced; "If I can forgive you for your sin, you need to forgive your husband for his." I hadn't been half as bad as he. I hadn't really done anything, while he had. My excuses continued only to trail off midway. I knew I was just as guilty as he. Until I forgave him, our marriage could not be what God had intended it to be.

My time in Chicago was filled with self-doubt and a desire to do God's will my way. I spent much time in prayer and, finally, as I forgave my husband, I felt my load lighten. I began to understand not only what God wanted of me, but that I, too, was a part of this marriage. Instead of blaming him for all the problems we had, I needed to be honest before God and let Him change *my* heart.

I returned home eager to start fresh with my husband and somehow salvage the mangled pieces of our marriage. Unfortunately, as it takes two to make a problem, it takes two to solve it. Try as I would, and as forgiving as I was, my husband wasn't interested in the resurrection of our dead relationship.

The troubled marriage wove drunkenly down the distressed thoroughfare until it finally came to a crashing halt at the doors of the divorce court. At the same time that I felt a failure, I also felt curiously relieved. Though the demise of my marriage was the most painful part of my life, I knew I had been the woman God wanted me to be. After the trip to Chicago, I truly forgave my husband and actively worked to make the changes in myself that God demanded. I no longer lived my life to save my marriage, but to draw closer to God. Regrettably, the closer I drew to God, the more my husband rebelled, until finally, our marriage ended.

Trying to pick up a priest certainly was one of my most embarrassing moments. But I like to think that eventually, it led me to one of my finest. I realized that living my life as Jesus would have done was the most important thing. Whether in marriage, or parenting, or work, or in other relationships, I can truly say that my in-flight antics marked the day I began to understand the phrase, "What would Jesus do?" Forgiveness was a near impossible lesson for me to learn, but learn it I did. Of all that I have learned in my years with the Lord, that was the toughest yet. It was also the lesson that has served me the most throughout my life.

Salt and Light In Church

"There is one body and one Spirit—just as you were called to one hope when you were called—one Lord, one faith, one baptism; one God and Father of all, who is over all and through all and in all."

—Ephesians 4:4-6

"The deeds you do may be the only sermon some persons will hear today." —Saint Francis of Assisi

Two Different Worlds

MARY J. DAVIS

Inside the building are fellowship, love, and sharing,
Outside the church are loneliness, hurting, and uncaring.

People flow into the building at meeting times each week,
Walking right past the downcast, those whom God would seek.

Why do they hurry to gather 'neath the steeple?
How can they ignore God's hurting people?

When will the two worlds finally meet and share?
When will the church-goers begin to care?

God sent us to be the salt and the light,
To reach out to others who stumble in the night.

So when will we realize that we are God's church,
Sent to minister, to love, and for lost lambs to search?

"Ingenuity, plus courage, plus work, equals miracles."
—Bob Richards

Ladies' First Thursday: A Light To the Community and the World

LINDA GILDEN

Over twelve years ago, the ladies of First Baptist Church, Spartanburg, South Carolina, recognized a need in their geographical area. There was a need for a means of hope and encouragement to other ladies, a way to reach out to their church and community. They began to pray, and thus began the Ladies' First Thursday ministry.

Each first Thursday of the month, October through May, the church dining hall is bustling. Ladies arrive early in the morning to begin wiping chairs, spreading tablecloths, decorating, folding napkins, polishing flatware, numbering tables, and filling salt and light—ahem!—I mean, pepper shakers.

Though the kitchen staff works to prepare food for the evening, they always have a special coffee area for those working, complete with bagels and homemade cinnamon rolls. By lunch time, preparations are complete and the dining room is beautiful, ready to feed five hundred ladies. The tables are adorned with decorations—fresh flowers, a seasonal basket, or a ceramic keepsake, and a Scripture card is included that carries out the theme of the evening.

All is quiet until about five o'clock. At that time, the dining hall springs into life again, this time with the "marvelous men" who are rolling up their sleeves as they enter the hall, ready for work. Then, glasses are filled with ice, bread baskets lined, salads put on tables, name tags made, and bins readied to receive dirty dishes in just a few hours. Many are whistling and most are smiling as they prepare for their job of serving the women.

"The men really enjoy this ministry. Even though it's hard work waiting on all those tables, the men approach it with eagerness and enthusiasm," says Ping Toney, who each month organizes the troop of sixty-five men of all ages. "God has really blessed me through this opportunity to serve. Participating in Ladies' First Thursday is also a good way for men to get to know one another."

The ladies begin to arrive shortly after six, all in fine feather (or in fine fettle) and ready for a special evening. The men attending to last minute chores greet them. If it is raining, those chores often include chivalrously shuttling the ladies from their cars to the church under umbrellas. They're also noted for carrying in the speakers' books, and parking cars. Each job is done with a contagious servant's spirit.

Many Sunday School classes converge at the tables. Some ladies buy a whole table of tickets and invite their unsaved neighbors. Others buy a table so that they can invite their co-workers or husband's office staff. Small churches that cannot have women's ministry programs bring their vans, full of women in need of encouragement.

Though different speakers and musicians are featured, the purpose of the evening is always the same; Ladies' First Thursday exists to provide a way for unsaved ladies to hear the gospel of Jesus Christ, and to encourage those who know Him with truth from God's Word. The speakers' stories are often unique, but their messages are unchanging as they share their joy, excitement, and hope in what God is doing in their lives.

But the ministry does not conclude with the clearing away of the dishes. The completed prayer cards, placed on each table beforehand, are collected for the prayer committee, who meets every Tuesday after Ladies' First Thursday to pray for whatever the ladies have indicated their needs are.

"This ministry isn't just any one person. It's about the whole group working together. If it weren't for everybody working together, it wouldn't happen," says Sara Hall, current ministry chairman.

Ladies' First Thursday has been the springboard for numerous similar ministries in North and South Carolina. Many churches, wanting to minister to ladies in their areas, have called. Some want to pattern their ministry closely after Ladies' First Thursday, while others need assistance in finding speakers or working out logistical problems. Two programs were started by Ladies' First Thursday supporters whose families have relocated to other places. They were able to begin similar programs in their new churches.

Ladies' First Thursday has also been the catalyst for numerous Bible studies. In its home church, hundreds of ladies have participated in these studies. There are currently six weekly groups in progress. Last year, the Bible study groups got together and bought materials to send with missionaries going overseas, and now small groups are participating in Croatia and Africa. Other groups have been started in Saint Louis and Thailand by ladies who have moved there.

"Women are hungry for the Bible. The Bible study that has grown from Ladies' First Thursday is really meeting a need. Our ministry is to put Jesus Christ first," says Ruthi Neely, Bible study coordinator. "It is exciting to know that God is using our Bible study as a springboard for groups all over the world."

So the prayers of a group of women many years ago have been answered abundantly. God continues to bless the faithfulness of this group of ladies and men who desire to be salt and light to their church and community. He has multiplied that desire and spread their efforts throughout the world. To Him be all the praise!

"When we do the best that we can, we never know what miracle is wrought in our life of in the life of another." —Helen Keller

The Bringer

CARMEN LEAL

Her gnarled hands grasped mine as she leaned on me for support. Her faded blue, watery eyes smiled her appreciation. "Thank you for singing this morning. You were blessed with the voice of an angel," she said. "I wish I had a gift, but I guess God didn't see fit to bless me."

I stared in amazement at this dear sister in Christ. She was over seventy years old, and had no comprehension of her own powerful gift.

"Why, you're a bringer!" I exclaimed. "There is not one Sunday that you don't bring someone to church with you, and often, more than one. Yes, God has blessed me with a voice, but who would listen to my voice if people like you didn't bring their friends and neighbors to church?"

A shy smile brightened her wrinkled face as she realized that she did indeed have a gift. She brought people to hear the gospel, and what better gift is there than to give someone the opportunity to hear about eternal life?

My friend is no longer here on earth, but I like to think of her as being in the heavenly choir, blessed with a beautiful voice. As she sings, I can see her eyes, now twinkling in excitement, as they land on newcomers to heaven and the choir. I wonder how many of them are in the choir because she first was a bringer on earth?

"The God who made the world has no trouble being seen and heard by those who honestly want to know Him."
—Martin R. De Haan II

The Divine Balloon

RON AND MARIE NEMEC

When the phone rang on that lazy Saturday afternoon in March, 1997, we had no idea of the amazing story that would soon be told.

"Hello? Is Kevin there?" It was a question we'd often heard in the past, but since Kevin, our twenty-six-year-old son, has lived in Aspen, Colorado, for five years, it was completely unexpected.

So on this day, the answer to that question was, "No, he's not. Who's calling?" The caller identified herself as Deborah Hall, from Mobile, Alabama, a fact easily confirmed by a southern drawl. With this, the stage was set. The incredible tale of God's incomparable timing and planning, of two families linked with the power of God by a little red balloon, began to unfold.

Deborah is a former alcoholic. Her battles with alcoholism were difficult, leaving wounds that threatened both her life and her family. It was then, at the end of her own strength to fight, that she met Christ, and was restored. Deborah changed dramatically after her conversion, something that happens to a person with a new life in Christ, and her husband, George, wasn't sure about this "new woman" he was married to. In fact, the change was so dramatic and noticeable that he was contemplating divorce. Topics like sin and righteousness hadn't been the common fare before, and he wasn't sure he liked them now. Things had reached such a point that he consulted a lawyer friend, Danny, about the situation and was advised to start divorce proceedings.

In an attempt to think things out, and to relax, George traveled from Mobile, Alabama, to the White River National Forest near Meeker, Colorado, to do some hunting. The calming effect of beautiful scenery, a successful hunt, and separation from wife and Scripture was sure to help his state of mind. He believed he would be better able to make the difficult decision of whether or not to continue with the divorce proceedings when he got back. What better way to relax than to spend Autumn in the Rockies?

Things weren't going to be that easy, though. While trying to make the trip a successful hunt, he did what every hunter dreads; he became completely disoriented in the woods. He was totally lost.

Looking around, he saw a clearing with a pile of logs in it that resembled a stack of children's "pick up sticks." And on the opposite side of the clearing, beyond the stack of logs, he spotted a string caught in a tree. Peering closely, he spotted what appeared to be a burst red balloon attached to the string. He was compelled to investigate.

While struggling to retrieve the balloon, George nearly hurt himself, but when he finally succeeded, he noticed a small tag with a hand-printed message written on it. It read, "If we confess our sins, He is faithful and just and will forgive us our sins and cleanse us from all unrighteousness." His first thought was, "How did my wife get this thing hung here?" This was one of the verses that he and Deborah had discussed back in Mobile, Alabama. Shocked, convicted, moved, he sunk to his knees under a tree and asked Jesus to save him. It was as dramatic as the Bible story about the appearance of Philip to the Ethiopian eunuch, in Acts 8:26-40. This was no coincidence! It was as if the Holy Spirit had carried this message on the wind, right to George.

This wonderful thing happened because in the spring of 1986, our son Kevin, along with the rest of the youth group of our church, had ventured into a project to put themselves into a position to be used by God. They each took a card, hand-printed a Scripture verse on one side, and on the reverse side they wrote their own names and phone numbers. The verse that Kevin wrote was 1 John 1:9. They then attached the cards to helium-filled balloons and released them from the parking lot of the church.

Do we really believe what Scripture tells us? Or do we sometimes trip and fall over its truth, pick ourselves up, and then hurry on as if nothing had happened? For instance, do the words of Isaiah 55:10-12 really have meaning in our lives or are they simply words of another time, another age, some other people? "As the rain and snow come down from heaven, and do not return to it without watering the earth and making it bud and flourish, so that it yields seed for the sower and bread for the eater, so is My word that goes out from My mouth: it will not return to Me empty, but will accomplish what I desire and achieve the purpose for which I sent it. You will go out in joy and be led forth in peace; the mountains and hills will burst into song before you, and all the trees of the field will clap their hands." I'm sure the trees in the White River National Forest were clapping their hands that day!

In the Spring of 1986, one certain red balloon, with one certain Scripture verse printed on it, was released from the parking lot of Red Lands Community Church in Grand Junction, Colorado. It traveled the seventy some miles from Grand Junction to the White River National Forest, near Meeker, Colorado. It then landed and was preserved through the summer on one certain tree near one certain clearing. In the Fall of 1986, one certain man, George Hall, from Mobile, Alabama, would find that one certain verse and give his life to Christ. We do indeed serve an awesome God!

"As the purse is emptied, the heart is filled." —Victor Hugo

Megan's Car

CARMEN LEAL

One year, a young single mother in our church found herself in desperate need of a car. The one she had was literally held together with duct tape and was not about to pass the safety check coming due the next week. But the young mom took the time to pray with her three-year-old about the car, confident that God would provide.

A few days later, a couple from the church arranged to visit her. The couple, themselves not wealthy, chatted for a while and then handed her a pretty little gift bag. In the bag were the keys and the registration for her new car! She was speechless, amazed at how God had provided the car that she and her son had prayed about.

After Megan had recovered a bit, the couple explained that, knowing of her need, they communicated to others how she could not go to school or care for her two children without a car. Thirty members of the church each gave $100.00 toward the purchase of a reliable car.

What a wonderful way for God to show His provision through this group of believers. Could one person have bought a car for her? Probably so. However, God allowed thirty people to experience the joy of giving as He provided, through them, for this young woman.

One hundred dollars doesn't go too far today. God can and did use thirty people and their dollars to demonstrate His love to Megan and her children in an exciting way.

Only by giving to others can we learn that God meant it when He said, "It is more blessed to give than to receive."

"I, being poor, have only my dreams; I have spread my dreams under your feet; Tread softly because you tread on my dreams."
—W.B. Yeats

Full Circle

SONDRA LARGENT

Our church choir had been selected to sing with the Symphony in the bandstand, located by a beautiful lake in the center of town. We were all delighted, and the drizzling rain couldn't dampen our excitement as we gathered together, awaiting performance time.

As the time drew near to enter the bandstand, I grew nervous and prayed that God would help me to remember the words. No one knew, not even I, that God had orchestrated all the circumstances of this day to remind me of a different, harder time in my life. He has never forgotten that other day, long ago.

We stepped on the platform and took our places, and I heard the musicians testing their instruments as they waited for the conductor to motion for silence. My eyes surveyed the crowd sitting on the white benches. It was then, as if God had briefly ushered me back into another time, that my eyes settled on the very seat where I'd sat many years before. The memory of that time rushed in, warming my soul and my spirit.

On that day, the laughter of my younger brother and sisters broke into my thoughts while I sat on the white bench, staring at an empty bandstand. I remember the wind, gently blowing through the trees, and the sun reflected in the shimmering lake.

If it had been a better time, I might have enjoyed the beauty of the lake and the park, but on that day I sat on the bench, discouraged, and wondered, "What next?" Our family was at the lowest point ever... we were homeless.

My parents had moved the family again. This time, we were four states away from all our friends and relatives. Like all young girls, I wanted to be with my friends. I missed my older sister and brother who had stayed behind, and I yearned to live in a house again. No matter how awful the house looked, or how cluttered it got, it was still better than having no home at all.

Oh, how I dreamed of someday being on that stage, of not being a homeless child, of having my own home, of never being homeless again, and of becoming somebody... someday! It was a dream so deep within my heart that I dared not speak it.

Where was this God I'd heard about? Was He listening? How could He let this happen? Didn't He love me?

On his second day of looking for a job, my father found one. Mom and the six of us children lived at the lake and the surrounding park during the day, and slept in the car at night. Everything we owned was in that car, and sleeping at night was not easy. Five children were crammed like sardines in the back seat; one child and our parents in the front. It was uncomfortable—to say the least. We sat up to sleep. I was fortunate enough to sit by the window, and I leaned my head against the glass, angry because we had no place to live. We ate bologna and dry bread for breakfast, lunch, and dinner, and we got our water from a thermos that Mom kept filled.

After my father was paid, my parents rented a broken down house, and my life went on. The dreams of a young girl were lost somewhere along the way. We were enrolled in school and I made new friends, but the memory of being homeless, and the emotional scars within me, remained.

As I grew older, it was hard for me to believe that God loved me. I went through so many things, some of my own doing, some beyond my control. Yet somehow, deep down in my soul, I knew God was beside me.

Years later, when I visited a friend and ultimately joined the church and choir, I never realized how much God had directed my path. Nor did I realize that He was about to prove His love to me in many unforgettable, tangible ways.

Suddenly, the sound of the music invaded my thoughts and I was hurtled back into the present. I realized that here I was, standing on the stage. I began to sing with all my heart, and as the words flowed from my lips, I knew that God had just given me proof-positive that He never forgot the day when a little homeless girl dreamed of singing on this very bandstand. The drizzling rain couldn't quench my excitement!

Today I am married to a man who loves me. I have one child that I was never supposed to be able to have, and I live in a beautiful home. It is because of God and His grace that I can write this story. I can say with confidence: You may have forgotten the dreams you dreamed and the hopes you hoped, but God hasn't. He hasn't forgotten you, and He hasn't forgotten your dreams. Let Him have your life now, and watch Him return to you anew all you ever lost.

"We will abandon it all, for the sake of the call."
—Stephen Curtis Chapman

Rejoicing On His Call

DENNIS WENZEL

It was the last chapel service of the year. That old familiar hymn, "On Our Way Rejoicing," rang out, sung by the students at seminary. Many would soon leave for appointments serving congregations. Others would resume their studies by serving as intern pastors for the coming year. Still others would be looking for jobs to pay for continued education. Me? I was heartbroken. Since the age of sixteen, I felt called by God; now I questioned whether my calling was to serve as pastor in a church.

Just weeks before, the examination board had asked me, "Dennis, in what ways do you feel called to pastoral ministry?" That question took me off guard. I knew the Lord called me to serve, but how did I feel called? I didn't know. It seemed that others could answer that question, they even had stories to back it up. I had no such experiences to share. Maybe I wasn't called at all. On their way rejoicing; others could sing, but I had no joy at all. I could hardly mouth the words.

That summer, when I was asked to serve as student pastor at a local congregation, I accepted, although I felt no particular direction of call. The pastor was very helpful and understanding. He delegated responsibilities, which lightened his work schedule considerably. At least for one summer, I would feel like a pastor of the Church.

As the summer melted past, my supervisor informed me that his two-week vacation was due; now I would be serving the congregation alone, as full-time pastor. With fear and trembling, I planned sermons and attended meetings, sharing those gifts I possessed.

The next Sunday morning, a council member knocked on the office door. "Pastor Dennis, Marge had a heart attack last night. Would you visit her after services today?" As I assured him that I would, the organist began to play the opening hymn, "On Our Way Rejoicing."

I'd never been in an intensive care unit before. I was excited, but fearful. Asking a nurse which room Marge occupied, I stepped boldly through the door. I was her pastor, at least for this hour.

But I was not prepared for what I saw. A woman so weak... so defenseless, and unconscious. Tubes and wires were strung everywhere, testing her vital signs and dispensing medication, while a ventilator kept her breathing. Would Marge be able to live without all these machines? I didn't know.

I peered nervously around the room. "What in the world am I going to do?" I wondered. My supervisor was not available, I knew no one in this hospital, and the chaplaincy staff was not available on Sunday. Marge was relying on me and I didn't know what to do. I recalled that Jesus prayed often at the bedsides of sick people, so I lifted Marge up before God's throne of grace. He would know what to do.

Two days later, I visited Marge again. This time she was awake and eating lunch. "Oh, Pastor Dennis," she said, "it is so nice to see you again. I really appreciated your visit the other day." I thanked her and asked how she was progressing. We had a fine visit, laughing at a number of jokes which she shared. I wasn't sure who received more benefit from the visit, Marge or me. I suppose we both did. I closed my visit with a prayer of thanksgiving and for continued healing for Marge.

As I prepared to leave, Marge thanked me again. "Pastor Dennis, thank you so much for praying for me on Sunday." I was puzzled. Sunday? Which prayer? "The one you prayed right here in the hospital." Puzzled even more, I asked if she remembered the prayer. Marge then repeated the prayer that I had struggled with. "Oh, that prayer. You're welcome, Marge."

As I left the ICU area that day, several thoughts flooded my mind. Marge had remembered my prayer, that was nice. She was very sick—I was delighted she felt better. All the tubes and wires that looked so intrusive were now gone, that was a sure sign of her recovery. She remembered my prayer, that was—*she remembered my prayer?* When I prayed, Marge was unconscious, yet she heard me speak. I was overwhelmed.

As I knelt at the altar of the hospital chapel, I asked, "God, what is going on?" Marge had been able to hear, without being conscious. How strange. My eyes gazed at the cross which displayed the word, "Forgiven." Forgiven? Me? For what? Then the words came to my mind: "For doubting Me, that I called you." Then, I understood. In Christian service, I am only the instrument; God's Word heals and reaches where the servant can't reach.

Yes, at that moment I felt called by God to serve in Jesus' name. The world seemed lighter and clean, there was not a care on my mind. Through a flood of tears, I thanked God for a valuable lesson learned; I knew I was called to serve others. I was truly "on my way rejoicing."

Twenty-one years ago, I met Marge as she lay in a hospital bed. My world had been dark and hopeless. Marge truly was a shining light for my spiritual journey. By repeating a prayer that a frightened student pastor offered for her, she gave me the vigor to rejoice in God's call.

"Anxious hearts are very heavy, but a word of encouragement does wonders." —Anonymous

A Note of Encouragement

CARMEN LEAL

After my divorce, I was a single mom with two sons. Eventually, I remarried, only to have my new husband become terminally ill soon after. Now I was back where I started, only with the challenges that face single parents added to those of caregiving a terminally ill husband.

But when I most need it, God invariably sends encouragement. Like one day, my family and I received a gift from a friend—a turkey, fresh fruit, and a modest check. I truly felt God working through this friend at a time when I was stretched to the limit.

This note was included with the edible gifts, and it encouraged me more than everything else.

"Dearest Carmen: We hope you will always feel comfortable enough with us to let us know what we can do to help you. We love you, Carmen, for your heart and your courage! The Lord is well served by your struggles and testimony for Him. Take care, dearest Carmen, and always remember how much we treasure you as a friend and a soldier for Christ."

Wow! In one note she assured me of our friendship, acknowledged my pain, and showed me how God was using my struggles in her life. She also gave me permission to let her know when I have needs. She didn't preach or try to diminish what was happening in my life. All that and the makings of a few meals for my growing teenagers.

My non-Christian friends often ask me why I go to church if it isn't a condition of salvation. Yes, I go to learn and worship and fellowship with others. But friends like this is one more reason.

Salt and Light In Ministry

"I thank my God every time I remember you. In all my prayers for all of you, I always pray with joy because of your partnership in the gospel from the first day until now, being confident of this, that he who began a good work in you will carry it on to completion until the day of Christ Jesus."

—Philippians 1:3-6

> *"Joy can be real only if people look on their life as a service, and have a definite object in life outside themselves and their personal happiness."* —Count Leo Tolstoy

The Size of a Mustard Seed

CARMEN LEAL

Carol woke with a start. It was the middle of the night, but she knew immediately that she wasn't alone. In awe, she peered at a wondrous sight; sitting at the foot of her bed, in deep discussion, were three identical angels. Try as she might, she couldn't hear what they were saying, yet she somehow knew they were not there to harm her. Not wanting to disturb them, she quietly got out of bed, and tiptoed away.

In somewhat of a daze, Carol went to the kitchen and opened the refrigerator, pondering all the while. Was this real, or was she dreaming? After a brief wait, she crept back to her bedroom and peeked into the room. There they were, still exactly as she had left them, beautiful beyond description.

They left as she entered the room, and Carol sank to her knees in prayer. "Please, Lord," she begged. "Please send me someone to love me and my children. I've been alone and I need someone to love and take care of us." With a sense of peace, Carol fell asleep.

The Grand Rapids, Michigan, native was far from home that night in her Central Florida bedroom. A young widow with five children, three of them still at home, Carol had been immersed in the busyness that comes with a move across the country. She had also waitressed, done pedicures, and volunteered at homeless shelters, including the Orlando Rescue Mission. She missed her friends and spent much of her time crying, wondering if she'd made the right choice by relocating.

It wasn't long after her night of angels that Carol met John Kane, and they were married a year later. After her marriage, Carol continued her volunteer work at the Orlando Union Rescue Mission and other agencies, always elated when she located affordable apartments for homeless families. But she soon discovered a painful reality. "I've brought these people to their new homes," she told John, "and now I realize they have absolutely nothing to put in them. There are no beds for the kids. They all huddle up on the floor with just an old jacket spread over them. I can't walk away from that."

So it was that, out of her own pocket, with God beside her, she helped set up a household for a single mother with three little boys. The young mother couldn't read or write and suffered from epilepsy. Carol persuaded neighbors and churches to donate household items, and even a used car.

Carol's passion for helping the homeless continued to grow, and John became her enthusiastic partner. He had a well-paying job, and Carol continued to work part-time, but still money trickled out of their bank account as they frequented neighborhood stores to buy necessities for a growing number of families.

Carol and John did not have an inexhaustible supply of resources. So Carol prayed and God answered, "Start your own program." Then she sat with a pencil and pad and waited for God to tell her how to proceed. Eventually, she created a list of three items. 1. A place to store furniture; 2. A truck; 3. People to know (Advertising).

Armed with her list and faith that God knew what He was doing even if she didn't, Carol got into her car. "It was as if my hands were on the steering wheel but I wasn't driving," she says. "I turned right and about a half-a-mile away I saw a blue sign that said, "Warehouses For Rent." I know the sign must have been there before, but I never noticed it until that day."

Then Carol got to work. First, she told her story to the warehouse manager who gave her a discount, and she signed the paperwork.

Heading back on the main road, she turned left and pulled into a U-Haul location. Again, she explained her business and told them of her goal to help the homeless. The manager there called their corporate office, and they arranged for a discount.

Next, she found the Treasure Chest office. This free, weekly advertising paper refused payment for an ad soliciting furniture and other household items. In less than ninety minutes, God had filled all the needs on the list!

Because they were not yet a non-profit corporation, Carol told people there would be no tax benefit by donating to the Mustard Seed, and still, many gave possessions they no longer needed. Though not a few people said it couldn't be done, Carol and John furnished ninety-nine families in the first year.

The paraphrased Scripture verse, *"If you have faith the size of a mustard seed, you can move mountains,"* became Carol Kane's foundation for the organization. Like the mustard seed, she began small, operating out of her own garage, financed by her own money, with the help of her husband and a few volunteers.

The Mustard Seed Furniture Bank provided household goods, furniture, appliances, clothing, toys, books, and games, free of charge, to the homeless and others in need. By working with local social services agencies, they helped people who demonstrated the desire to rebuild their lives and become self-sufficient.

Then disaster hit. Just as the ministry was growing, John's company down-sized, and he lost his job. "We have a situation here," John said. "This would be a good time for you to work full-time while I job hunt. There's no way I can pay all these bills by myself."

But Carol knew she had to continue helping those in need.

"Carol, the only way we can keep the Mustard Seed open is to sell the house. Is that what you really want?"

Carol was totally at peace with selling all they had to continue helping others. Her remarkable husband agreed. With only enough for one house payment, Carol asked God to arrange for a quick sale of their home or to find a job for John. God chose the first option, and with only twenty-five days to vacate, the house was sold.

When Carol realized how much she'd given up, she felt torn apart inside. She wept harder that night than she ever had before. Cried out and exhausted, the Lord moved Carol and John to a rental house, and later, into an even smaller apartment. From the sale of their house, Carol and John lived and continued to operate the Mustard Seed.

Eventually, John found a job. Armed with a remaining $5,600 and needing to buy a house or pay significant capital gains tax, the search began.

On one of their house-hunting forays, a wonderful Christian realtor and Carol stopped in front of a two-story house that was reminiscent of buildings in Michigan. They placed an offer on the house, and though much lower than the asking price, the owner accepted it. Two days before Thanksgiving, their "no money down VA mortgage" was approved.

Owned by a builder, the house had never been lived in. As if waiting for them, it had stood empty the entire time John was unemployed. They were able to decorate, and as they had previously given their own away, they now bought new furniture, too. In fact, God had given them a better, brand new house and furniture, and allowed the Mustard Seed to remain open.

From a vision of wishing to help one family per month, the Mustard Seed has grown into an organization that helped over 1,200 families receive complete households of furniture in 1998. Thousands more received clothing, food, and holiday meals and gifts. Everything is donated, and all goods are given to the needy, free of charge. A small paid staff of five, numerous volunteers, and countless prayers have made it possible.

Since 1986, the Mustard Seed has operated either in the Kane's garage or in a rented warehouse. Two acres of industrial warehouse zoned property, a most generous donation, is making it possible for the Mustard Seed to finally have their own 20,000 square foot facility. And, thanks to a matching grant from United Way, along with dozens of in-kind donations, the new warehouse will open in 1999, debt free.

Today, Carol says, "I love the *people* part of running the organization. My dream is to hire others to handle the paperwork. Certain people come in who need love; that's what I'm the best at."

Carol often thinks of her three angels. She knows they're still watching over her as she continues doing what God asked her to do.

People wonder how she could give up her house and furniture for strangers. But she wonders, "How could I not?"

"The greatest use of life is to spend it for something that will outlast it." —William James

The Greatest Is Aloha

CARMEN LEAL

There are moments in our lives that are destined to forever change who we are. They alter the way we view our purpose in life, and how we measure our effectiveness. Sometimes, these moments are planned for and eagerly anticipated. Other times we stand almost paralyzed with fear and doubt, scared for them to happen but afraid they won't.

The latter was the case that bright, sunny morning on Waikiki Beach. It was the early 1980s, and I'd just become a Christian. Though I'd been a singer for years, with the exception of parochial school growing up, my performances were always in the secular realm. Now here I was, scheduled to sing three songs in a ministry I really didn't understand.

The owner of the local Christian bookstore had asked me to sing in a concert at Kaimuki High School. In the audience that night, my first public appearance as a Christian, sat Ruby Nobles, secretary of the Waikiki Beach Chaplaincy. Ruby approached me after the concert with tears still glistening on her cheeks. She briefly explained the ministry, which took place on the beach of all places, and asked me to come—prepared to sing three songs.

In a daze, I agreed. But later, after I realized I only knew one Christian song, I raced off to Rhema Bookstore to buy and then learn two more songs.

Wondering just what I was getting myself into, I arrived at the Hilton Hawaiian Village, dressed in my best muumuu. The dazzling sun on the brilliant blue Pacific ocean was blinding on that postcard-perfect day. Diamond Head peeked out from behind the high rise hotels and condos, and people lounged in skimpy bathing suits and other beach attire. Tourists and locals alike crowded the beach; some worshipping the sun, others waiting to hear about a different Son.

As the sound of Hawaiian slack key guitar hymns filled the air, Chaplain Gene walked out to greet tourists from around the world. I can't tell you what Gene talked about that first Sunday, but I can tell you I was petrified of facing the crowd, forgetting my music, and making a fool of myself.

It was my turn to say a few words and sing my carefully prepared numbers sooner than I expected. I guess I'd have described myself that morning as "an inadequate fraud," but somehow, I kept singing. Midway through my first number, a man hesitantly walked onto the beach, and sat directly in front of me. He might not have been homeless, but he was certainly dirty and tattered.

His smile encouraged me to continue, though, and I sang those three songs with a heart filled with gratefulness that after over thirty years, that God-shaped void inside of me was finally filled. This was an opportunity to express my feelings about a God I was just getting to know and love.

Gene ended the service with an explanation of what being a Christian means and an invitation to follow Christ. Then the people began to approach the book table, to compliment me and share how much the service and my singing had touched them. Finally, as the equipment was being broken down, I felt a hand on my shoulder. I turned to see the man who had sat at my feet.

"I just wanted to tell you it was your singing that brought me here today," he said. "I was way down by the Ala Wai Yacht Harbor and I heard the most beautiful music. I just had to come. I also wanted to tell you that I asked Jesus into my heart today, too. Thank you."

With that, he slipped away, leaving me stunned. Never did I think I would see such results from my three little songs! Of course, now I know God hand-picked me that day. He allowed me the privilege of ministering with the Waikiki Beach Chaplaincy for over twelve years.

Founded by Bob Turnbull on February 8, 1970, the Waikiki Beach Chaplaincy is an independent interdenominational Christian ministry. It is an evangelistic outreach funded solely by individual contributions and not affiliated with any one church. Their mission is to sensitively present the message of Jesus Christ in a refreshingly unique manner, using local talent in the process.

As a youth minister with Prince of Peace Lutheran Church, Bob Turnbull had a burning desire to reach out to the thousands of visitors to Waikiki Beach who might never enter a church building. A year after he founded the ministry, Bob resigned as youth pastor so he could devote himself full-time to reaching people in the internationally known resort area. Each year, over six million tourists from seventy different countries flock to the sands of Waikiki. There are also residents and an ever changing group of military personnel. Truly the fields are white and ready for harvesting.

Bob served as Chaplain until November 1980, at which time he was succeeded by Gene Ozbun, and in June of 1988, by Alex McAngus.

Using Christian hula and talented local musicians, the Chaplaincy continues to go where the people are—on the beach, in the hotels and entertainment areas, in the streets and by-ways. The ministry has grown since its beginning in 1970 and now includes E Ho 'Omana, a time of Sunday worship in three hotels, Ekalesia Iluna Kahakai, the church on the beach each Sunday morning at 10:30, Pule Aina Kakahiaka, a Monday morning fellowship breakfast, and Po Lama, a midweek concert by the Duke Kahanamoku statue on Kuhio Beach. There is also a sister ministry called the Kona Coast Chaplaincy led by Chuck and Doni Antone.

A distinctive cover, featuring a sun-kissed beach, graces the New Testament appropriately titled, *The Greatest Is Aloha*. Over five thousand of these are given away annually.

Alex and Ruby continue to develop their own support as missionaries. Dozens more volunteer each week doing office work, providing music, running the sound system, and a host of other jobs.

Over the years, thousands from around the world have accepted Christ as their personal Savior on that beach in Waikiki. Jeff, from Australia, wrote the following in a letter to the Chaplaincy.

"While I was in Honolulu investigating a number of matters relating to the fraud, I decided that suicide was a real option and definitely in the best interest of my family. I was staying on the thirty-first floor of the Ala Moana Hotel, and on the night of Sunday, July 12, 1981, I decided to jump off the balcony to the alley below. To cut a long story short, the Lord miraculously intervened and I did not jump, but for the first time in my life I recognized the reality of the unconditional love of God as I found myself following the selected Scriptures in *The Greatest Is Aloha*."

Jeff continues sharing that God not only saved him, physically and spiritually, but restored his marriage.

Simply put, that's the ministry of the Waikiki Beach Chaplaincy—saving lives. Each day, the staff and volunteers share God's Aloha with people, they give mahalo (thanks) to a God who loves us enough that He gave His only Son for our sins, and they graciously accept kokua (help) from those who have somehow been touched through this special ministry.

I no longer live in Hawaii, but not a Sunday goes by that I don't long to see the fluid hula dancers lifting their praises to God. Nothing has ever felt so "right" as my time of speaking and singing in Waikiki and helping to grow a ministry that is life-changing. Maybe one day I'll be a part of it again, but until then, I, like thousands of others around the world, will always hold a piece of "Aloha" in my heart because of the Waikiki Beach Chaplaincy.

"Whoever is spared personal pain must feel himself called to help in diminishing the pain of others." —Albert Schweitzer

Topper's Very Best Christmas Gift

PAT VERBAL

"Hello, Ministry To Today's Child," I said cheerfully as I picked up my business line. "This is Pat."

"Mrs. Pat Verbal?"

"Yes, I'm home for the holidays, and it's nice to answer my own phone once in a while."

The young caller evidently knew I travel a lot. "I didn't expect to get to talk to you personally," she replied with a soft, halting voice.

She went on to say how much she'd enjoyed one of my teacher training seminars in Greensboro, North Carolina, in October and was interested in getting a copy of my new picture book.

"As soon as I saw *Topper's Very Best Hat*, I wanted to get it for my seven-year-old son Joshua." Her voice cracked. I wondered if she'd been crying.

"Even before November fourth, when he was diagnosed with a malignant brain tumor, I wanted to give him your book for Christmas. Now, I know it will have special meaning for him."

The caller was referring to my book about Topper, a lovable, six-year-old hat lover, who refused to take his hat off on his first visit to church. During the Bible story, he noticed that Jesus wore hats too. One of them (the crown of thorns) led Topper to invite Jesus into his heart so that someday he could wear a gold crown in heaven.

Debbie Langston, a home school mom with clear strength of conviction and a gentle poise, quietly told me about her son. Joshua Langston had just finished a painful series of radiation treatments, while his family stayed at the Ronald McDonald House across the street from the hospital.

To his delight, they enjoyed Thanksgiving at home, but now he was back to face chemotherapy during the Christmas season.

"We realize now that God had been preparing our family for this for some time. It stops you cold and causes you to examine everything in your life," said Debbie. "Joshua is so trusting. He loves the Lord and is a brave boy for his three-year-old sister Rachel, who adores her big brother." Debbie then gave me her credit card number to place the order.

Reaching for a box of tissues, I assured Debbie she didn't need a credit card. The book and a gold crown to go with it would be a gift for Joshua with my love and prayers. We prayed together on the phone and I promised to put her family on our e-mail prayer line.

I returned the phone to the receiver and sat, motionless, at my desk, staring out the window at the lush Florida landscape. Thoughts of the many months of writing, searching for a publisher, editing, waiting, contracts, illustrators, and marketing strategies faded into the distance. My nagging anxieties, about being good enough as a writer, stopped for a moment. To be a tiny part of one hurting child's comfort and confidence during this Holy Season was gift enough for me. This was such a blessed Christmas gift from Topper!

"The value of compassion cannot be over-emphasized. Anyone can criticize. It takes a true believer to be compassionate. No greater burden can be borne by an individual than to know no one cares or understands." —Arthur H. Stainback

From Crisis To Blessing

LINDA ROOKS

Adoption is a clear example of God working in wondrous ways through adversity and the mystery of Romans 8:28. Through adoption, we see how God causes "all things to work together for good to those who love God and are called according to His purpose."

Shepherd Care Ministries is a Christian adoption agency where, in three major ways, God's love is the healing agent. This is true 1) for women going through the trauma of a crisis pregnancy, 2) for children who were not planned or wanted, and 3) for couples struggling through the pain of infertility. Each one in this adoption triad serves as light and hope to the other two. God uses them in their own affliction as instruments by which He breathes new life into the lives of the others.

Here's an example. A young woman calls, her life seemingly come to a screeching halt as she faces a life-changing decision. She is pregnant. The situation is completely unexpected, and reality hits her like a truckload of cement.

There are no easy answers. Her first thought is to "undo" the pregnancy. "I can't be pregnant," she thinks. "I can't deal with this." Abortion comes to mind as a way to reverse the pregnancy, but then she realizes it is self-deceiving to think of an abortion as just becoming "un-pregnant." She knows all too well that a life has already begun within her. There's too much information out there now to ignore the fact that a baby has a heart beat at twenty-one days, brain waves at forty days, and is entirely formed at eleven weeks.

But to keep the baby, and to raise it, will change her life! This isn't a short-term commitment; parenting a child is a lifetime undertaking. Is she ready for this? What will this do to her future? Her dreams?

Adoption? She's heard people talk about it, but that seems too hard. Carrying the baby for nine months and then letting others raise it as their own?

Then another woman calls. She's been crying all morning. She and her husband had tried to have a baby for four years, even gone to infertility doctors, and nothing has worked. The idea of going through life without ever having a child to raise and love is more than her heart can bear. She asks what the process is to adopt a baby. How long will it take?

The reality to one—a baby wanted, but seemingly out of reach for the other. A baby, alive and growing, fearfully and wonderfully made by the God of the universe, his days ordained and already written in God's book of life. A baby whose life and future hang in the balance. Will the child live? And if so, who will raise it? A sixteen-year-old girl or a husband and wife in their early thirties?

This is the triad, with three painful circumstances. People whose pain God can use to be the healing salve for each other's wounds.

Shepherd Care Ministries is more than an adoption agency. It is a center for healing and hope for each member of this adoption triad. Shepherd Care brings these people together so God can work His miracles.

Young women who find themselves in a crisis pregnancy situation often have been mired in confusion for an extended period of time. When they find themselves pregnant, they can no longer ignore their turmoil. Shepherd Care helps these women put their lives back together with continued counseling and practical help. Shepherd Care began as a pregnancy center in 1980; then became a licensed adoption agency in 1985.

When Paige first came in, she'd run away from home and had been living with her boyfriend. With her parents divorced and her mother remarried, Paige was in complete rebellion. Her mother, a Christian who was active in her church, was beside herself. A few months after she'd come in, after months of counseling and working with Shepherd Care, Paige placed her baby with a beautiful family who was present with her during the delivery of the baby and with whom she'd instantly bonded. She reconciled with her parents, recommitted her life to the Lord, and although she experienced times of sadness, she had complete peace that she'd made the best decision.

Robin and Paul were two nice kids whose relationship was out of control. They, of course, thought they were in love, and were supportive of each other through the pregnancy. Paul wanted to be an officer in the Air Force, Robin was headed for college and a teaching career. Having a baby would have seriously altered the course of their lives. A few years after placement of their baby, Robin called to say she and Paul were getting married, but not to each other. Their high school romance had prematurely produced a baby, but with the freedom to enter adulthood unhampered, their lives had gone in different directions.

Trudy called Shepherd Care from a half-way house facility. She was twenty-nine, with five children, and just released from jail, where she'd been imprisoned for selling drugs. She and her husband were separated, the children were in the state's foster care program, and she was pregnant by another man. She decided to place her baby for adoption and was able to select a family who already had an adopted four-year-old. She met with them, asked questions about issues close to her heart, was thoroughly impressed with their sincere love for her baby, and chose them as her baby's adoptive parents.

After a few months of counseling at Shepherd Care, Trudy recommitted her life to the Lord and was back in church, was gainfully employed, and living with her reconciled husband and five children in a house she was renting. The baby was born with serious medical problems, and although the doctors predicted she would probably have to be on machines for an extended time, God heard the many prayers of her Christian adoptive parents and Shepherd Care workers. Her stay in the hospital only lasted a month.

It was almost too late for Ginger and Ted, a tender-hearted couple in their mid-forties who were in the ministry. She had had a physical condition requiring surgical removal of an ovary, and was infertile because of it. They could not imagine having to go through life never being parents, and when they realized Ginger could not get pregnant, they went through an intense period of grief. But Shannon was impressed with their solid marriage, and their commitment to each other and the Lord. She herself had made a series of bad choices throughout her young life and told her counselor that placing her baby with this couple for adoption was the first good decision she felt she'd ever made. She also made a first time commitment to the Lord.

When young women first come in for counseling, they're confused, but they know they're taking responsibility in choosing what they believe is best for their child. Some ultimately choose to parent the child themselves. Some choose to place the baby in a Christian family for adoption. If adoption is chosen, the young woman begins by choosing the child's parents. Often she elects to meet them and talk to them about their plans for the child. This is considered a semi-open adoption as names and cities of residence are kept confidential. If she wishes, the family will agree to send pictures and letters for a certain period of time after placement. The birth-mother is also invited to send gifts and a letter to her baby so she can express her feelings in her own words. The agency attempts to help her with practical needs if necessary, and counseling is available for as long as she needs it.

The workers at Shepherd Care won't try to tell you that girls who place their babies for adoption don't experience grief. They will. But this grief will come to a final resting place with the peaceful recognition that with God's help, they turned a crisis into a blessing.

"A person does what they must—in spite of personal consequences, in spite of obstacles and dangers and pressures—and that is the basis of all human morality." —John F. Kennedy

The Shaws of Restore Orlando

SUSAN CHESSER BRANCH

What leads some people to make drastic changes in their lifestyles, give up luxury and comfort for a cause? For David and Bonnie Shaw, it was the strong and unmistakable call of God.

"We felt God was calling us to help in the inner city, to be 'salt and light,'" says Bonnie. But she and her husband needed a sign from God before they took their six children, left their spacious, country club home complete with a swimming pool, and moved to the inner city of Orlando, Florida.

For months before their decision, David, the Pastor of Distributed Ministries at Northland Community Church of Longwood, Florida, had been disturbed by the plight of the inner-city, the deserted section of America. He began reading books about these areas and was intrigued by the idea of middle-class families moving into the inner-city.

The Shaws were drawn to the Holden Heights neighborhood, an inner-city, neglected area of Orlando. Their daughter, Megan, had been part of a youth group from Northland who volunteered at "Restore Orlando," a non-profit group working to transform the Holden Heights area. She and other teenagers were working in the soup kitchen, youth center, and thrift store, and interacting with the families of the neighborhood. The rest of the family came to volunteer, and before long, they had fallen in love with the people of Holden Heights.

The thought of a call to the inner-city would leave some people shaken, but the Shaws embraced God's grand idea. Instead of fear, they were excited about the possibilities.

"We have no problem doing something radical as long as God ordains it," says Bonnie, recalling their decision. She wanted God to make it really clear. "Send me a gold-leaf letter and sign it 'God'!"

So the Shaws put "the sign" in front of their house, and waited for God's "gold-leaf" sign. They got it. Without a realtor, and with a high asking price on their home, their house sold in six days.

And so they left their fashionable, suburban subdivision and moved into a two-story older home, in the middle of a neglected area of Orange County. On a two-acre plot of land, they are encased in their own little farm with gardens all around them, a pond on one side, muscadine vines in rows, playground, and even animals.

The major difference between this house and other farmhouses is that outside the perimeter lies a community with prevailing problems. The neighborhood is run-down, lawns full of weeds and garbage, the streets are dirt, and the beautiful pond is polluted. Prostitutes, drug dealers, and the homeless roam the streets. The sound of gunfire and sirens is not uncommon.

The community has been ignored, literally, by the city. The neighborhood is in unincorporated Orange County even though it is less than two miles from Orlando City Hall. "This is like a third world country right here in the middle of Orlando," says David. "Dirt streets, open sewer, and a polluted lake."

As they've lived there, their prayers for the neighborhood have changed. When they first moved, they had specific ideas of who they would help and what they would do. They believed their main ministry would be to the youth. They didn't expect to become the important voice for the community, especially for some of the older families, that they are. Dave attends public county meetings and helps the neighbors state their concerns. For instance, the community would like to see the county install sewer lines, a storm-drainage system, and paved streets.

"Who says that just because you're poor you don't deserve to have sidewalks, street lights, and paved streets?" he asks.

One of the main accomplishments for the Shaws and "Restore Orlando" has been a partnership formed to purchase and renovate twenty-six homes in Holden Heights. These homes can then be sold to residents who otherwise would not qualify for funding.

"We have not moved in to make this a middle-class neighborhood," says Bonnie. "We want to help these inner-city families, who are mainly renters, to own their own homes." In the Restore Orlando area, eighty-seven percent of the homes are rentals.

The people of Holden Heights have had a huge impact on the Shaws' lives and lifestyle, too. Like their neighbors, they are adopting a simpler lifestyle. They grow many of their vegetables, and have learned to walk whenever possible instead of driving. And their favorite thing is to gather their family on the front porch, often with their neighbors.

"Our front porch is where it happens in our neighborhood. That's where we have our theological and political discussions," says David. "It's where we live instead of in the family room."

In their Tuscawilla, country club home, most often the neighbors came home from work, went into their air-conditioned homes, and never even saw each other. But the people of Holden Heights don't hibernate within their homes. "They are out on their front porches, or they walk everywhere because they don't have cars," says Bonnie.

Of course, there are safety concerns for their family, and they've taken proper precautions. They installed an alarm system, and keep their dogs in the backyard. They've seen transients in the street or near the pond, prostitutes roaming the streets, drug deals going down and drug dealers busted. Once, a neighbor awakened them in the middle of the night to get help because of a drug deal gone bad.

The children's bicycles were stolen once, too. Not long afterward, a man attempted to steal the new ones off the back porch in the middle of the day. At first, her children wanted to blame it on the neighborhood, but Bonnie reminded them of when their bicycles were stolen at their upscale, Tuscawilla home, and even in the small town of DeLand, Florida.

Bonnie sees these troubling incidences as learning experiences for her children. While suburbanites get a glamorized view of dangerous lifestyles, her children are seeing the truth.

"They see a twenty-year-old prostitute, all wrinkled and dirty, who looks like she's in her forties," she says. "And they saw a drug dealer thrown on the ground and handcuffed."

Yes, the Shaws are seeing a lot of things they never saw in their sleepy, middle-class subdivision. But now, they are experiencing how God can take a family and send them to be salt and light to people in need. The irony is, they are receiving more from the people in need than they ever expected.

"More important than a work of art itself is what it will sow. Art can die, a painting can disappear. What counts is the seed."
—Joan Miro

Life in Christ Circus

RANDALL WILLIAMS

For me the application of clown make-up is more an experience than a process. The sweet smells of mineral oil, powder, and spirit gum float up from the tubes and jars scattered on the counter before me, evoking memory flashes of distant events. The face in the mirror returns my gaze, eyeball to eyeball, never quite ready to subjugate itself to the imminent rebirth of a character who is at the same time foreign and yet wells up from my own being deep inside.

The character is a Christ clown, a stumbling clod of the earth who sees with the eyes of a child, accepts life with a shrug, and freely tenders acts of love and service without any expectation of return.

It's a pretty far stretch from the real me. I've often wondered about the differences and why it takes a face full of red and white grease paint, a spongy red nose, and a tangle of red curls to enable me to share the Good News. I wonder about it now in these strangely quiet preparations for a production of the Life in

Christ Circus, just moments away.

The Life in Christ Circus has been opening hearts to the joy of God's love for over twenty years—close to fifteen in Central Florida—and has traveled as far as East Germany and Poland with its rollicking messages of God's love and acceptance of our human follies. It's a loosely organized assortment of Christ clowns, the majority of whom were trained by Dr. Richard Hardel, a Lutheran pastor, and more recently Executive Director of the Youth and Family Institute of Augsburg College, Minneapolis. Dr. Hardel, himself an accomplished Christ clown, created Christ Clown College to teach the biblical foundations of clown ministry and encourage Christian outreach built on a framework of circus clown traditions.

My graduation certificate says I'm a "Clown of Christ," class of '87. A certificated fool, along with half a hundred area Christ clowns dedicated to falling down so that others may be lifted up. Make-up applied, costumes adjusted, lines (I hope) memorized, a dozen of us wait in the wings for the start of another production. We have several tasks ahead of us, not the least of which is to fill the air with the healing power of laughter. Another challenge is to help our audience discover meanings by seeing things in a different light.

Pastor, poet, and philosopher Herb Brokering, in the book, *Tag, You're It!*, co-authored by Dr. Hardel and Penne Peterson-Sewell, uses parables to encourage this discovery process. We like to think of each of our clown skits as a kind of parable that, as Brokering puts it, "breaks through the senses, seeing old things in a new way or just seeing new things." That's really been the clown's job, Christian or not, right down through the centuries: to help others discover truth by looking from a different angle.

So here we are, a dozen otherwise normal human beings hiding behind these dusty curtains ready to pretend to be buffoons so that Truth might be revealed. The noise from the "house" sifts through the heavy fabric. It's an unintelligible din of conversations about who knows what punctuated by an occasional shout from excited children as they maneuver for a good spot at the foot of the stage.

With the pre-performance butterflies fluttering around in my stomach—or was it the hamburger hastily eaten on the way over here?—I venture a peek at the audience through a sliver of opening in the curtain. It's a sea of faces, all ages, shapes, and sizes. Some are still finding seats, many, as the noise had indicated, turning to talk to one another. They're mostly smiling, waiting to see what's in store. It's a casual crowd come to see the Christ clown show, expecting to see—what? Bible stories? Tedious morality plays set to circus music? Hope we don't disappoint you, folks. We're here to make you laugh, and in the process, break down a few of the barriers between you and the love of Christ.

As the squeals and occasional shouts had indicated, the children are gathering at the front of the audience. They don't worry about the theological or philosophical implications of clown ministry. They just want to see clowns, those colorful living cartoons who do silly things just for kids and who give out plenty of attention—and plenty of balloons. Not satisfied to sit back with the adults, the kids are always right down front. They scoot and surge closer at every opportunity as though they somehow, by some magical spell, will be swept up by the clowns and merge with the colors and light, to swirl 'round and 'round in a zany dance of brightly painted characters.

I've been spotted. A child with curly brown hair and sparkling green eyes, wide with surprise, is pointing my way, shouting, "Look! A clown!" Startled, I duck quickly back into the secret backstage world denied to spectators. I didn't expect to be spotted, but I also didn't expect to see the fear in the child's eyes. I didn't go into this business to scare children, like some crazed Halloween monster lurking in the shadows.

My foolish need to preview the audience and this child's discovery have unexpectedly begun the show. I hadn't intended it to begin this way—this turn of events is certainly not written in my script—but now I'm part of it. I'm obligated, now, to carry on and complete the scene. I need to rescue this situation from an outcome I didn't expect and don't want.

Carefully, I once again part the curtain, peering with wide eyes at the little faces now giggling with delight. I duck back again, change position and again peek out. I know this game well, having played it with my own children, and I get the expected reaction. Most of the children squeal with laughter at my unexpected appearances. Adults in the first few rows are chuckling, too, mostly at the joy they see in the children. Farther back in the audience, people are bending forward to see what is causing the commotion. The sea of random conversation begins to form ripples of laughter and it wraps itself around me, tugging at my heart.

But—there's something wrong with this picture. The child with the curly brown hair and bright green eyes has backed into the center of the crowd of children. I can feel her tension welling up from some unknown black depth, feel its icy tentacles piercing deep inside me. Even before the opening curtain, I've begun the process of breaking down the walls surrounding this group of people, releasing them from the prison of the every day and opening them up to the healing power of mirth. But one cell remains to be opened. It's a tiny cell surrounded by dark walls of fear.

Now, I know, it's time for choices. There's a show ready to go on, a whole houseful of "paying" customers who've invested the time and the effort to be here. Little Curly Hair will get over it, sooner or later. But the fear in those eyes cannot be ignored. I decide to do something about it—now.

I duck back behind the curtain, frantically searching for something to give. But what? Backstage has become a hubbub of commotion with last minute arranging and rearranging of props and clowns running back and forth. There's nothing—nothing!—available to solve my problem.

The pressure from the audience out front pounds in my ears. I can't leave them hanging while I stroll around looking for some doodad to thrust upon that child. My inclination is to escape backstage, to fly from this accidental encounter, but the crowd wills me back. I'm a rag doll pulled back and forth by two demanding children: first one way and then the other until my arms and shoulders ache and I expect them to, at any moment, burst out of their sockets with a flurry of feathers and stuffing. The crowd wins this tug of wills and I step back out from behind the curtain with nothing but an idea.

With a white-gloved finger to my lips, I carefully sneak out in front of the people, as though by my exaggeratedly stealthy movements I have become invisible to them. With careful steps I tiptoe toward the children. Their eyes are wide with anticipation, their upturned faces a sea of rosy cheeks and smiling teeth. Little Curly Hair is in the middle of this crowd and we lock eyes. This performance is for her alone. To get down to her level I drop to my knees, the floor beneath me cold and unforgiving. I reach back into my memory for the least threatening facial expression I can muster up. There's not much time here— always the time pressure—and timing is all important.

I'm agonizing for the movements, the face, the body language that says it all: "I know you're afraid. So am I... a little. But I'm really just a person like you, painted up and wearing these silly clothes. This is all given for you. To fill you with joy. Here, touch my hand. It's OK."

The other children instinctively seem to understand what I am trying to accomplish and cease their incessant jumping up and down and grabbing for my clothes, hair, and nose. The grownups in the front rows are at the edge of their seats now. They are with me. They want me to win this one. Even with the noise I can hear the coaxing, the whispers of "It's all right, dear…. Go ahead…. The clown won't hurt you…. Don't be afraid."

The little girl edges forward, but starts a little when I reach forward with upturned palm, fingers relaxed and unthreatening. She reaches forward hesitantly, grasping a gloved finger. Her eyes dart to the hand and back to mine. I give a little shrug, tipping my head slightly as if to say, "Hey, not so bad, huh? Not so scary after all."

Slowly, some of the shadows of fear pass from her face. In her eyes I can see she is working hard to sort out all the contradicting evidence: my strange face, my soft expression, the wildly intimidating colors, the softly gloved hand. As she continues to cling to my fingers, unwilling to release her grip on the fear she seems to be overcoming, I decide to risk it all and go for a hug. I hold out my other hand and she hesitates. I can see by her expression that she is weighing everything, trying to decide whether to trust me. No, not me, but this character thing I have become.

Now I'm wondering what this image I have so painstakingly constructed out of colored grease paint and ill-fitting clothes actually says to others. Have I done it right? Have I properly assembled all the lines, connected all the dots through the years? Is this clown inside me—the me inside me—communicating what I intended?

I want to give her the opportunity to end this encounter on her terms. "Accept me," I want to say. "Accept me for what I am. I have nothing to offer but this foolish, stumbling, parody of myself."

Carefully, hesitantly, she draws nearer, into the circle of my arms, and wraps her tiny arms around my neck as all her fear washes away in the warmth of this intimate embrace, this pow-erful mutual surrender. And as I cling to the warmth of this tiny body, I feel my own fear and uncertainty wash away as the waters of a spent wave slip gently down the sandy shore.

At the edge of my consciousness, I hear a light patter of applause.

"Look on other lives besides your own. See what their troubles are, and how they are borne." —George Eliot

Joy Town

DOUGLAS W. SONDERDAHL, M.D., FACS

At 7 a.m. on Friday, March 13, 1998, my wife, Nancy, and I joined a team of ten gathered in front of Kijabe Medical Center. We were there to load several crates containing the day's supplies into two Land Rovers. We prayed that this day we would both be a blessing and be blessed as we ministered to the crippled children at Joy Town, one of two Salvation Army schools in Kenya for an incredibly needy, and probably mostly neglected, group.

As volunteer urologist and nurse, we had no idea what to expect. The one-and-a-half-hour journey to northeast Nairobi went quickly as we admired the beauty of early morning in east Africa and watched the shopkeepers preparing for another arduous day. We threaded our way through increasingly thick traffic, lurching over unmarked speed bumps at forty-plus miles per hour. We arrived at Joy Town's lovely campus, a boarding school for approximately five hundred students in grades 1-12, in time to enjoy chai (tea) while being briefed by the Assistant Principal. The school, founded in 1980, offers not only education and medical care, but love and hope and a strong Christian upbringing to its students. The $400 tuition/year covers operational expenses for the school, but capital expenditures come from donations to the Salvation Army. After being briefed by the Assistant Principal, "tea time" closed in another time of prayer for power and wisdom in ministry today.

We moved to a large, open physical therapy building in another area of the grounds, where we saw crippled children on crutches and in wheelchairs, many assisting one another, moving to their assigned places. Most were to see the orthopedic part of our team, but nineteen had appointments to see the first urologist to consult at Joy Town—me.

First, Christine, one of our Kenyan staff, brought a dynamic message from God's Word... the account of Jesus raising Lazarus from the dead. She emphasized repeatedly how we are intended to live for the glory of God, no matter what our circumstance. Just as Jesus instructed the newly-alive Lazarus to remove what was binding him, we, too, must remove from our lives whatever it is that might hinder our living to glorify God.

A graduate of Joy Town, Daniel, now one of the Kijabe team members, translated either into English or Swahili, depending upon which language Christine happened to speak! The patients for the day listened with rapt attention. Assigned to assist us were Kenyans: Sister Nancy, the lone Joy Town school nurse, Jennifer, a new member of the team from Bethany Crippled Children's Hospital (an arm of Kijabe Hospital), and Mwangi, one of two physical therapists at the school. From time to time, a dorm mother (in charge of twenty-two five-year-olds, (four of whom have no bladder/bowel control) appeared in order to learn how to provide better care.

We held clinic in the dispensary, a room about ten by ten feet complete with table, a couple of chairs, a few boxes of supplies, medicines scattered among papers on the table, and a bit of light coming in from a small window near the ceiling and a 25-watt light bulb, mostly decorative during daylight hours. A tiny sink did supply running water, while a plastic container held perhaps an ounce of liquid "soap." It looked more like dirty dishwater, if the truth be told.

One after another, we interviewed and examined nineteen patients with an abnormality of the spine (spina bifida); they had either poor or no lower limb function, and little or no bladder or bowel control, as well. While they managed as well as they could, with rags for diapers, with their socks and shoes urine-soaked, the odor, intensified by the small, hot room, defied description. That day we saw spinal deformities, children with crutches, others in wheelchairs... and Helen, a teenager, who slid out of her wheelchair to shuffle across the urine puddles on the floor in order to reach the exam table. Some bedsores, caused by the constant soiling, were craters over two inches in diameter and extended deep into bone. Lack of self-esteem and shame does not begin to describe what undoubtedly must have been their recurring thoughts: Why? Why? Why?

Our little team worked for nearly six hours straight without a lunch break— other than sharing the few cookies Nancy had the foresight to bring. Not having a clue of what we faced, we'd brought few supplies: catheters, gloves, lubricant. Amazingly, Joy Town's nurse, Nancy, had the exact number of catheters necessary, permitting us to contribute as much as possible. We wore only a couple pairs of gloves all day, washing them between examinations. All patients all lay on the same, undraped examination table. Flies located us quickly, too. Fulfilling our bottom line objectives, we trained the caregivers (even some of the older patients) in techniques to achieve dryness, hopefully impacting issues of poor self-image and disgrace, too. As we taught, Mwangi took copious notes and kept records, and Sister Nancy, Jennifer, and the dorm mother showed keen interest as well. It is quite challenging to attach three feet of plastic tubing and an adult-sized urinary drainage bag to diminutive girls who either walked with crutches or shuttled in and out of a wheelchair without assistance.

But, incredibly, the children all smiled, apparently in a joy incomprehensible to the healthy. Immanuel Kant, German philosopher, said it well, "We are not rich by what we possess, but rather by what we can do without." (We didn't see any toys.)

Did the children see Jesus in us? We pray that they did. Did we see Jesus in the children? A resounding *yes*. Jesus said, "In as much as you have done it unto the least of these my brethren, you have done it unto Me" (Matthew 25:40).

It is thrilling to see God so obviously at work... in the joy of the disabled children, in the love of the staff, in the unity of fellow Christians ministering "a cup of cold water " in Christ's Name, in the work He did within us. We experienced deeply-felt love for and desire to minister in such heart-rending circumstances. Truly, we returned richly blessed, and broken and grateful. May we be faithful to use our gifts and skills to work where He leads. "Delight yourself in the Lord and He shall give you the desires of your heart" (Psalms 37:4).

Follow-up: Five of the children were admitted for various reasons to Kijabe Hospital four days after our consultation visit. They were delivered by Leonard Mwangi, one of the Joy Town's two physical therapists. As eighteen of the patients lacked any bladder control, and we'd placed them on a catherization program in order to achieve dryness, I asked Mwangi how our training in catherization was coming along.

Mwangi's face lit up. He told me that all of the eighteen are now completely dry. In fact, most of them have learned to perform the technique by themselves without supervision! I was astounded, since even in the States this program is not one hundred percent effective, and it does have a "learning curve" before it is mastered.

He went on to say that the lives of these children have literally been transformed before his very eyes! He can scarcely believe it, and of course, he is so thankful to us for having come with this solution to an extremely distressing problem.

In turn, we praise God for the privilege of serving Him in this way. And we thank you for enabling us to serve a cup of cold water in Jesus' Name. We are humbled and grateful.

"Faith is building on what you know is here, so you can reach what you know is there." —Cullen Hightower

The Z

EVA MARIE EVERSON

Jim Hoge, General Manager of radio station Z88.3, says that he is not a theologian by any stretch of the word. Some may call him a visionary. After speaking with this humble servant of God, I'd have to say he would deny that title as well. The fact of the matter is that ten years ago, on his way to Sunday School, God planted within his heart an idea that would metamorphosis to a pang, and eventually to a passion.

"I was listening to a Sunday morning Christian music program on a local secular station, and I wondered why Orlando didn't have a twenty-four-hour FM Christian music station."

Hoge grinned. "And with that thought," he said, "Z88.3 was conceived."

But between the thought and the actual establishment of the radio station is a lot of time, an abundance of prayer, and thousands of dollars. Jim Hoge's background was in commercial radio, and finding a lucrative commercial frequency in or near Orlando was a near impossibility.

"There were times I thought this was hopeless," Hoge says. "It wasn't until I broached the idea to a friend, who pointed out the success of what was, at that time, WCIE, in Lakeland—a non-commercial FM Christian music station—that I saw it wasn't."

The idea of a non-commercial station was foreign to Hoge. "But it is FM, and FM is made for music. But I had no idea if, or how, it would support itself."

In the 1940s, the Federal Communications Commission, the agency that oversees broadcasting in the United States, reserved the bottom twenty channels of the FM band for non-commercial "public" stations that would promote educational and cultural programming to the citizenry. In 1987, Hoge tried to sell his idea to his employer, who had no interest in non-commercial radio. The result: he launched out on his own in 1988.

"It had to be God," says Hoge, "because in the early days I didn't have a clue as to what I was doing!"

After finding and buying a defunct application for 88.3 MHz for the community of Union Park, in east Orange County, Hoge, using $6,000 of his own, formed a not-for-hire corporation. But the 88.3 allocation was confounded by recent FCC rule changes relating to interference with TV Channel 6, located just below 88 MHz on the FM band, meaning that some FM radios can pick up audio from local Channel 6, WKMG at 87.7 MHz. Additional stumbling blocks came when the FCC process allowed other groups to file for the same frequency once the initial application was placed on file.

"When the smoke cleared after the application cutoff date in November of 1989, we had five applications filed on top of us and we were, by far, the weakest!"

"What happened after that was God," Hoge continues. "'The Z' was eventually approved, but the real story here is not how Z88.3 got on the air. It's how God taught an average 'non-theological Joe' how to walk by faith! I thought, surely if God's in this thing, it will be smooth sailing—no trials. Boy! Was I wrong!"

From day one, true to Murphy's Law, everything that could go wrong did go wrong. "The engineering in the application was flawed. The FCC attorney I had retained didn't want to go to the hearing with such a weak case and strongly suggested I withdraw the application. Channel 6, after granting the initial permission to use their tower, rescinded it. So, I lost the proposed tower site and on top of that, I lost my job!"

In fact, Channel 6 did this several times before "The Z" went on the air. Each time, Jim Hoge would get in his car and go down to see them, his wife, Eunice (whom he affectionately calls "the praying wife"), would get down on her knees and pray it through. "I would go into these meetings with usually very hostile TV execs, and always come out with an agreement. Now that's the power of a praying wife!"

Reeling from the last shock of the lost tower site and his job, Hoge and his wife re-evaluated the situation. "There was a small glimmer of hope. The FCC hadn't dismissed the application. With that, we still had a chance," Hoge continued. "If God truly wasn't in it, the door would slam shut, and at that point it hadn't. So, putting God to the test, I continued to try to fix the 88.3 application. But," he adds with a smile, "just in case I was out of God's will, I began looking for work in other states."

Years of daily walking by faith followed. "It was amazing!" says Hoge. "The doors closed on all out-of-state jobs and God opened a door at a local Christian station, WTLN. They not only became an employer but also a much-needed financial partner. God supernaturally moved at Channel 6, allowing a novel proposal to 'diplex,' or combine, the 88.3 frequency into their television signal to eliminate interference. God also provided a seasoned Christian FCC attorney to litigate our case. Through it all, there was God's hand."

It took eight faith-testing years before "The Z" experienced its first day in August of 1995. "We were flat broke when we finally got on the air. We won the FCC hearing just to have it appealed in Federal court. If the cost of litigation wasn't enough, problems in diplexing the signal into Channel 6 had mushroomed construction costs threefold. We were roadkill—flat broke when we got on the air. But God is absolutely faithful. Donations began coming in as soon as the signal was up, and they met the need. From there, we slowly bootstrapped ourselves into business. What God taught me are the simple truths of the Gospels: 'He who is faithful with little will be faithful with much,' and 'Don't worry about tomorrow, for tomorrow will take care of itself.'"*

In the early days, in order to run the station as cheaply as possible, the station tied into a network from Colorado Springs, Colorado. There were no local disc-jockeys. Eventually, Scott W. Smith was hired to do the morning show. Then, one by one, radio celebrities were hired as the station could afford them. Finally, in December of 1997, the station became local twenty-four hours a day.

"Our mission statement is this: 'To promote the Christian life by playing positive Christian music, expounding Christian beliefs, and promoting edifying activities twenty-four hours a day,'" says Hoge.

By uplifting the body of Christ, being a light for the lost, and sharing the saving knowledge of Christ, "The Z" keeps listeners focused on the Lord all day long. "It meets an age-old need of redemption with a modern method; evangelism is now heard in the form of contemporary Christian music."

The popularity of "The Z" is inspiring. Like most radio stations, Z88.3 encouraged listeners to call the station and request bumper stickers for their cars. Hoge says that the response was overwhelming. "Any station can buy a billboard, but a driver must feel passionate to put a sticker on his car. We receive tons of calls for stickers. In fact, I received one call from another station manager who asked me, 'What is it that you people do to get so many people to place your stickers on their cars?' I repeated to him what I just said to you. Our listeners support us because they feel passionate about what we are doing for the Lord."

It doesn't stop there. With the bumper stickers in place, Z88.3 held a radio share-a-thon to raise money for billboards. The staff and listeners prayed for enough money to purchase two—one to be placed on I-4 and one to be placed on I-95. What they got was a bigger miracle than they ever expected. In eighteen hours, $133,000.00 was raised. They asked God for two billboards; they received eight.

According to the latest figures from Arbitron, the company that measures radio listening, 76,400 Central Floridians are listening to Z88.3 each week.

"From our research, approximately thirty percent [of listeners] are not churched," says Hoge. "With the Z stickers and the billboards, we feel that number will grow. We have a tremendous opportunity to impact thousands with the Gospel!"

Carry on, Z88.3. In the Name of our Lord, carry on!

*Matthew 25:21; Matthew 6:34

"Although the world is full of suffering, it is full also of the overcoming of it." —Helen Keller

The Union

WENDY CHANG

It's an impressive structure when you first see it—a large, colorful, contemporary building standing brightly among blocks of decaying warehouses, low-income hotels, and makeshift tents. From the looks of it, the edifice could be that of a museum or an ad agency. Who would guess that it's actually a rescue mission? On the streets, it's known as "the Union."

I had never been down to Los Angeles' Skid Row until 1997, when I visited Union Rescue Mission, the largest mission in the United States. As we drove through the neighboring streets, I saw too many homeless men and women with fear, suspicion, and despair in their eyes. Then, when I observed how the Mission served the poor and homeless, I realized that the size of the building wasn't just a façade. It reflected the scope and vision of Union Rescue Mission's outreach to the surrounding community.

Shortly afterwards, I had the opportunity to work directly with homeless women and children at the Mission. At first, I was scared. What would I say to them? What would we have in common? Would they even speak to me? But as I spent time with them, talking and playing games, I realized that we were fundamentally the same. We all laughed when someone told a joke. We cried when we were sad, and we yelled when we were angry. During those afternoons together, we weren't "the haves" and "the have nots;" we were fellow card players, lamenting over bad hands and celebrating wins. The homeless were no longer a conglomerate of people standing by freeway exits, asking for money. They had faces and names. Yazmine laughed and played like any other three-year-old, not yet aware of the grim circumstances around her. Stephanie preferred to sleep on the streets as opposed to the Mission, because the streets were all she'd known since childhood. Ruby, an older woman, was unable to work because of a physical disability. Pat held a master's degree and knew twelve languages but was frustrated by mental illness. Diana, a runaway now in her forties, never stayed in one place for very long. And twelve-year-old Mario wasn't in school because he had no permanent address.

Through these and others, I've learned that the homeless face an array of issues, including poverty, substance addiction, mental illness, domestic violence, and broken relationships. Often times, with *homelessness* comes *hopelessness*. Hope is the driving force behind living life. When it is stripped away, there is a loss in the will to try. Why try to get off the streets if there is no hope for a better life? Indeed, studies show that the longer a person is homeless, the harder it is for them to believe that their present actions will result in a better tomorrow. The only hope that is eternal is the hope in the Lord Jesus Christ. Once people, with or without homes, are able to identify themselves as children of God—loved, worthy, and valuable—they find the motivation to make every day count. That's one of the reasons the homeless are "guests" at the Mission. All day long on the streets, they are frowned and looked down upon. At the Mission, they are cared for and served.

Union Rescue Mission's long history can attest to its effectiveness and importance to a city with one of the highest homeless populations in the country. Founded in 1891, the Mission began its ministry on horse-drawn "Gospel Wagons," which wound through the streets offering food, clothing, and the Word of God to the poor. More than a century later, from its 225,000 square-foot facility, the Mission serves more than a million meals and shelters thousands of people each year. Its longevity is due in part to its ability to adapt to the circumstances around it.

During the Depression years of the 1930s, Union Rescue Mission supplied forty-two percent of the free meals provided by the city's private charities.

From World War II through the Korean War, the Mission served millions of servicemen. Now, Union Rescue Mission is expanding its services to meet the unprecedented surge in the numbers of homeless women and children.

In addition to emergency services, the Mission offers biblically-based recovery programs for men and women and transitional housing for families. Free health care is provided through the Health Center, and dental services will be available in the near future. If that weren't enough, the Mission's annual Christmas Store supplies homeless and poor parents with free Christmas toys and gifts, which they are unable to purchase. Unlike mass toy giveaways, where parents are randomly handed gifts, the Christmas Store allows parents to retain the dignity of choosing gifts within a store-like setting.

From the roof of Union Rescue Mission, I have often watched men and women congregating on the sidewalks. A man who used to sit across the street and twirl an iron rod like a martial arts master is no longer there. A small woman nicknamed "Shorty," who used to stand on the corner shaking the loose change in her gallon milk container, was recently found stabbed to death in a dumpster. Familiar faces, they became like neighbors. Now that they're gone, I find myself missing them. In the midst of this seemingly overwhelming setting, the Lord works miracles every day at Union Rescue Mission. It happens in a man who finds a new job, a battered woman who laughs for the first time in years, a child who comes to know the Lord, and a family that moves from the Mission into their own apartment. The Bible says, "There will always be poor people in the land" (Deuteronomy 15:11). As long as that is true, Christians will always have work to do, and ministries like Union Rescue Mission will continue to be havens of hope to all those who seek refuge from the storms of the world. Thank God.

"The rewards for those who persevere far exceed the pain that must precede the victory." —Ted Engstrom

Fortunate Sufferer

MICHELLE AKERS

In 1991, I was named the best women's soccer player on this planet, and my team, the United States of America, became the first ever Federation of International Football Association (FIFA) Women's World Champions. We went undefeated in the tournament; I scored an unprecedented ten goals in five games.

My name is Michelle Akers. I am 5'10" and weigh 150 pounds. I am muscular. I am tan. I have wild, sun-bleached, curly hair. My teammates call me Mufasa, from *The Lion King*. I love to laugh.

On vacations, I love to hike in the Cascade Mountains near Seattle, Washington, with my dad and brother. I am the starting center forward for the World Class American Soccer Women's Team—a 1996 Olympian. If you saw me today, you would see a healthy, physically fit, elite athlete.

But I am not. I am sick. I have chronic fatigue and immune dysfunction syndrome (CFIDS), and I am hanging on by the very will and courage that helped me attain my status as an elite athlete. Some days, it is all I can do just to get through the day... let alone be an elite athlete.

On those days, the only way I can even step on the field is to stop, close my eyes, take a deep breath, and gather every ounce of strength and will. Then, the thing to do is focus solely on surviving the hour and a half of practice ahead of me. Most days, I survive the practice. Sometimes, I do even better than merely survive. Sometimes I can actually see glimpses of the player that I used to be. Those days are glorious.

To feel good, to have energy, to be light and strong—this is what it's supposed to be like. To have fun, be carefree. I revel in the feeling and the gift of good health.

On the very bad days, on the days when it is all I can do to survive, I walk off—drag myself off the field, light-headed and shaky. With labored breathing, blurred vision, my legs and body leaden, it is all I can do to get to the locker room, change my clothes, and keep from crying in utter exhaustion and weariness. My teammates ask me if I am okay, and I nod yes. But they see the truth in my empty, hollow eyes; dull and lifeless eyes. It scares me to look in the mirror when I get like this. I shake my head, knowing I overdid it again. I crossed that invisible line between functioning and being very sick. How long would it take to recover from this one?

I tell you these things not to gain sympathy, but so you, too, can experience a day in the illness—the pounding migraine headaches, the insomnia, and the overwhelming fatigue, the "fogginess" that causes me to lose concentration, forget where I am. Sometimes I forget how to get where I've been a thousand times before.

This illness demands attention in every detail of my life,

and if I don't pay attention, it punishes me without remorse. It is a difficult experience to explain because it encompasses so much of my being—of who I am. There is grief in realizing you will *never* be the person you were before. CFIDS becomes who you are, at times leaving you—the old you—a mere shadow of yourself.

I have always believed that anything can be accomplished through hard work and perseverance, through dedication and commitment. This is how I became a World Champion, an Olympic athlete. That is the irony of this illness. The harder you work, the more it drags you down. The more it disables you. It is the first time in my life I have been beaten. It is the first time I may have to quit before I have accomplished my goal. I cannot defeat this illness through hard work or pure drive and desire. For the first time I have realized that I cannot overcome on my own terms, in my own strength.

And I am a fortunate CFIDS sufferer. Because I am an elite athlete, I have access to the best doctors, the best care in the United States and therefore the world. I have an incredible support system through my team and family. My family, friends, coaches, and employers are sympathetic and flexible regarding my health and limitations. They have never doubted that I am sick—not depressed, mentally unstable, or, God forbid, faking it.

Yes, I have lost a lot. Yes, CFIDS is a devastating disease. And no, I am not the same person before I was stricken with CFIDS, and probably will never be again. But this is not a message of hopelessness, of defeat. It is a story about courage, growth, and challenge. This is a story about overcoming. I have gained a lot from this illness. Nothing that can be touched or measured, but through the suffering and heartache, I have gained a strength and purpose that carries me when I cannot do it myself. I have seen and experienced God's grace and peace only because I have been in the "valley." I now know that it took this long visit in the depths of this illness to open myself to a more meaningful, purposeful life.

I live by the verse in 2nd Corinthians which says, "My grace is sufficient for you, for My power is made perfect in weakness.... This is why for Christ's sake, I delight in weakness, in hardship, in difficulties. For when I am weak, then I am strong" (2 Corinthians 12:9b,10).

God's power is made perfect in me. I will overcome, but not through my own efforts. That is the final irony. The more I struggle to save myself from this disease, the more it takes my life away. The moment I just rest—rest in the strength of God's perfect grace—is the moment I begin to overcome, the moment I am whole again.

I have learned to accept CFIDS as an opportunity to make a difference. I have turned this weakness into a strength, and even though it is still raging inside me, I refuse to be beaten by it.

I will overcome. And I will show others how to overcome also.

EDITOR'S NOTE: In 1996, Michelle started the Michelle Akers CFIDS Fund to support youth and athletes with CFIDS, as well as friends and family of persons with CFIDS.

Salt and Light In Cyberspace

> [Jesus] said to them, "Go into all the world and preach the good news to all creation."
>
> —Mark 16:15

"If I can put one touch of rosy sunset into the life of any man or woman, I shall feel that I have worked with God."
—George MacDonald

Welcome to Debbie's Place

EVA MARIE EVERSON

Within the cyber world of America Online, somewhere between the numerous and extremely varied "chat rooms" and the well thought out channels, is a place where Bible scholars and Scripture enthusiasts can go to play Old Testament Bible Trivia. About a year ago, I happened to meander there, ready to impress the other players—and myself—with my competitive spirit and with what I thought I knew about the Word of God.

As it turned out, I won the game... not because of any great knowledge, but rather because they just happened to ask questions with answers I was familiar with. The game over, I'd already returned to my exploration of cyberspace when I was greeted by an instant message from a man named David.

"Good game," he wrote. "You really know your Bible."

I recognized his screen name as being one I had seen in the game. "Thanks," I wrote back. "I love the Bible, don't you?"

Thus began an on-line friendship. At some point, David told me about another frequent player to OTBT named Debbie. He said he'd told her about me, as well. Within a few days, I "bumped into" Debbie in the trivia game and we, too, became cyber-buddies.

Debbie's zeal for the Word of God was bar none! I soon became blessed daily with little antidotes, short devotions, jokes, etc. from her. She shared with me her love for writing (after she discovered my work in the field), but said that she'd never finished anything she started. That may have been true of her writing, but it certainly wasn't of her witnessing to others. Debbie had made countless contacts through the Internet, those she had brought to the Lord and those she met as brothers and sisters in Him.

One day, I told her about an infection, caused by an ant bite, on my daughter's left ring finger. The doctor was quite concerned about it and had even expressed the possibility of surgery. I was anxious, too, both for my daughter's health and because we don't have medical insurance. Debbie wrote: "Do you want me to share this with my prayer team?"

"What prayer team?" I wrote back.

"I started an Internet prayer team," she said. "Your prayer will go all over the United States in a matter of seconds."

Wow! I thought. "Sure."

Two days later, Debbie wrote me again. "Several members on the prayer team want to know how the finger is."

About that time my daughter walked in. "Honey, let me see you finger," I said. Imagine my delight when I saw that her finger was almost healed! When I shared this with Debbie, she was ecstatic. This was a woman whom I'd never met face to face, yet I felt totally at one with her.

Several months later, I discovered a Verse of the Day link on AOL. I read it, copied it, and sent it to a few friends. Naturally, Debbie was on the list. This became a daily ritual, followed by friendly comments from everyone. Except for Debbie; her comments were different. She'd write detailed discussions concerning the Scripture verse, and I'd respond likewise.

Then one Thursday, Debbie did not respond. Nor did she respond the following day. A quick chat with David informed me that Debbie was supposed to be going out of town soon, and perhaps this was the weekend for her trip. I agreed; it probably was.

That Saturday night, after my husband and I returned home from a dinner with friends, I decided to check my e-mail before going to bed.

I walked into the office at the end of the hall, signed on to AOL, and listened for the "You've got mail!"

The first e-mail was from David.

"Hey," he wrote. "I had no idea Debbie was this sick, did you?"

What sick?

I clicked down the page to find a letter written by Debbie's husband. In her forties, Debbie had died unexpectedly the previous morning from heart failure.

I was physically ill. How could this have happened? Why would God take someone with so much work to do and so much love to give?

But who better to receive the reward that comes with dying? I reminded myself that Debbie is no longer gazing into her Savior's eyes with her heart; she is now doing so with her eyes.

My "verse of the day" soon took on a new personality. I felt compelled to continue Debbie's work of sending prayer requests, devotionals, and jokes. My daily e-mail, which now goes out to hundreds of people each morning, became Debbie's Place.* Within the mail, a reader will find Verse of the Day Hall, The Prayer Room, Dad's Den, A Woman's Place, The Teen Tavern, etc. The responses have been overwhelming! Nothing thrills me more than to learn that someone to whom I send Debbie's Place forwards the site to others.

Debbie took The Great Commission seriously. I dare say she spent hours each day on-line, ministering to believers and non-believers alike. What I do takes a matter of minutes. But it's something I can do....

For more information about Debbie's Place, or to become a member of Debbie's Place mailing list, write to PenNhnd@aol.com

⟡

"It's a small world after all."
—Richard M. Sherman and Robert B. Sherman

Using God's Tools

APRIL BOYER

Can such a worldly media as the Internet be used of God? It's been called the devil's tool, Satan's domain, a tool of the antichrist. Perhaps these things are true, maybe true only in part. Probably they're only true in the hands of those who are willing. I was a skeptic for two or three years while being pushed to buy a computer and get on the 'net.' All I'd seen on television and in other media was negative. Aside from the educational advantages, which I viewed as an excuse to read less, what I saw was more of the violence, immorality, and greed I'd had enough of on television and in publications.

But the idea of faster research, unlimited resources, and additional tools grew on me. I decided that if I used a computer and the Internet, I would manage what I saw and heard, I would have good sense and self-control.

I've done that, by the grace of God, and perhaps even by the direction of God. But what I saw in the Internet surprised me. I found an endless supply of information about Christian organizations, books and supplies, information, and world-related concerns.

I also found Christians. They reached out to other Christians in support and concern; they reached out to seekers, confused in their hearts and about who God is, and they reached out to people in trouble and pleading for help.

What I saw were people praying for one another, seeing their prayers answered, sharing in grief, in triumph, and in blessings. Christians in many different websites were sharing Scripture that charged the unsure, enlightened the unlearned, and uplifted the stumbling. Many sites provide Bible lessons. Some provide information about missions. E-mail exchanges provide a place to ask and receive prayer and support. In one short week, I saw people saved, lives changed, and even a suicide prevented.

It bothered me at first to think that people were neglecting important parts of their lives to stare at and talk to a screen. Then I realized that they were seeking, just as people in our face-to-face encounters are seeking. Christians were making themselves available in a way they might not have otherwise, and seekers were seeing words they might not have seen.

In God's world, everything has its purpose. In spite of Satan's influence and our desire to please ourselves, God still rules. Our Lord has used television, films, magazines, and books to help people reach people. As our Father, He understands the difficulty of living in this world without becoming a part of it. I'm glad He gave me the opportunity to use this tool in the world, for Him, with the words He gives me.

"Lord, give me the determination and tenacity of a weed."
—Mrs. Leon R. Walters

In His Strength

JoAnn Zarling

I was ready to throw in the towel about three years ago. Retirement seemed inevitable. Handicapped for nearly thirty years, I'd managed to keep my writing and editing career active throughout multiple surgeries, accidents, heart attacks, and increasing pain—until then. Over the last year or so, the pain had accelerated to unbearable heights. I'd gradually pulled away from my highly active roles in the writing club I'd started and maintained for years, the local Press Club, teaching and board memberships in several writing and art guilds, and most painfully, from writing itself. I could no longer sit at my trusty computer, even in my wheelchair. Gone were the days when I could hop into a car and keep going all day long. There I was, seemingly appendaged upon my lounge chair, useless and almost mindless with pain and frustration—mostly frustration.

Medications helped me cope, yet I still could barely move. Okay, I thought. Maybe now is when I yield totally to upholding others in prayer. God had supplied all my needs for many years, He wouldn't stop simply because I'd had to give up writing. I'd always asked Him to use me, use my work, my all, to glorify Him and to edify others. For years, He'd given me talents in writing and editing, now He was changing my course, steering me into other areas. I'd always loved to pray anyway, and now I would do it exclusively. Who was I to complain? So I resigned myself to retirement, informed my friends and colleagues that we'd no longer be working together, and sank deeper into my lounge chair. Funny how we can talk ourselves into things—good *and* bad.

But no, that didn't sit well with a couple of the dearest friends I've ever known. T.K. Cassidy stormed into the house one day with her old Mac under one arm, and hauling a small computer desk with the other. She was closely followed by Jenni Rush.

"Ha! You think we're going to let you sit there and stagnate, and leave us to do all the work?" T.K. said, grinning. "Think again, old chum!"

Then Jenni piped. "You got *that* right, kiddo! I've prayed, and I know God isn't going to let you off the hook that easily. Neither are we!"

They went to work, rearranging furniture, me, and YumYum, our cat. Finally, I was set up with the desk and computer next to my chair, and those two working wizards were busily conniving to get me on the Internet. The Internet? I didn't even know what that really was. Neither had I ever heard of "on-line lists," "surfing" or "cyberspace." Boy, did I learn fast! Before I could properly protest, I was propped up, on-line, and introduced to a new way of life.

Oh yes, I'd heard about it. But my husband and I had put it off every time the subject came up. We were just two tired old dogs who didn't care about learning new tricks. And I was retired. Wasn't I?

Not according to Jenni and T.K.! Together we started a business called "Masters Editorial and Writing Service," and my life was once again buzzing. I was back in the swing of things, writing, editing, and even editor of an "ezine," another word I'd never heard before. I latched on with everything I had, having the time of my life and loving every minute of it.

A whole new world opened up for me the day I was introduced to the Internet. By God's grace I am useful again, working in a field that I love, using the talents He gave me. Since my arrival in cyberspace, God has placed authors, His missionaries, in my life, and impressed me with the fact that it is *my* mission to edit their written words. That is what I live for, to glorify God through helping others glorify Him—with words. By His grace and in His strength, I now work on manuscripts He brings my way, sometimes for only the wages He pays me—the unspeakable joy of being His tool—and sometimes I even earn a little money.

The Internet was God's way of bringing me back, restoring my life, my usefulness to Him and to others. I learned once again that "I can do all things through Christ, who strengthens me." In all ways, on and off the Internet, I live and work in His strength, in His will, with His love, by His grace.

"Education is too important to be left solely to the educators."
—Francis Keppel

The Hope Chest

VIRGINIA QUARRIER KNOWLES

Honestly, a home schooling mom with six young children just can't expect to fly around town doing good deeds, ministering to the poor and needy. I fully believe that being a mom is the most important thing I can do during this hyper-busy season of life. Nevertheless, I wanted to do something that made a difference beyond my own walls. It had to be something I could do from my home, something I could pick up and set down between diaper changes, spelling tests, science experiments, and the never-ending loads of laundry. Fortunately, the answer wasn't too far away, because I have a passion for writing.

By the beginning of this year, this passion overflowed into home school newsletter features, church advent devotionals, newspaper editorials, a few freebie magazine articles, and an unpublished book manuscript. I had scores of new ideas, bursting out of my brain, and the flood just wouldn't stop! Then, the Internet arrived at our house. So I satisfied my writer's urge by answering questions on the home school message boards. After a while, though, I noticed I was answering the same questions, over and over and over. It seemed such a waste of time; just a few people would read it!

That's when the crazy inspiration hit. To be truthful, it seemed more like a happy whim. I decided to start a free e-mail home school newsletter and send it to a few dozen families. I wouldn't have to wait around to see if someone would print my articles; I could be my own instant publisher, without worrying about advertising revenue, or printing and postage costs.

Maybe I'm naive about the power of technology and the effectiveness of word-of-mouth advertising, but I wasn't prepared for the response that came into my e-mail address, HOMENEWS@JUNO.COM. After just six months, The Hope Chest was reaching about six hundred families around the globe, and articles had been reprinted in newsletters throughout the US and even in New Zealand. Readers often forward it to their friends, who write in for their own subscriptions. Numbers alone don't tell the story of how God has used The Hope Chest. I often get comments about how the newsletter "seems to fill a lot of need in me that I didn't even know was there!" or, how it came at just the right time with a word of encouragement or advice for someone who felt overwhelmed. It has also brought joy to a lonely retired school teacher, who sent an announcement offering help to parents with special needs children.

Each month, I try to include inspiration, practical teaching tips, web links and recommendations for great educational resources. I often share poems by "salt and light" poets like Amy Carmichael, Edgar Guest, and John Greenleaf Whittier. I try to encourage the moms to reach out in cross-cultural ministry through hospitality. To give us a more balanced perspective, the readers write large sections of the newsletter.

In the issue about American History, I shared how I became a believer in Jesus during the 1976 bicentennial celebration. I also told how spiritual liberty is the foundation for national independence. Our Easter issue even featured a poem that just might explain why I'm so eager to share the abundant life through service to Jesus.

Knowing that The Hope Chest is read by many who are not yet Christians, I try to display the graciousness of God in a winsome way, making a clear presentation of the Good News without turning people off by religiosity.

"Without friends no one would choose to live, though he had all other goods." —Aristotle

Carmen and Me

JoAnn Zarling

Some of God's most precious gifts to us are friends and friendships. They are often the tools He uses to care for us. We ask for encouragement, He sends a friend; we plead for comfort,

He sends a friend; we need counsel, He sends a friend. Godly friends provide the "touch," the visual perception of the only part of our Lord we will *see* (apart from His Church and His Word), until He returns or we go to Him, whichever comes first.

Friendships are normally formed by contact and interaction. It grows by the give and take of confidences, by sharing everyday victories—and failures, too. Friends laugh and cry together, they work and play together, travel, shop, and sometimes just walk in the park together. Friends are visible lifesavers to cling to in the sometimes turbulent waters of life. Someone whom we identify with—that's a friend.

For the disabled, the homebound, making life-enriching friendships can be nigh on to impossible. These relationships can be profoundly difficult to come by when one can't share life with another. Many "physically unchallenged" people find it difficult to be in close proximity to us; almost as though they're afraid the contact will somehow taint them. Like maybe our handicap is catching. Some find us unattractive, perplexing, or even repulsive. But mostly, the fact that they are so much more active then we are eliminates even the chances of their meeting us. This is why we frequently lead very solitary, lonely lives. Even the hale and hearty beautiful, if life is spent out of sight and company of others, are lonely. You have to be with people before you can interact with them. Isn't this what melds two people into a vibrant entity called "friendship"?

When I first arrived in cyberspace, I discovered otherwise. When I was introduced to the Internet, it boggled my mind that all of a sudden, I was sharing my "space" with millions of others. Here I thought I was doomed to spend the rest of my days in my lounge chair, praying for others, reading, cross-stitching, but always alone. Cyberspace proved me wrong. It can be as lonely as we like, or as crowded as we like. And, in cyberspace I had my chance to flourish, to use the talents God has given me without my handicap to hold me back. That great "space" is an equalizer to end all equalizers.

I have made many precious, lasting, sweet friends in cyberspace. One of them is my friend Carmen. Without ever setting eyes on each other, our friendship blossomed into a wondrous, blessed, and permanent relationship. From the very beginning, God impressed on us both how blessed this friendship was destined to be; He is at the pinnacle of our friendship, our director, our overseer, our leader, who blesses wherever our fellowship wanders.

I'd no sooner been introduced to a Christian "writer's list" before Carmen Leal exploded into my life, and I've never been the same. Her dynamic personality burst through every cyberword she wrote. I remember thinking how "alive" this woman was. Never in a million years would I have thought of the ways God was going to use Carmen in my life. Recently introduced to the Internet by two other dear friends, my life had taken a dramatic turn. My body simply couldn't be active anymore, and I'd thought my career was over. Jenni and T.K., my friends, had different ideas. Since going on-line, I was busier than I'd been for years, and I was doing more writing and editing than ever.

But when God brought Carmen into my life, we both almost heard His voice: "You haven't seen anything yet, my children!"

Soon after we "met," Carmen and I were "talking" through personal e-mails, and I learned about my new friend and the horror she lived with daily in caring for her husband, a victim of Huntington's Disease. I'd always believed I knew more than the average person about medical matters (with my problems, I'd made it my business to know), but I'd never heard of this dread disease called "HD."

I don't remember exactly how God worked it, or the words that were used, but all of a sudden, Carmen knew she had to write a book about HD, one that would encourage and comfort the countless victims of that horror. And I can't remember exactly how God told me I needed to edit that book, but He did. He gave me the desire to help my friend, and to help the thousands of HD victims I'd never heard anything about just months before. And He gave us both the tool to accomplish His will—the Internet.

I prayed, hard. At the moment, I was swamped with work, and when God instilled in me a desire to help this amazing woman with her book, I argued intensely with Him.

"Lord, I can't possibly!"

"Says you!"

"I can't!"

"I said, 'Tell her you'll edit the book for her!'"

"Rats! Oh, all right, I'll edit her book!"

And that's what I did. We worked hard, fast, and we worked well together. Before we knew it, the book was done. Praise our glorious God!

I will thank Him for as long as He permits me to live on this earth. He blessed me with so many cyberspace friends! But with Carmen, our special working and fellowshipping relationship sets her apart. While I have never met her in person, I treasure her, and love her dearly. It was to Carmen that I cried out in distress when our youngest daughter Stacey Jean was sick and shortly after went to the Lord; it was Carmen (she has Internet contacts of mind-boggling proportions) who placed the prayer requests for our Stacey and me that flew around the world, via the Internet, which comforted me more than I can say. And it happened all over again when I needed delicate surgery a few months later. It's Carmen who is there whenever I need her via e-mail or the telephone, who seems to know exactly what I'm feeling through my voice, or my words. God has used her in so many ways!

I laugh when I think of my splendid husband, too. Dennis has learned to love Carmen, and to respect her abilities, through watching us work together. He's almost as thankful as I am for her, for the oodles of godly friends I've met in cyberspace, and for the Internet, which has been my lifeline to the rest of the world.

When Carmen and I first met, we were both homebound, but for different reasons. She was a caregiver, while I was a "care-needer." The Internet brought us together and God used us in ways that, without the Internet, would have been out of the question for us both.

The Internet, like every other wonderful invention that God enables man to create, is sometimes taken over by our "enemy" and used for evil purposes. But God also uses it to bring about the "impossible," as it is used for Him and for His glorification. Like everything else, just how it is used in our lives is our choice.

Cyberspace is a place for the disabled as well as anyone else. More so, I think. Without it, I wouldn't have the contacts I need for my work; my life would be the solitary, lonely one that I envisioned. Instead, I am a useful, busy worker in God's ready-for-harvest field; a worker with a vast number of friends.

> *"A kind heart is a fountain of gladness, making everything in its vicinity freshen into smiles."* —Washington Irving

The Poet

MARY J. DAVIS

I met him on the Internet—in a Christian chat room to be exact. The first time I met Poet, I knew he was a very special servant of God.

The unique thing about Poet is that he isn't able to get out like most of us. He has a rare allergy and has to be very careful. But he's not depressed because he spends his days at home and can't attend church or fellowship with other Christians in person. He's an upbeat, encouraging person.

Poet picks up on situations in chat rooms that most of us would ignore. Anyone needing a friend, a prayer, or a word of encouragement is sure to hear from Poet, either in the chat room or through e-mail. All the "chatters" in one particular Christian chat room have come to love this man dearly. We all wait for the late-night hour when Poet pops into the room with his big "God bless ya, friends." He makes the room a big family, and takes it upon himself to encourage every person in the room.

Poet, of course, writes poetry. He shares his words of comfort in the Christian chat room, on Christian message boards, and recently, in his own ministry website. Many of his new Internet friends are privileged to receive a book of his poetry; poetry that reflects an unwavering trust in an awesome God.

Truly salt and light is this precious, gentle, man. Truly a servant of God in a very unique situation. Poet ministers to others, giving all the credit to his wonderful Lord. My life, and countless others' lives have been blessed by "The Poet."

Poet was recently blessed with the answer to his most frequent prayer—God sent him a beautiful Christian wife, who will share in his ministry to others.

"Friends are those rare people who ask how we are and then wait to hear the answer." —Ed Cunningham

A Heart As Big As Alaska

CARMEN LEAL

I discovered a treasure named Marie one year before I met her. Actually, I met her on-line, in a Christian Writers' Group, before I finally saw her face-to-face. To some people, meeting on-line doesn't qualify as the real thing, but though Marie lived in Colorado, and I in Florida, we had a strong friendship even before we hugged each other at the Denver airport.

In 1997, I decided to get more serious about my writing. Yes, I had succeeded in selling a few magazine articles, but I didn't feel as if I knew the craft of writing. Having recently moved to a new state over 5,000 miles from home, I didn't have a church or any type of support system; I felt disconnected. Being the only caregiver for my terminally ill husband made it difficult to get out of the house and meet people, much less take a writing class.

The Christian Writers' Group, started as a ministry by a dedicated writer and pastor's wife, is a forum for writers who communicate with each other via e-mail. People from all over the world join together to discuss writing and publishing, and support each other in prayer for both personal and writing requests.

Unlike myself, Marie is what is called a "lurker." In Internet terms, this means she rarely posts messages but reads them all. In December of 1997, I asked for prayer; my brother, Merrill, was dying in Kansas. It was such a hard time. Also, I really wanted to see him while he was living and I wanted to take my sons to the funeral, too. But with little income, no medical insurance, and mounting bills, there was no money for airplane trips, no matter how important the cause.

Marie is not a wealthy woman, but her heart was touched. She gave me a gift that not only allowed me to see Merrill during his final days, but also to bring my sons back a week later for the funeral. While I was grateful to others who gave me modest gifts for the trip, I was overwhelmed when Marie sent her paycheck to me. She reasoned that she works because she likes to bless people, not because she needs the financial rewards of being employed.

Our friendship grew as we talked about our writing projects. *Faces of Huntington's* was my first book and was I ever excited. In her quiet, unobtrusive way, Marie began asking questions about Huntington's Disease. Information was exchanged as our friendship grew.

As the book release date drew near, Marie's husband got a job transfer. Since they live in Grand Junction, Colorado, this meant a temporary separation while her husband, Ron, found an apartment in Colorado Springs. Ron moved about the time my books were ready for shipping from the publisher in Canada. The national Huntington's Disease Society of America's had its convention in Denver, and Marie graciously offered me space in their apartment so I could have my publisher send a quantity of books there, in Colorado Springs. This represented a huge savings; I would not have to lug eighteen boxes from Florida. All this and we'd never met!

Marie drove all the way from Grand Junction, picked up the boxes, then met me at the airport and became my personal assistant for the next three days. Marie sold books, made change, answered questions, and soon became indispensable. All the while, she quietly soaked up information about Huntington's Disease and made several friends. I could never have made it without Marie, but each time I said thank you, she said, "No, thank *you*!"

Recently, she told me that her life has never been the same since attending the HDSA convention. A few brief months before she had never heard of HD, and now her life is changed. I knew it could be a life-changing experience for those with HD or in an HD family, but Marie is not affected personally by Huntington's Disease; she has never even met my husband, Dave.

An avid biker, Marie has decided to raise funds for HD through biking. She and two friends, Charlotte Reicks and Evelyn Logan, will make a trip that is destined to change not only their own lives, but thousands more. These three women will ride their bicycles over 3,000 miles.

Marie Nemec is a woman with a heart the size of Alaska. She told me she wants to play an active role in finding a cure for the thousands of people who daily live with this devastating disease.

Marie and friends plan on following the old "Route 66" through California, Arizona, and New Mexico. They will continue through Colorado, Kansas, Missouri, Kentucky, West Virginia, Maryland, and into Arlington, Virginia, for the 1999 HDSA convention. By averaging approximately fifty miles a day, the trio hopes to reach their goal of 3,000 miles in two months.

I know that Marie will create HD awareness and raise much-needed research funds. But, as much as I appreciate her willingness to ride 3,000 miles for Huntington's Disease, there is something else I treasure even more. Besides sharing her friendship with me and biking for a cure, Marie does something even more important. Marie prays.

Sometimes, the burdens of the world seem overwhelming. She aches for those who hurt and wants to solve the world's problems single-handedly. Marie probably wishes she had millions of dollars to help those in need. She doesn't have the money and she can't solve all the world's problems, but she can and does pray. There is really nothing more significant that anyone can do for others than to pray for them.

I'm so proud of Marie. And I'm honored to call her my friend. I'm thankful that God led both Marie and I to the Christian Writers' Group. While I've learned much about writing and Christian publishing through the list, I've also learned that God does care and does provide friends for us in creative and timely ways. One reason I know this is because He taught me—through Marie.

"The nature of God is a circle of which the center is everywhere and the circumference is nowhere." —Enpedocles

Website

ROBERT DIACHEYSN, JR.

Sunday a.m.: After a week of sleepless nights and struggling with our one-year-old son, Dakota, my wife, Sharon, and I decide to take him to the emergency room. He is crying out in pain and has, at this point, lost the use of his legs.

Sunday p.m.: After a long day of blood tests, prodding, and probing, the doctor decides to admit Dakota for further testing. Diagnosis: unknown.

Monday a.m.: The doctor informs us that Dakota may have contracted any one of a number of neuromuscular diseases, some considerably more serious than others. We are told he must undergo an E.E.G. (electroencephalogram), an M.R.I. (Magnetic Resonance Image), and a spinal tap. We are warned that there is "cause for concern." Diagnosis: still unknown.

Monday p.m.: Upon arriving home, I am greeted with a barrage of phone messages, offering sincere concern and prayers from dear friends. I go on the Internet to send messages to a few friends explaining why I will not be available to fulfill my obligations to them this week. "Coincidentally," I bump into a dear friend from New Jersey. I tell him the situation and he promises to spread the word to our friends up North, so that they may pray. Suddenly, I remember a close friend here in Florida who has a daily devotional that reaches hundreds. I fire off a quick e-mail asking for prayer.

Tuesday noon.: Dakota is diagnosed with Guillain-Barre Syndrome: a rare neuromuscular disorder in which the immune system attacks the protein in healthy cells, resulting in temporary paralysis. We are relieved to have a diagnosis and to know that this syndrome is never fatal. It does, however, call for constant monitoring of the heart and lungs and can last for weeks, months, or even years!

Tuesday p.m.: Again, upon arriving home I am bombarded with phone calls and e-mails from praying Christians as far away as New Hampshire, Kentucky, even California! The entire country is in prayer for our baby's healing! I send an update and return countless local calls from people asking, "How can we help?" Sharon and Dakota are inundated with hospital visits, gifts, meals, love, and prayer, prayer, prayer!

Wednesday p.m.: Dakota's condition takes a dramatic turn-upward! For some reason, he is sitting up, kicking his legs, eating, laughing! Coincidence? Or is God sending an "Instant Message" of His own?

Friday p.m.: Dakota's condition continues to improve remarkably. Our family continues to be blessed by the love and care and constant intercession of God's children everywhere!

Saturday p.m.: Dakota comes home! The doctor is pleased and amazed at his rapid recovery. He tells us, "He may be completely cured in as little as a week or two!" I go to the computer once more; this time to report the good news: God still hears and answers our prayers! He is a God of miracles!

Thought: In this age of fast-paced, cyberspace technology, we can communicate faster than ever before. God uses the Internet to carry needs, answers, and messages of hope around the globe in just seconds. Yet He knows the desires of our hearts before the words ever leave our lips. He inhabits the prayers of His people. I am thankful that I am "connected" to a God who never goes "off-line," and I am grateful to all those who were "linked" with us prayer.

Biographies

EVA MARIE EVERSON grew up in a rural southern town in Georgia. She is married, has three children, and lives in Orlando, Florida, where she currently writes for several ministries and publications, including Life Devotion Ministries, Inc. She teaches Old Testament Theology at Life Training Center, Longwood, Florida, and home schools her youngest daughter, a senior in high school. She publishes a daily Internet devotional ministry, Debbie's Place. Eva Marie is a noted speaker on a variety of subjects designed to develop intimate relationships with God. She is a contributing author in a number of publications, including works by Kathy Collard Miller, Peggy Munson, and Lynn Morrissey. Eva Marie is currently working on her second novel, a gift book, and a devotional book. She may be contacted at PenNhnd@aol.com or (407) 695-9366.

CARMEN LEAL is the author of *Faces of Huntington's*, a book for and about people with Huntington's Disease, and others who care.* She has been published in Focus on the Family's *Single Parent Family Magazine*, Simon and Schuster, and numerous local publications. Her writings will be appearing in Linda Evans *Shepherd's Heart—Stirring Stories of Romance* (Broadman and Holman Publications), and a new book of miracle stories published by William Morris and Co. In addition to her writing, Carmen is a professional speaker and singer. As a companion to the book, *Faces of Huntington's*, her musical CD was released in May, 1999. Carmen is married to David Pock, who has Huntington's Disease and is the inspiration for her book on that subject. She is also the mother of two teenage sons. In addition to speaking at churches and conventions, Carmen speaks in the community on behalf of the Mustard Seed Furniture Bank and the Heart of Florida United Way. Carmen may be contacted at Carmen@Leal.com.

JoANN ZARLING, born and raised on the Big Island of Hawaii, has written and edited for publication for the past thirty years. Now residing in the beautiful state of Wisconsin, she is the proud mother of four, grandmother of five, and wife of one. JoAnn has primarily written and edited non-fiction for numerous newspapers and magazines, a few children's fiction stories, and Bible studies for women. Today, she concentrates on editing and working on her book of devotions. JoAnn founded and led the Guam Writer's Guild, and was active in helping to develop writing talents among the youth of Guam. Her life's priority is to glorify God in whatever small ways that He allows her.

ESTHER HORVATH is a professional artist who enjoys paintings ranging from easel to mural size. She resides in Orlando, Florida. Esther has been painting since early childhood, and has done everything from portraits to large scale murals. Her work is all in private collections. If anyone is interested in contacting Esther regarding acquiring prints of the cover artwork, she may be contacted at (407) 671-5963 or fax: (407) 671-5463.

MICHELLE AKERS is a 1996 Olympic Gold Medalist, World Champion, and starting striker for the United States Women's Soccer Team, founder of Soccer Outreach International, and speaker for various world organizations. She is the co-author of *Standing Fast* (with Tim Nash), *Face to Face with Michelle Akers*, and a columnist for *Soccer Jr.* magazine. She lives in Orlando, Florida. Her website is http://www.michelleakers.com.

JULIA ARRANTS is a counselor in private practice near Savannah, Georgia. Her recent publications include a poem in an upcoming issue of ProCreation literary journal and *The Dancing Christmas Tree*, a story in *The Solstice Evergreen*, by Sheryl A. Karas (Aslan, 1998). She is a former "honorable mention" in the Writer's Digest Short Fiction competition, and for the past several years has served as editorial consultant for Quick Brown Fox publishers in Athens, Georgia.

SHARI LEE BEYNON is a creative, business, and technical writer living in Longwood, Florida. She has been working as a full-time freelance writer for the past three years. Known as "Lee" to her friends, she has three daughters and eight grandchildren.

TANDY CHILES BARRETT is the eldest daughter of the late governor of Florida, Lawton Chiles. Tandy is an active intercessor and is currently writing a book about the insights God has given her. She is also working on a Christian adventure novel. Tandy and her husband, Boe, live in Winter Park, Florida. They have two adult children, Tandy Gay Barrett and Joe Lawton Barrett.

CHUCK BATES AND HIS WIFE, BETTY, grew up in the Chicago area and have been married for over fifty years. They have five living children and ten grandchildren. Chuck co-owns and operates Custom Communication, Inc., a small family communications business, in Winter Park, Florida.

MARY BEASLEY, a native of Ohio, is a retiree from thirty years as high school teacher and media specialist in Florida, North Carolina, and Darmstadt, Germany. She spends her retirement proofreading and writing, and enjoys music and art.

MARGIE BERRY has been disabled since 1987. Prior to that, she worked for Torrington Bearings Plant for twelve and a half years. She is active in her church where she has taught Sunday School for twenty-three years. Margie is also the Mission Study Coordinator of Women On Mission in her church. She is very active in and attends regularly the Screven County Seniors Center where she is a member of their "band."

RABBI EDWARD S. BORAZ presently serves as the Rabbi of Dartmouth Hillel and the Upper Valley Jewish Community in Hanover, New Hampshire. Ordained from the Hebrew Union College-Jewish Institute of Religion in 1993, he entered its School of Graduate Studies and received his Ph.D. in rabbinics in 1998. He is the author of *Understanding the Talmud: A Modern Reader's Guide for Study*. He is married to Shari and has two children, Joshua and Rebecca.

APRIL BOYER calls herself a late bloomer, having started writing only six years ago. Before that, she was busy raising her children. She enjoys writing profiles, backyard stories, and inspirational poetry. She self-published a small book, *Perceptions*, in 1998.

SUSAN CHESSER BRANCH, a former journalist, is staying home to tame her three children. She is a contributing writer for the adult Bible study curriculum of Northland, A Church Distributed in Orlando, FL.

G.W. FRANCIS CHADWICK is originally from Jamaica, but has lived "the world." He holds a BA degree in English and French, a BS in Nursing, and an MS degree in psychiatric nursing. He enjoys ballroom dancing, gardening, and writing. Currently living in Atlanta, he works as a day trader and individual investor. Francis was featured in a 1998 *Wall Street Journal* and recently collaborated with Eva Marie Everson on a Christian intrigue novel.

WENDY C. CHANG is a second generation Chinese-American. Raised in Denver, Wendy graduated from the University of California. She enjoys traveling and writing.

KATIE L. DAVIS gave her life to the Lord at age sixteen. She is from Liberty, Missouri, active in her church youth group, enjoys writing poetry and short stories and hanging out with her friends. Katie's work has been featured in four previous publications.

MARY J. DAVIS is author of over thirty books, including the popular "My Journal" series for children. She specializes in Christian Education writing, and loves to write for children. She has spoken for many women's, children's, and church groups. Mary also develops and presents free writing workshops for children. She and her husband, Larry, reside in a small Southeastern Iowa town, where they raised three children.

ROBERT DIACHEYSN has been a performer for over 20 years, most recently acting in a children's show at Universal Studios. He writes puppet sketches, children's devotionals, science fiction, and stand-up comedy. He and his wife, Sharon, are raising their five children and aging quickly.

VICTORIA GAINES writes about life. Not what she thinks life should be, but as God reveals it—through her family, friends, children, and personal struggles. As a wife, home school mom, nurse, and lay minister, she enjoys writing devotionals, articles, and stories that reflect her faith and bring hope to the trouble-hearted.

NATALIE NICOLE GILBERT is the Morning Show co-host for WQFL 101FM in Rockford, Illinois. She lives with her husband, Phillip Golden, and their two guitars. Her writing accomplishments include *Southeast Outlook*, *Natalie's Nook*, song writing, devotions, and poetry.

LINDA GILDEN is a wife and mother of three. She is the author of over one hundred articles and has contributed to several books. Her favorite pastime is reading while floating in the lake, surrounded by splashing children. She has been involved with Ladies' First Thursday since its beginning.

JO HUDDLESTON is the author of *Amen and Good Morning, God*, *Amen and Good Night, God*, and *His Awesome Majesty*. Her stories and devotionals have appeared in such national magazines as *Guideposts* and *Decision*. Jo is a book reviewer and conference workshop speaker.

MARGARET JOHNSON is the author of *18, No Time to Waste*, seven non-fiction books for Zondervan, and four contemporary novels. She and her husband, Vern, live in Southern California where they have raised five children.

TIFFANY JOY JOHNSON lives in Orlando, Florida. She is a student at Judson B. Walker Middle School where she is on the Honor Roll, a member of the National BETA Club, and on her school's Peer Mediation Team. Tiffany is also the student editor of her school newspaper. She considers her relationship with God and her bonds with her large extended family to be the most important things in her life.

CAROLYN JONES grew up as a preacher's daughter in Georgia. She was a high school teacher, worked in missions, and owned a wholesale business. She and her husband raised five children, have ten grandchildren and three great-grandchildren. Carolyn enjoys writing, speaking, art, and music.

VIRGINIA KNOWLES AND HER HUSBAND, THAD, are the home-schooling parents of seven children. When she is not homemaking, teaching, or writing, she enjoys reading. The Knowles family lives in Maitland, Florida.

SONDRA LARGENT currently lives in Orlando, Florida. She is a wife and mother of three. She works as a freelance writer, speaker, and vocalist, and is a small business owner.

ELLY LEBLANC was born and raised in South London, England. She immigrated to the United States in 1984. She enjoys writing poetry and songs, and is currently working toward a Bachelor's degree in Psychology. She lives in Southern California with her husband, Stephen, and they are expecting their first child, Miles Anthony LeBlanc, in July 1999!

M. ELDRED MANN is from Glennville, Georgia. He is presently writing a novel and teaches piano. Eldred is a retired school teacher.

SAMANTHA MARCHANT is a native of Sylvania, Georgia, now living in Blairsville, Georgia, where she is employed at

North Georgia Tech Blairsville Campus as System Technician/Computer Information System Instructor. She is the mother of five daughters and one son. Samantha's education includes a Bachelor of Science degree in Home Economics and a Master's Degree in Education.

KATHY COLLARD MILLER is the author of over thirty-five books, including the best-selling *God's Vitamin "C" for the Spirit*. She speaks fifty times a year and has addressed audiences in over twenty states and three foreign countries.

LYNNE MIXSON, a public relations and marketing professional with a special focus in sports, enjoys freelance writing as a sideline. She writes poetry, prose, and non-fiction articles on a variety of subjects, but always featuring the strength of the human spirit. Lynne can be contacted at lmixson@netpass. com.

SKYLLA MOON says that God took a heart of stone and created a heart of gratitude when He freed her and her husband from the slavery of the new age occult. Skylla is employed as a nurse in Alabama. She has been writing since age twelve.

RON AND MARIE NEMEC have been married for over thirty years and have two sons. They enjoy soccer, bike riding, and hiking. Ron is the director of a small Christian ministry, HIS Ministries, which focuses on Roman Catholic evangelism. Marie is a retired elementary school teacher.

ESTHER PHELPS loves writing songs and stories about love, hope, and triumph over adversity. She and her husband, Jon, have four sons and one newly-adopted daughter and are founders of Full Sail Real World Education, a media/recording arts college in Winter Park, Florida.

PHIL PIATT is a husband and father of three children and three grandchildren. He retired after twenty-one years as City Engineer of Overland Park, Kansas. He now enjoys writing and has had several poems published.

CHARLES AND SANDRA POCK are actively being salt and light in San Antonio, Texas. Charles is an engineer, while Sandra works with the state of Texas as a CPA.

BARBARA PUGH is an accomplished writer who enjoys praising God through her poetry. She resides in Orlando, Florida, and works in the banking industry.

BETTY PURVIS lives in Sylvania, Georgia where she works for the Screven County Board of Education and is active within her church and community. She is the mother of two grown children, including Eva Marie Everson.

MARION ROBBINS, JR. served with the 8th Air Force in World War II. He operated a state-wide cold storage construction company for twenty years. He now works part-time, and grows amaryllis and garlic. Marion enjoys writing stories about life experience, composing and reciting poetry.

LINDA ROOKS has been writing and publishing for over twelve years. She was an editor for *Center Stage Magazine*, an Arts and Entertainment Magazine in Central Florida. Among her credits is Cameo Best of Show Award for her nationally distributed commercial, "Testimony of an Unborn Child." She has worked at Shepherd Care Ministries for five years. Linda is married, has two daughters, and is a member of Northland Community Church.

Becky Russell has written Easter and Christmas devotionals which have been published in church booklets. She has also written devotionals for use in church groups such as the Stephen Ministry. She has taught elementary school for thirty years where she has helped teach students to write and express themselves.

Carolynn J. Scully is a wife and mother. She is a graduate from Colorado State University in Child Development and Family Relationships. Writing has been a long-time hobby which she is making into a career. Her poems, devotions, and stories are now being accepted by various publications. She is a member of Potter's Wheel, a group dedicated to the encouragement of creative expression.

Laura Sherwood has been married for twenty-one years to Joe, has three teenagers, and lives in Longwood, Florida. She is involved with FCA, Student Venture, Bible Studies, Sunday School, and has run four Disney Marathons. She is a member of The Metro Church of Christ.

Ruby Slater died on her birthday in October, 1998, shortly before acceptance for this publication. She lived in Newington, Georgia, where she and her husband raised four children. She is fondly remembered for the many cakes she baked and delivered to others, along with her Christian testimony.

Nina Snyder began writing at age thirteen. She has ghost-written two books, *Around the World in 80 Years* and *Eight Eyes to Spiritual and Physical Health*. She has edited numerous works and contributed to two of Northland's Life Training Center courses: "Panoramic Tour of the Bible" and "God's Plan for Successful Living."

DOUGLAS W. SODERDAHL, M.D. was born in Rockford, Illinois, in 1941. He is married and has three children. Dr. Soderdahl is a prolific writer and a popular speaker at medical seminars and conferences. He enjoys jogging, tennis, and water sports. He and his wife, Nancy, currently work as a surgeon-nurse team in volunteer medical mission work in developing nations.

NANETTE THORSEN-SNIPES, a freelance writer since 1981, has had over 250 articles, columns, stories, devotions, and reprints in over thirty publications, including: *The Christian Reader*, *Positive Living*, *Breakaway*, *Home Life*, *Honor Books*, *Georgia EMC Magazine*, *Accent on Living*, *Southern Lifestyles*, *Experiencing God Magazine*, *The Upper Room*, Publications International Ltd., and others.

CARLA TRETHEWAY has been a nurse for twenty-three years and is currently working in a rural emergency room setting in Georgia. She states that the incident she writes about in this book has touched her deeply, and that she says a prayer daily for the safe keeping of "Mutsy" and her owner.

CHRISTEL TURNER attends Central Michigan University where she majors in secondary education. She has been an active volunteer in her community since her childhood. She is the president of the American Red Cross club of CMU, and teaches first aid/CPR classes. She is in leadership position with Alternative Spring Break, and volunteers with the United Way.

MARY VON PLESS is the author of many poems and short stories. Her poem, *A Lifetime In Small Boxes*, has been published and appreciated as far away as Arabia. She is completing her first novel.

SUSANNA VELASQUEZ hails from Kansas City, Missouri, and has been in the entertainment industry for *fifteen years*. Some of her theater credits include *The King and I* (with Shirley Jones), *West Side Story*, *Seven Brides for Seven Brothers*, *Singin' in the Rain*, and *Hello, Dolly*. She also has multiple film and television credits.

PAT VERBAL is a speaker, author, and founder of Ministry To Today's Child. Along with Shirley Dobson, she co-authors the best selling *My Family's Prayer Calendar*. She travels thirty weeks a year, drawing on her rich background as children's pastor, teacher, and school administrator. Pat may be contacted at (800) 406-1011.

DR. DENNIS WENZEL has served our Lord in Pastoral Ministry for twenty years, serving as Hospital Chaplain and Parish Pastor in several locations in the United States and Canada. While in Canada, he earned a Doctor of Ministry degree, working with church leaders and pastors who experienced "spiritual burnout." He now serves as pastor in Southeastern Michigan.

MABEL WILKINSON is a retired school teacher living in Glennville, Georgia. She is married, has two children and one grandchild. She is the author of *My Link to the Past*, her memoirs of life during the depression. Currently, Mabel enjoys being a member of a local quilting club.

KATHY SEVEN WILLIAMS is a Consultant/Writer specializing in "Access to Information" for the visually impaired. She enjoys the beauty of Utah with her husband, teen son, and increasingly independent daughter. She is currently writing a book that will assist blind people with purchasing computer equipment for their needs.

RANDALL WILLIAMS has written, edited, and designed marketing and public information publications for over twenty-five years. Since 1987, the year he graduated from Christ Clown College in Orlando, he has donned make-up and costume to help spread the Gospel through the medium of laughter. Randall and his wife, Valerie, attend Northland, A Church Distributed, where he is helping to rewrite A *Panoramic Tour of the Bible* for the Internet.

Appendix

FEATURED MINISTRIES

Dr. Doug Soderdahl
dsoderdahl@worldnet.att.net

Life in Christ Circus
c/o Nita Zimmer
1414 Tusca Tr.
Winter Springs, FL 32708
407-695-2620

Michelle Akers
http://www.michelleakers.com

Ministry To Today's Child
(800) 406-1011
MTTC@aol.com

Mustard Seed Furniture Bank
P.O. Box 915223
Longwood, Fl 32791-5223
407-578-4565

Northland, A Church Distributed
530 Dog Track
Longwood, FL 32750-6546
407-830-9840
http://www.northlandcc.org/

Restore Orlando
Contact: Jerry Appleby
1030 W. Kaley Street
Orlando, Florida 32805
http://www.restoreorlando.org

Shepherd Care Ministries
251 Maitland Ave.
Altamonte Springs, FL. 32701
(407) 265-9549

Union Rescue Mission
545 South San Pedro Street
Los Angeles, California 90013
Tel: (213) 347-6300
Fax: (213) 612-0260
http://www.urmusa.com

Waikiki Beach Chaplaincy
P.O. Box 15488
Honolulu, Hawaii 96830
(808) 923-3137

Z88.3
P.O. Box 607883
Orlando, FL 32860-7883
1-888-297-8080
(407) 869-8800
zcrew@z883.com
http://www.z883.com

There are an abundance of salt and light opportunities in cyberspace. For a list of salt and light links on a variety of topics, please go to http://Carmen@Leal.com/saltlinks.com. If you have a site you would like to recommend, either visit the links page or send an e-mail to Carmen@Leal.com.

For more information or to order additional copies
of *Pinches of Salt, Prisms of Light,*

please visit our website at
http://www.Carmen.Leal.com/salt.html
or call 1-800-356-9315

or contact:
your local Christian Bookstore

or

P U B L I S H I N G

44 Moira St. West
Belleville, ON K8P 1S3
Phone (613) 962-3294; Fax (613) 962-3055
1-800-238-6376
E-mail: info@essence.on.ca
Internet: http://www.essence.on.ca

Essence Publishing is a Christian Book Publisher
dedicated to furthering the work of Christ
through the written word.